Wakefield Press

What have the French ever done for us?

What have the French ever done for us?

French contributions to
Australia's cultural life

edited by

JOHN WEST-SOOBY

Wakefield
Press

Wakefield Press
16 Rose Street
Mile End
South Australia 5031
www.wakefieldpress.com.au

First published 2024

Cover design by Michael Deves, Wakefield Press
Designed and typeset by Michael Deves, Wakefield Press

ISBN 978 1 92304 234 6

NATIONAL
LIBRARY
OF AUSTRALIA
A catalogue record for this
book is available from the
National Library of Australia

Wakefield Press thanks
Coriole Vineyards for
continued support

Contents

Acknowledgements

Most of the essays presented here began life as public lectures presented as part of a programme of events organised in April – November 2018 to commemorate the centenary of the French Department at the University of Adelaide. That series of events, the overall theme of which gave this book its title, would not have been possible without the support provided by the University of Adelaide, through its School of Humanities, Faculty of Arts, University Collections (special thanks to Mirna Heruc!) and Elder Hall, as well as by the other hosting institutions, the Art Gallery of South Australia and the State Library of South Australia. I gratefully acknowledge that institutional support, which provided the opportunity to celebrate a major milestone, namely 100 years of the teaching of French language and culture at the University of Adelaide. Long may that tradition continue!

I am particularly indebted to those who have contributed to this volume. Their thoughtful work and the patience they have shown as this publication project has progressed are sincerely appreciated. I would also like to express my gratitude to the other speakers and presenters who participated in the 2018 programme of events: Pierre Serna (Professor of Modern History at the Université de Paris 1), who gave so generously and graciously of his time during his stay in Adelaide; Nick Fletcher (Head of the Military Heraldry and Technology Section at the Australian War Memorial in Canberra) and Amy Milka (ARC Centre for the History of Emotions at the University of Adelaide), who both joined Pierre on a panel to discuss animal rights at the Adelaide Festival of Ideas; Roy Howat (Royal

Academy of Music, London) and Adelaide soprano Rosalind Martin, who, together with Emily Kilpatrick (also of the Royal Academy of Music) and Adelaide bassoonist Josie Hawkes, provided us with some memorable performances at our musical *soirée* hosted by the Elder Hall; and Julie Rapebach, whose French poetry readings beautifully complemented the music.

A key feature of the programme of events was the second conference of the Institute for the Study of French–Australian Relations (ISFAR), hosted at the University of Adelaide on 27 September 2018 on the theme: 'French Contributions to Australian Life'. The conference included a panel session devoted to a critical appraisal of the commemorations in Australia and France of the centenary of the Great War. My thanks go to the panel participants: Sharon Cleary (co-author of *Valour and Violets: South Australia in the Great War*, Wakefield Press), Romain Fathi (Flinders University), Colin Nettelbeck (University of Melbourne) and Robin Prior (University of Adelaide).

Last but by no means least, I would like to thank Michael Bollen and the team at Wakefield Press for their support in bringing this book project to fruition. It is hard to imagine what our artistic and intellectual landscape would look like without the vital contribution Wakefield Press makes through the many wonderful publications it produces and the events it organises and sponsors. It is greatly to be hoped that one day someone will write a book celebrating WP's own centenary!

John West-Sooby

Introduction: What exactly have the French done for us?

John West-Sooby

When John Cleese's character Reg asks his fellow Judean activists in Monty Python's *The Life of Brian* (1979) what the Romans have ever given them, the answers to what was intended as a rhetorical question come thick and fast. At the conclusion of this series of exchanges, an exasperated Reg memorably sums up by asking: 'but apart from the sanitation, the medicine, education, wine, public order, irrigation, roads, a fresh water system and public health, what have the Romans ever done for us?'

If we transpose that scene to contemporary Australia and ask the same question – minus its rebellious flavour – about the French, we might expect the list to be more modest. And yet, there are some surprising similarities: water and waste management (with Suez and Veolia as major players); medical products (Servier, Pierre Fabre, to name just two); education (dual French–Australian postgraduate degrees in areas as diverse as marketing, engineering and acoustics); wine and spirits (Pernod Ricard); and road construction (Colas). We could also add energy management to the list, thanks to the presence in Australia of French companies such as Schneider Electric and Neoen, not to mention industrial gas, Air Liquide having been established in Australia as far back as 1957. Furthermore, insofar as defence and cyber security might be construed as contributing to a form of (international) public order, any number of major French companies now have a presence in Australia (Thales, Dassault

Systèmes, SEGULA Technologies, among others). Naval Group and its submarines were set to occupy centre stage in that defence partnership, but we all know what happened there ...

Despite that *contretemps*, the extent of French engagement and investment in Australia seems destined to continue to grow into the future, notably in areas related to science and technology. As reported on the website of the French Embassy in Canberra, a number of French research organisations are currently seeking to expand their activities in Australia, in fields as diverse as energy transition, space science, health science, oceanography, sustainable agriculture, biodiversity conservation and digital technologies. Given that France is at the forefront in these domains and is also an industrial powerhouse capable of building planes, trains and automobiles, in addition to warships and cruise liners – a fact which the country's reputation as a tourist destination and as a centre of gastronomic excellence can sometimes lead us to overlook – any expansion of French research and development in Australia can only be of mutual benefit.

In economic terms, official statistics give a good indication of the breadth and depth of French investment 'down under'. According to the website of Australia's Department of Foreign Affairs and Trade (DFAT), France's total investment stock in Australia in 2021 was around A$43 billion and on an upward trajectory. Furthermore, during 2020 (the most recent year for which statistics are available), Australia imported from France goods and services to the value of almost A$7.15 billion, with pharmaceutical products and medicaments featuring prominently, valued at over A$1 billion. Investment and trade naturally function in both directions: Australia holds significant investment stock in France (A$64 billion in 2021) and exports many goods and services there (valued at a little over A$2.5 billion in 2020). If France is investing heavily in Australia, Australia is doing likewise in France.

With respect to this latter point – that is, Australia's contribution to France – the same DFAT website makes special mention, and rightly so, of the great sacrifices made by Australian soldiers on French soil during World War I, the centenary of which in 2014–2018 featured many joint commemorative events in both countries. This is an important legacy which, together with Australia's involvement in France in the Second World War, plays a vital and enduring role in the bilateral relationship. These historical connections, as one of the essays in this volume reminds us, extend even further back in time to the era of French maritime exploration in the Indo-Pacific, which pre-dated the establishment of the British colony in Sydney in 1788 and continued well into the nineteenth century. With a new chapter in the history of French-Australian relations now being written, through the developing defence and security relationship between the two countries, it is perhaps fitting that it should likewise have a strong maritime theme. The cooperative agreement with France that aimed to deliver Australia's Future Submarine Program may have been torn up, but other significant partnership arrangements remain in place, such as the agreement officially signed by both countries in 2018 foreshadowing an extension of operational level collaboration in the Pacific and Southern Oceans – through joint exercises designed to coordinate the provision of regional humanitarian assistance and to combat illegal fishing, for instance.

France's involvement in all of these domains is undoubtedly important to Australia and it looks set to become even more so. For all that, if we were to ask a random group of Australians what the French have ever done for us, it seems safe to assume that, alongside episodes highlighting our historical ties, examples from the arts and culture would feature prominently among their responses, and most likely towards the top of their list. Moreover, this would surely also be the case if the 'us' were understood not just in the specifically Australian context but in a more global sense. The notion that France is synonymous with culture is indeed something of a *cliché* (a French term which derives, interestingly, from the noise made when using a metallic plate to reproduce images or type). But clichés come from somewhere. However trite such stereotypical characterisations may be, they have currency precisely because they spring from a shared and oft-repeated understanding. Looking at it another way, as Jack Kerouac put it in typically succinct fashion in *Big Sur*, 'cliches are truisms and all truisms are true'. Whatever its origins and however well-founded it might be, the association of France with 'culture', understood in general terms, appears to be deeply entrenched in our collective imaginary.

Separating the myth from the reality in this case is a daunting task. It may indeed ultimately prove to be an insurmountable one. It is nevertheless a question that has exercised the minds of generations of scholars of all stripes. The motivations behind their questionings of the stereotypes are neither trivial nor esoteric. For in order to draw genuinely meaningful lessons from our engagement with another society and culture we need to have a level of understanding that can only be achieved by challenging the clichés and interrogating the assumptions on which they are based. Hence the need for sophisticated and critical appraisal. There can be no denying the appeal of France's rich history and traditions, of its picturesque towns and villages, of its cultural institutions and monuments. But the picture postcard image of France masks a more complex reality and is partial, in both senses of the term. It also tends to spawn a kind of Francophilia which is often superficial and which can in fact be a barrier to developing a deeper and more nuanced understanding of the French-speaking world – and thus of what we might gain from engaging more purposefully with it.

Herein lies the value of the scholarly work undertaken by historians, sociologists, literary critics, cultural commentators, film critics and musicologists, among others, whose research has for many years provided important insights into the complexities and subtleties of French society and culture – past and present – and continues to do so. Much of this work has also served to heighten awareness of the history, society and cultural productions of the Francophone world beyond metropolitan France – in the French-speaking parts of Africa, Asia, the Pacific, North America and the Middle East. And if the geographical scope of this scholarly interest now extends well beyond the Hexagon, so too are the objects of study more diverse than was traditionally the case. In more recent times, for example, researchers have extended their critical analyses to a wider range of cultural phenomena such as popular music and the Francophone comic book tradition. There is, in short, no lack of thoughtful and informative material available to anyone wishing to add depth and breadth to their understanding of the French-speaking world.

This volume seeks to contribute in its own modest way to that collective undertaking. It aims to do that by revisiting some of those aspects of France's culture and heritage which have contributed in a major way to the country's current position and reputation. There are essays on art and music, literature and cinema, food and wine, as well as book history, diplomacy and maritime exploration. There is also a chapter on language – arguably the most fundamental of all the various means of cultural expression and commonly viewed as a cornerstone of modern French national identity. Each essay attempts in its own way to illustrate the impact France has had and the legacy it has left in the particular field on which it focuses. The chapter on language, which opens the volume, examines the historical and contemporary relationship between French and English, highlighting the contrasting attitudes of the traditional cross-Channel rivals towards the evolution of their respective languages. The 'us' in question here is therefore the English-speaking world, taken broadly. Of the following essays, some respond to the question posed by this volume's title from a specifically Australian point of view, while others adopt a more global perspective. Either way, in focusing on the question of impact, and despite the necessarily selective range of domains it covers, this volume aspires to provide an opportunity for readers to add to their appreciation of certain key aspects of French history and culture, and thus to develop the deeper level of cultural understanding advocated above.

While the emphasis in this collection is on what the French have done 'for us', it would be interesting to see what a companion volume on, say, Australian contributions to French life and culture might look like. Readers would perhaps be surprised to learn of the depth of interest the French have, for example, in the culture of Australia's First Peoples (during the 1990s it seemed that everyone in France had read Bruce Chatwin's *The Songlines*!), or of the success of films such as the quintessentially Australian *Crocodile Dundee* and *Young Einstein*, among many others, in a country where cinema is revered as the seventh art. It is also worth noting that, while the focus in the essays presented here is on metropolitan France and its cultural and historical impact, an additional and equally rich companion volume might be compiled if the purview were extended to the wider Francophone world. There is, in other words, ample scope for future publications of a similar ilk that might want to adopt this kind of intercultural perspective.

For the time being, however, it is hoped that readers of this present collection of essays, all of which have been compiled by leading experts in their field, will derive great pleasure from learning more about France's rich cultural heritage and its legacy beyond that country's own shores. Perhaps these accounts will also serve as motivation for discovering new French films, books, music, artworks, recipes or stories – or for reconnecting with older ones that have left fond memories. After all, as pointed out by André Malraux, the French novelist and Minister of Cultural Affairs under President Charles de Gaulle, 'culture is not inherited, it must be won'. For without culture, according to the eighteen-century French royalist and writer Antoine de Rivarol, we are nothing more than 'a tree without fruit'. The fruits of France are many and varied. And while this volume provides an opportunity to savour a number of them, it still only offers a sample of the possible responses to the question provocatively chosen for its title. As Reg found with his band of rebels, it is a question for which there is no shortage of possible answers.

On Language

One of the abiding images of the French is that they are deadly serious about their language. This deep – some might say obsessive – regard they are said to have for the French language seems indeed to rank almost on a par with the baguette, the beret and the Eiffel Tower as a marker of French national identity. The French language itself has likewise earned a level of notoriety bordering on the mythical: for many an 'outsider looking in', its supposedly impenetrable intricacies, coupled with the reverence it is presumed to engender among those who speak it, have imbued the language with a certain mystique. Much mileage is certainly made of this (alongside other cultural stereotypes) in portrayals of cross-cultural encounters with the French, both in books – of the 'My Year in France' variety, which seem to be in endless supply – and in film or on television screens – the Netflix series *Emily in Paris* being a recent and particularly rambunctious example.

There is, it must be said, some substance behind the myth. The French language has, after all, been an affair of state ever since the Renaissance, when King François 1 became the first ruler of France to make a major public policy decision relating to language use, implicitly linking it with the national interest. In similar vein, successive regimes, from the absolute monarchy through the French Revolution to the Third Republic and beyond, have all in various ways harnessed the French language as a unifying force. As a result, the national language became a projection of the nation itself.

The prestige enjoyed internationally by France during

much of that long time span led, logically enough, to a certain acknowledgement of the preeminence of the country's language and culture. This view did not remain uncontested, both within France and beyond its borders, but it was keenly held and promoted by many. The eighteenth-century royalist Antoine de Rivarol, for example, was moved to compile an essay in 1784 on the 'universality of the French language'. This was his winning entry to a competition, the first question of which – 'What has made the French language universal?' – was admittedly loaded. History therefore suggests that there is some justification in asserting that language has for centuries been a central marker of national identity and sovereignty in France. As the author of a 2013 article in the *Guardian* put it, the French are as protective of their language as the British are of their currency!

Of course, linguistic diversity has always existed in what we know today as metropolitan France, despite the centralising historical policy decisions mentioned above, and it is as much a feature of modern French society as it is of most other nation-states. It is interesting to note, in that context, that in recent decades there has been a renewal of interest in France's regional languages (Breton, Occitan, Corsican, Alsatian …), whose status as 'national treasures' has recently been enshrined in a law – the 'loi Molac', passed in May 2021 – designed to protect and promote them. This new legislation necessitated a revision of Jacques Toubon's protectionist and restrictive 1994 law, the dispositions of which were rewritten to specify that the Toubon law (for which he became ironically referred to in France as 'Jacques Allgood') was 'not an obstacle to the use of regional languages or to public and private actions undertaken in favour of them'. There are nevertheless limits to the formal recognition of such linguistic diversity. The 'loi Molac', for instance, had initially included a provision for immersive education in regional languages, but this clause was controversially removed by the Constitutional Council on the basis that it was contrary to Article 2 of the French Constitution, which declares that 'The language of the Republic is French'. The primacy of Article 2 thus enshrines as a principle that the French language must remain a key marker of French national identity.

But in what sense can it be said that their national language is something the French have given *us*, in particular those of us in the English-speaking world? Anyone who has attempted to learn French and negotiate its intricacies might feel that they have been bequeathed little more than an endless potential for embarrassment. But it is worth reminding ourselves that, despite the global spread of English, French remains an important world language whose historical interconnections with English have influenced the development of both languages, in a process of ebb and flow which endures to this day. As Roly Sussex demonstrates in the following essay, this interaction between French and English raises some interesting questions regarding the evolution of the French language and the role it plays in a rapidly changing world.

JWS

1

Roland Sussex

French and English: Deluge, reversed deluge, and what comes after us

To the memory of my father, Professor Ronald Sussex, a lifelong connoisseur of France and things French

Introduction

Over the years the French and British have experienced *ententes* which have not always been *cordiales*. After the Battle of Hastings in 1066, when William the Conqueror defeated Harold and established French domination in England, the English have in fact done somewhat better than the French in war – think of Agincourt or Waterloo – and certainly as a colonial power. But the key factors in their relationship have involved ongoing bilateral cultural interchange, which was almost always asymmetrical, and until about 1900 was weighted very much in favour of the French. The English bore this inequality with varying degrees of equanimity. The French, on the other hand, have tended to feel more actively defensive, and sometimes apocalyptic, about the possible inroads of English into the citadel of French.

It is with this sentiment of impending doom that I start this chapter, though on this occasion the trigger is political and historical rather than cultural. We do not know for certain, but it may well have been Louis XIV who said *après moi, le déluge* (after me, the deluge). Another account, less regal and egotistical, and more inclusive, is ascribed to Mme de Pompadour: *après nous, le déluge* (after us, the deluge). Both of them were right, in the sense that the Revolution did indeed constitute one kind of deluge. But it is also instructive to apply this metaphor to the cultural and linguistic to-and-fro between French and English over the centuries. These reflections address the theme of these essays as formulated by John West-Sooby: 'What have the French ever done for us?', to which I shall add a slightly rephrased rider: 'What have the French done to us?' I will then turn this dictum on its head: 'What are we doing to the French?'

I begin with the first deluge, from French into English, dating from the Norman Conquest. We will then pause for an interlude to consider French language policy and planning, especially as it asserted its preeminence over the speakers of many languages who inhabited France. After policy comes the second deluge, this time reversed, from English to French. And we will conclude with a consideration of a recent and prescient analysis of the current and future prospects of the French language, presented to the Académie française by none other than the President of the Republic, M. Emmanuel Macron. He addresses a question which is unusual, even somewhat confronting, for the French: 'What is going to happen to the French language after us?' The political and historical elements have come back to shed their light on culture and language.

The first deluge: French to English

Melvyn Bragge, in his suggestively titled book *The Adventure of English: The Biography of a Language,* muses about 'what was to become English's most subtle and ruthless characteristic of all: its capacity to absorb others'.[1] These metaphors are striking and idiosyncratic. The adventure of a language? Could one without disrespect conceive of an *aventure de la langue française*? But Bragge is deliberately personifying the language, proposing to write its biography. And the personality so described as a language differs quite fundamentally from the profile of French. As we shall see, English is the ultimate mongrel language, absorbing material wherever it goes, and forming a new identity as it does so, on-the-fly. As James D. Nicoll noted, in a *bon mot* widely disseminated on the web:

> English doesn't borrow from other languages. English follows other languages down dark alleys, knocks them over, and goes through their pockets for loose grammar.

(Not to mention vocabulary, as we shall see.) What could be less French? But in the case of English, it also provides something like a linguistic analogue of a phenomenon which is already known in genetics: diversity can make one remarkably, and competitively, robust.

But I anticipate. English, of course, is not a British language. In the fifth century AD, law and order were breaking down in England, and an invitation was sent by the resident Celts to the Angles, Saxons and Jutes to come across the Channel and help. They came, and helped, and stayed. As is documented by Bede (672–735) in his monumental *Ecclesiastical History of the English People,* the new arrivals were given land in the south-east of England in return for their peace-keeping. They were illiterate. They helped to push back the Celts and Picts westwards and northwards. And the Angles, who spoke a language called Englisc, gave us the beginnings of the language as well as its name. That language, as Old English, began to flourish exceedingly.

In the ninth century, Alfred the Great, the outstanding early champion of the English language, its written monuments and translations, established in a very short time the beginnings of a sophisticated literary culture. Alfred had to struggle with incursions from the Vikings in the north-east of England, who took possession of the Danelaw and left a number of lexical borrowings behind.

But they were not a cultured invasion, and did little to threaten the growing vitality of the young Anglo-Saxon written medium.

Nevertheless, Old English had already learnt how to assimilate. From the Vikings English adopted words like:

nouns:	*law, root, birth, sky, egg, window*
verbs:	*are, call, die, cast, want*
adjectives:	*wrong, loose, ugly, flat, low*

all of which form part of the core vocabulary of Modern English. Even part of the Old English pronoun system yielded to the invaders: *they, their* and *them* replaced the Old English pronouns *hie, hiera* and *him*.[2]

All this came to an abrupt halt, or rather an intermission, in 1066. William the Conqueror defeated Harold and the English at the Battle of Hastings. Norman French became the language of the court, Latin continued in the Church, and English entered a period when it was not a major written vehicle. But while some of the English learnt French, there was no wholesale shift to the language of the conquerors – as there had been, for instance, when the inhabitants of South-East England took on English from the Angles, Saxons and Jutes. Such assimilations are not uncommon: the Turkic-speaking inhabitants of Bulgaria were speaking Slavonic a century after the Slavs conquered them.[3] In contrast, English persisted, but with a difference. The English language assimilatory sponge was already both active and efficient. David Crystal reports that, by the end of the thirteenth century, 10,000 French words had entered English.[4] And 75% of them have persisted into modern English.

And in so doing they created and grounded the typical lexical layers of modern English, where the Germanic word is for the concrete and everyday, and the French word is more stylish and educated. A typical modern example involves the pairing *flat – apartment*, where the French *apartment* has taken over the top end of the real-estate market. Of older provenance, however, are examples that persist to modern times – pairs of synonyms like:

> *lively – animated*   *reach – arrive*   *shame – disgrace*
> *mild – gentle*   *napkin – serviette*

There are near synonyms like:

> *unlawful – illegal*

and the characteristic word order of noun + adjective Noun Phrases:

> *governor-general*   *body corporate*

The novelist Sir Walter Scott famously observed in his novel *Ivanhoe* (1819) that while the names of food animals are Germanic – *ox, bull, cow, pig, sow, sheep, deer* – the names of the corresponding meats are from French – *beef, pork, mutton, venison*. Unkind commentators have drawn negative conclusions about the quality of Middle English cooking.

English also adopted technical-medical terms from French:

> *finger – digital*

as well as the tendency, already present in French, to use Greek roots for medical and technical terms. When grafted on to English this produced the three-level pattern of:

> *tooth – dental – periodontist*
> *hearty – cordial – cardiac*

The last of these contrasts with the German use of Germanic roots:

> *Herz* 'heart'   *herzlich* 'hearty'   *Herzinfarkt* 'heart attack'

Nonetheless, it is significant that all of the 100 most commonly used words in English are Germanic. The first Romance word is *just*, at position 105, followed by *people*, at position 107. The words in the first 100 are predominantly monosyllabic. But the picture is very different when we consider word formation and word-forming suffixes. Out of a selection of 45,000 words, the French contribution to English word formation is dominant:

Suffix	Number	Variant	Number
-tion	6,200		
-sion	600		
-age	1,400		
-ment	1,900		
-ant	1,900	-ent	1,900
-ance	1,000	-ence	900
-ic	8,000		
-ism	3,000	-ist	3,400
-ity	3,100		
-cy	1,300		
-able	3,900	-ible	600
-ive	2,500		
-ise	1,200	-ize	1,400

This helps to explain why so much of the abstract vocabulary of English shows not only French roots, or at least Romance consisting of French from Latin, but also patterns of Romance suffixation. True, there were attempts to promote Germanic roots over Romance, as in the fourteenth century work *The Ayenbite of Inwit*. This title is a calque – a morpheme by morpheme translation – of what would otherwise have been *The Remorse of Conscience* (*re = again* [*ayen*], *morse = bite*, *con = in*, *science* [*knowledge*] = *wit*).[5] In retrospect, we can see how different this approach is from the lexis of modern English.

This overwhelming French input was very evident to English commentators in the eighteenth century. Joseph Addison, founder of the *Spectator*, the first English newspaper, commented in 1711:

I have often wished, that as in our Constitution there are several Persons whose Business it is to watch over our Laws, our Liberties and Commerce, certain Men might be set apart as Superintendents of our Language, to hinder any Words of a Foreign Coin from passing among us; and in particular to prohibit any *French* Phrases from becoming Current in this Kingdom, when those of our own Stamp are altogether as valuable.[6]

Addison was not without sarcasm:

when we have won Battels which may be described in our own Language, why are our Papers filled with so many unintelligible Exploits, and the *French* obliged to lend us a Part of their Tongue before we can know how they are Conquered?[7]

But French was indeed omnipresent in the English of the day, and the balance with English elements was unstable and ill-defined. It was not until 1755, when Doctor Johnson published his monumental dictionary, that there was an authoritative central point which people could use for reference. The problem of assessing the limits to the language, however, turned out to be beyond even the substantial powers of Johnson:

Those who have been persuaded to think well of my design, will require that it should fix our language, and put a stop to those alterations which time and chance have hitherto been suffered to make in it without opposition. With this consequence I will confess that I flattered myself for a while; but now begin to fear that I have indulged expectation which neither reason nor experience can justify.[8]

But the sensitivity with respect to French was also omnipresent. Johnson himself noted archly (and unfairly – he had assistants) that a single Englishman, working for eight years, had produced a two-volume dictionary of 43,000 entries. Whereas the comparable task for the dictionary of the French Académie – to be sure, its publication in 1694 had antedated Johnson's by 61 years – had taken 40 Frenchmen no less than 55 years of work. Johnson's strategic decisions on many matters of spelling have persisted to this day. He followed the French model for the spelling of *programme, colour* and *theatre*, all of which were changed by Webster (to *program, color* and *theater*) in his dictionary of the American language of 1828.

The influence of French is fundamental to modern English, particularly its vocabulary. The exact proportions depend on how one counts roots and suffixes, but in broad terms 75% of the vocabulary of modern English comes from elsewhere, especially French (29%), Latin (29%), Germanic (26%) and 'other' (16%).[9] And as we have seen above, French was the channel through which many of the Latinisms arrived in English. An analysis of 10,000 words of business letters shows an even more impressive impact of French, with 41% of the tokens, as against 33% for English.[10] The Latin contribution has dropped to 15%, which is indicative of its specialised and bookish or intellectual overtones. But the 'higher' stylistic register of French-derived vocabulary nonetheless persists, as we saw in relation to Scott's *Ivanhoe*. Generations of Anglo school students would have gone through my experience of being told to avoid short and undignified words like *get, good* and *nice* in favour of longer and more Gallic vocabulary. In a more public sphere, Winston Churchill well knew the value of Anglo-Saxon vocabulary when appealing to the nation to defend itself against the Nazis in 1939:

> [...] the <u>odious apparatus</u> of Nazi rule, we shall not flag or fail. We shall go on to the end. We shall fight in France, we shall fight on the seas and <u>oceans</u>, we shall fight with growing <u>confidence</u> and growing strength in the air, we shall <u>defend</u> our island, whatever the <u>cost</u> may be. We shall fight on the beaches, we shall fight on the landing grounds, we shall fight in the fields and in the streets, we shall fight in the hills; we shall never <u>surrender</u>.[11]

Here the vocabulary of Romance origin, indicated by underlines, is down to 8%, if we allow that the word *air* was already standard in Middle English.

The precipitation of French

The trajectory of French, at least until the twentieth century, appears far more linear, incremental and organic. Until recently the visitor to metropolitan Paris saw principally a Gallophone nation, and this impression was only modified when one visited places like Brittany or the Basque region. But France is not only a multicultural, multilingual country; it has always been so.[12] However, the monolith profile of French has a very sound pedigree of more than five centuries. When François I promulgated the *Ordonnance de Villers-Cotterêts* in 1539 he made French the official language, ahead of other potential contenders like Latin and Occitan. The *Ordonnance* launched a growing sequence of work designed to establish and enhance the elegance, status and dignity of French, and the maturing of the literary language, elements which are amply illustrated in Joachim du Bellay's *Deffense et illustration de la langue francoyse* (1549), and which were formalised in the creation of the Académie française by Louis XIII and Richelieu in 1635. The Académie's *Dictionnaire* of 1694 codified and centralised the French language in a way which became the benchmark for such endeavours in Europe. The French language was henceforth a monolith, the citadel of French culture, and the home of a growing authoritarian and prescriptive list approach to language. Article 24 of its *Statuts* specifies that:

> *La principale fonction de l'Académie sera de travailler, avec tout le soin et toute la diligence possibles, à donner des règles certaines à notre langue et à la rendre pure, éloquente et capable de traiter les arts et les sciences.*[13]

> The principal function of the Académie will be to work, with all possible care and diligence, to give our language definite rules and to render it pure, elegant and able to handle the arts and sciences.

The model of the Académie, in fact, provided the empirical basis for the development of the policy and practice of language planning, where 'planning' includes the notion of management. In other words, by doing language planning in practice, the French created a set of principles and practices which were later built into both an intellectual discipline, and guidelines of language policy and its implementation, both in France and globally.

Language planning

The contemporary discipline of Language Planning incorporates three main branches.

Corpus Planning deals with the forms and usage of the language, its norms and the regulation of the language by means of prescriptive policy, dictionaries, grammars, orthographies, and the propagation of prestige models by prestige people. The *Dictionnaire* of the Académie was one of the first and most influential contributions to the Corpus Planning of French, a tendency which reached even the royal house: Henry IV, a Gascon, was subjected to language standardisation in order to purify his speech.

The French have a long history of conceptualising language in political terms.[14] In the Corpus Planning of French the centrifugal model of educated Parisian usage became the touchstone of cultured discourse throughout Europe for roughly three centuries. The aesthetics of the language was strongly carried forward by French literature and science, with goals like clarity, purity and precision. Denis Diderot, the compiler of the *Enyclopédie*, expressed the view that, while one might write tragedies in English, as Shakespeare had done, doing philosophy required one to think and write in French. And one was expected to write in a particular type of French, purified from foreign pollution. The defensive and purifying approach to French is evident as early as du Bellay, and found a more recent expression in the Loi Toubon of 1994, according to which writers using foreign elements, especially the despised Anglicisms, could be taken to court and fined, in order to excise from French the *'gangrène du français par des termes étrangers'* (gangrene of French by foreign terms). Not everyone agreed, including prominent feminist and human rights activist Françoise Seligmann:

> *Vous voulez édifier une sorte de ligne Maginot de la langue derrière laquelle le français serait à l'abri d'intrusions étrangères ...*[15]
>
> You want to erect a kind of Maginot Line for the language, behind which French would be sheltered from foreign intrusions.

The battle continues unabated, where a car salesman, offering a vehicle with *un airbag*, will be corrected and encouraged to say *coussin gonflable*.[16]

Status Planning specifies the standing of a language in relation to national and official status, and the political positioning of the language in relation to the geopolitical concept of the country. Here the *Ordonnance de Villers-Cotterêts* was one of the first instruments which established a top-down, centrist and authority-driven approach to establishing one variety of language rather than another in an official role. The status of French as the national language of France is enshrined as the first clause of Article 2 of the Constitution of the Fifth Republic:

> *La langue de la République est le français.*[17]
>
> The language of the Republic is French.

The French were one of the first nations to use language planning for explicit political centralisation. It is not widely known that, at the time of the French Revolution in 1789, only 50% of the population of France could speak any French. And even by 1871 only 25% of the population spoke French as their native language. It took time, but the French persisted, using language as a vehicle of national unification, identity, citizenship and sentiment. And, at home and abroad, as a mechanism, both centripetal and centrifugal, of elitism.

The French took this a major step further. They built what amounted to an ideology of the language, or perhaps an ideology of French nationalism with the French language as its capstone. The language became a symbol, and national index, a link to state, education, media and – in spite of the formal laicity of the French state – to church. French language became indissolubly linked to the French idea of nationhood. And this kind of symbolic, almost spiritual fusion was then imitated in many of the emerging states of Europe during the nineteenth and twentieth centuries, especially but not only among the Slavs.[18]

As a consequence of the upgrading of French in France, dialects and non-French languages were relatively suppressed, or at least defocused. Corsican, Breton, Gallo, Basque, Franco-Provençal, Occitan and Catalan are accorded 'official' status, which means that they can be used for public purposes within their own jurisdictions, without in any way infringing on the rights of French as the national language. But it is significant that France has signed, but not ratified, the European Charter for Regional or Minority Languages of 1992,[19] which would have accorded these languages and language varieties more substantial protection.

In the eighteenth and nineteenth centuries, and well into the early twentieth century, French was the international language of prestige, diplomacy, culture and society. The aristocracy, upper classes, intellectuals and cultured people in most countries of Europe were expected to know French, and to know it well. In the early nineteenth century, for instance, upper-class Russians learnt French first. Alexander Pushkin, Russia's greatest poet, only learned Russian from his nanny around the age of eight. The French language in France was monocentric, in the sense that it had only one focal point of prestige,[20] and it was managed, top-down, by the powerful instruments which projected French language and culture across Europe and beyond. Where French was administratively present it was either the national or an official language, as in Canada (and it is the sole language of Québec), Pacific islands like New Caledonia and Tahiti, and most particularly in Africa. The Organisation internationale de la francophonie (the French-speaking world), created in 1970, has 84 member states. And while French speakers amount to only 2.5% of the world population, French is the second most spoken language in Europe and the United Kingdom, the third most spoken in the European Union, the third most numerous on the Amazon website, and the fourth on the World Wide Web. 136 million people have French as a first language, and 84 million have it as a second language. French is spoken in 57 countries, on five continents, and is an official language in 29 countries.[21] French is an official language of bodies like the European Union and the International Court of Justice. At the Olympic Games it is a co-language with English, an appropriate recognition of the role of the Baron de Coubertin who was responsible for the revival of the Games in 1896.

Language in Education Planning is a more recent emanation of Language Planning, particularly in relation to countries with multilingual profiles, and to international languages which are considered to be necessary or important for political, economic, diplomatic, cultural and other purposes. French is either a first or a co-first language in many countries. In France, consistent with the policies of the European Union, the then Minister of Education, Jack Lang, officially recognised bilingual education in 2001. And for those for whom French is not a mother tongue, there is the industry of *FLE – Français langue étrangère* (French as a foreign language) – the French version of ESL or English as a Second Language. Overseas, French is promoted by the network of Alliances Françaises and the Institut Français.

The English deluge
Nonetheless, over the course of the nineteenth century the omens for the continuing pre-eminence of French were less and

less positive. The imposing outreach of the British Empire, the economic and mercantile success of Britain, particularly after the Industrial Revolution, and the slow but increasing rise of the United States of America on the world stage, all pointed to a showdown. Towards the end of the century the German Chancellor, Otto von Bismarck, noted that the dominant emerging factor of world politics was the 'inherited and permanent fact that North America speaks English'. And it was of immense significance, both practical and symbolic, that the official text of the Treaty of Versailles at the end of World War I was written not only in French, but in both French and English. The thin end of a widening wedge had publicly arrived.[22]

As Bragge noted (see above), English early developed its 'most subtle and ruthless characteristic of all: its capacity to absorb others'.[23] The French have been no less subtle and ruthless in their approach to promoting their language. Indeed, the French have often exceeded the English in their imposition of their language and culture. But their capacity to absorb others has not been one of the characteristics. And since the earliest days of their language planning in the sixteenth century, they have had a particular allergy to Anglicisms, which have been seen as various varieties of 'contamination' of the 'aggressive Anglo-Saxon elements'. This tendency accelerated enormously in the twentieth century. The ubiquitous *le weekend* made its appearance in French as early as 1926. Attempts to push back, like the introduction of the term *Baladeur* for the Sony Walkman in 1985, pale in comparison to the approaching English wave. René Étiemble's *Parlez-vous franglais* (1964) was something of a *succès de scandale*. The extent of English incursions has been documented in many lexicographic studies.[24] And the invention of Globish, a cut-down version of English for international communication, was the work of a Frenchman called Jean-Paul Nerrière working for IBM, an American international company.[25]

It is instructive to inspect the range and depth of this English penetration into French vocabulary. Had French developed Bragge's absorption capacity somewhat earlier, it might have been better adapted in evolutionary terms to cope with the influx of English items. We will consider here not outright borrowings, which are enormously abundant. I will address instead various forms of borrowing-with-adaptation, which show how English language material, both groups and affixes, have become embedded in French to the extent that French creates new words from English material in ways which could not have been the result of mere direct borrowing. Some of these lexical adaptations – it would not be appropriate to call them 'borrowings' – have been around for quite some time. Others are relatively newer.

1. *Borrowing with semantic slippage*

The first group (French examples in italics) concerns words borrowed from English but undergoing semantic re-assignment in French. The new French meanings are usually metonyms of the English originals, where there is some semantic association along a number of different possible vectors:

catch	wrestling
slip	underpants/briefs
stop	hitchhiking
snob	follower of fashion

This kind of semantic slippage is familiar when words pass from one language to another. It is what happened when English borrowed the French word *éditeur* without also borrowing the sense of 'publisher'. All the above examples are grammatically masculine. But in some cases the new French word is feminine, in this case referring to *chaussure* (shoe):

baskets	trainers, sneakers
(*baskets montantes*	high-top trainers, high-tops)

2. *Clipping with semantic slippage*

A second group involves clipping or removing the second root of a two-root English compound word or phrase:

foot	football (the game, not the ball itself)
golf	golf course, also the sport
spot	spotlight; advertisement
snack	snack bar, also something to eat
goal	goalkeeper
pull	pullover, sweater

3. **The suffix -*man***

It is significant that suffixes like the English -*man* transfer into French not only in ready-made borrowings like *caméraman,* but also in new formations which do not exist in English:

tennisman	tennis player
rugbyman	rugby player
recordman/woman	record holder (male/female)

and, with semantic shifting,

sportsman, sportswoman	jockey, also sportsman

4. **The suffix -*ing***

The very productive English suffix -*ing* has taken vigorous root in French, being morphologically productive to produce words, all masculines, which do not exist in English. They form several semantic groups:

LOCATIONS

dancing	dance hall
camping	campsite, also camping
bowling	bowling alley
parking	car park
living	living room
skating	skating rink, also roller skating

ACTIVITIES: SPORTS

footing	jogging
forcing	sports = intensive attack

ACTIONS

lifting (1955)	face-lift
zapping (pre-1986)	television channel-hopping
shopping (early 19th C)	leisurely browsing

CLOTHES

smoking	dinner jacket/tuxedo
training	tracksuit, also training
jogging	tracksuit, also jogging

SUBSTANCES

shampooing	shampoo

This list is incomplete, and to some extent impressionistic. But it illustrates ways in which English roots, suffixes and word formation processes have become embedded in French, to the point where they are creating forms which could not have been directly borrowed from English. Furthermore – and this observation is equally true of English, where people outside North America often rail at the importation of Americanisms – this process is a pull and not a push. In other words, the motivation and activity originate almost exclusively from the receiving language. From the perspective of French, in other words, this is actually a form of self-Anglicisation.

And there is push-back from the Académie, whose website – apart from providing access to the Dictionary – has a page entitled *Dire, ne pas dire* (to say or not to say: can this be an echo of *Hamlet?*) devoted to neologisms and Anglicisms, and how to approach them in a rational and French spirit.[26] On 30 June 2020, the most recent Anglicisms under criticism were *Click and collect, liker, drive, followers* and *choose France*. The Académie is working with the Commission d'enrichissement de la langue française (Commission for the Enrichment of the French Language), a body which reports to the

Prime Minister, to monitor and manage lexical and grammatical additions to the French language. They have recently proposed the replacement of *smartphone* by *mobile multifonction*, *fake news* by *information fallacieuse*, and *wifi* by *accès sans fil à l'internet*. These suggestions are long and uncomfortable, to a degree artificial, and are unlikely to succeed. But the Commission has proposed an alternative for *information fallacieuse* in the form of *infox*, a combination of *information* and the word *intox*, an informal word for disinformation. That might just work. And the pushback comes not only from the Académie. There is a good surge of outrage and resistance in the French speaking community from authors like Jean Maillet, whose 2014 book *Langue française – arrêtez le massacre!* (French language – stop the massacre!) inveighs against words like *cool* and *hashtag*, the over-enthusiastic presence of English in French advertising, and the combination of laziness and misguided snobbery, especially among younger speakers, which is seriously diluting the French content and nature of the French language.

Enter the President
On 20 March 2018 M. Emmanuel Macron, President of the French Republic, in his capacity as president and patron, visited the Académie française on the occasion of the Journée internationale de la Francophonie. He addressed a large and assembled gathering, not just the 40 *immortels* (the 'immortals', members of the Académie), on the subject of Francophonie, its current standing, where it is going, and how its forward trajectory could be managed for the benefit of the expansion and consolidation of the international status of the French language. Such a scenario would not be thinkable in the context of English, and not only because the English language has no Academy. But even if it did, even several Academies, it would be difficult to conceive of a head of state visiting to read the riot act about the current nature and future trajectory of the language. English-language politicians do not involve themselves with the

English language in such a culturally-politically engaged manner.

Nonetheless, President Macron's substantial address – consisting of nearly 9,000 words – was, as far as I can determine, the first occasion on which a French President had addressed the Académie on questions of the French language in global language policy. And though he does not use the academic jargon of language policy, his speech shows a penetrating understanding of what it is, what it does, and how it can be pressed into service to promote the renewed status of French as an international language. The President's tone is upbeat, and not without elements of *aux armes, citoyens!* (to arms, citizens!) of the 'Marseillaise'. He uses the word *bataille* twice, and *combat* no fewer than 11 times. This is not a hand-wringing piece deploring the way the French language has fallen from grace, but a proactive, reformative call to arms.

The thrust of his address was thoroughgoing, direct and directive. He presents a radical reorientation of French language planning in terms of corporate planning, status planning, and language in education planning, which constitute a redefinition of Francophonie in language, cultural centralisation, and geopolitical-economic influence. And it is this redefinition which shapes the implications for French corpus planning, French status planning and French language in education planning.

French Corpus Planning

It is fair to say that the traditional stance of the Académie has been broadly conservative, prone to xenophobia, puristic and elitist. It has also been both Paris-centric and monocentric, in the sense of sociolinguistics where there is one designated prestige variety of the language, supported by instruments of policy to implement its application.[27] This model worked well during the eighteenth and nineteenth centuries, when the status of French, and this variety of French, were accepted and propagated outside France with little overseas imposition by the Académie itself. The Académie and the

French language merely had to exist and be eloquent, elegant and authoritative, all of which they self-evidently were.

But the Francophonie that President Macron is addressing has a different topology. He talks frankly about *décentrement* (decentralisation), and how French, having formerly been *un jardin aux allées rectilingues* (a garden with rectangular paths), has now *épousé progressivement les inflexions de la planète* (progressively espoused the directions of the planet) to become a *langue archipel* (language-archipelago) in what he calls the *immense aventure de la langue française* (immense adventure of the French language). Francophonie, instead of being on the outskirts of European French, is now the entire expanse of the language. It is a community where the work of the outliers has its own existence and rationale, not just through the prism of the norms and practices approved by the Académie.

And if the *aventure* has not been a picaresque journey, but one with an articulated centre and governing instrument and apparatus, the Académie, it has its down sides too:

> *on a torturé en français, on a fait des choses merveilleuses en français et on continue à faire des choses merveilleuses et terribles en français. Il y a toujours des tyrans qui pratiquent la tyrannie en français [...].*

> people have tortured in French, done marvellous things in French, and they continue to do marvellous and terrible things in French. There are still tyrants who practise tyranny in French [...].

But behind this stands the *volonté de la liberté* (wish for freedom) which has been associated with French for so many centuries, together with its resonant and rich traditions:

> *Parler le français, l'écrire, c'est entrer dans une immense communauté d'expériences et de regards.*

> Speaking French, writing it, is to enter into an immense community of experiences and views.

It is at this point that I respectfully demur from one of the President's key points.

As we have seen, Article 24 of the Académie's *Statuts* specifies that the Académie's role is to *donner des règles certaines à notre langue et à la rendre pure, éloquente et capable de traiter les arts et les sciences* (to give our language definite rules and to render it pure, elegant and able to handle the arts and sciences) – in other words, to promote the viability of French as a language of culture and knowledge, with the implied further step of emancipation from the former dominance of Latin in these domains. There is a clear role for codification and regulation in this statute, and it is one which the Académie has sedulously applied throughout its history, especially in its constant campaign against the inroads of Anglicisms. And not only lexical Anglicisms. The movement towards gender equality in language, which began with early steps towards Political Correctness in English, has impinged on the grammar of French. What should one do with masculine nouns for the roles of public figures when that public figure is female? The Spaniards bit the grammatical bullet out of courtesy to Margaret Thatcher and added *primera ministra* (Prime Minister-female) to the former *primer ministro* (Prime Minister-masculine). But the Académie has pushed back in some of these areas, for instance in ruling against *Mme la juge* (Madam judge-feminine) in favour of the conventional *Mme le juge* (Madam judge-masculine). In this context it is curious that the President's salutations at the start of his address contain two (presumably inadvertently?) inconsistent formulations:

Madame le Secrétaire perpétuel ...

Madame La Secrétaire générale ...

Madam perpetual Secretary [masculine]

Madam general Secretary [feminine]

But that is, in one sense at least, history. The President is firm and consistent in his insistence that the rules of the Académie should be *adaptées à l'usage* (adapted to usage), and not the instrument of this or that ideological or political tendency. And by *usage* he specifically includes the whole range of French as practised in Francophonie:

> *la francophonie est une sphère dont la France avec sa responsabilité propre et son rôle historique n'est qu'une partie agissante, volontaire mais consciente de ne pas porter seule le destin du français.*
>
> Francophonie is an area of which France, with its particular responsibility and its historical role, is only one active party, willing but conscious that it does not bear the destiny of French alone.

And that deceptively simple statement has enormous implications for the content and conduct of the French language. Given that there may be 700 million speakers of French in the not distant future – a figure quoted by the President – and most of those will be in French West Africa, the balance is about to undergo a decisive shift. Under the traditional model, Francophonie was a broad area surrounding a core of European continental French, and especially Académie-French. In the new model, the privileged position of France-French is subsumed in a new decentralised international, and indeed supranational, language space:

> *Le français s'est au fond émancipé de la France, il est devenu cette langue monde, cette langue archipel [...].*
>
> French has fundamentally become emancipated from France, it has become this global language, this archipelago-language [...].

The metaphor of the archipelago is striking and destabilising. It invokes an extended, potentially discontinuous, space, one which is no longer specifically centrifugal with authority and influence emanating from Paris. And in this space the norms of the French language of Francophonie will be pluricentric and distributed. The parallelism with the international profile which English has achieved is not articulated, but it is inescapable. We will potentially be dealing with *langues françaises* (in the plural), just as there is already a scholarly journal called *World Englishes*.

French status planning
Within this new and enlarged Francophonie the French language will – with the corpus adjustments that we have considered – be the de facto dominant language. Here the President is talking not only of status in the conventional sense, but also of functionality in terms of activity and roles, both nationally but especially trans-nationally.

There are issues of European Union language policy to be sorted out in France, but these receive no coverage from the President. The numbers of French speakers will doubtless continue to grow, especially in Africa. And French will continue to offer the benefits of its long and rich traditions. Here there is an indisputable problem in the form of English and its dominant position, not least as the international lingua franca. Here the President is discreet. He refers to English, the elephant in the room, only thrice, and in a strategic rather than a combative way:

L'anglais n'a sans doute jamais été aussi présent à Bruxelles au moment où nous parlons de « Brexit ». Cette domination n'est pas une fatalité, il nous appartient simplement de retrouver là aussi quelques règles, de réinvestir certains lieux et de refaire du français une langue par laquelle on accède à ces opportunités que j'évoquais.

English has doubtless never been as wholly present in Brussels as at this time when we are speaking of 'Brexit'. This domination is not inevitable; it is simply incumbent upon us to rediscover several rules there as well, to reoccupy certain domains and to re-make of French a language through which people have access to the opportunities that I was referring to.

But there is a problem here, which has two main aspects: the need to retain language functions for first-language French speakers, and the need to tackle head-on the dominant position of English, at least with the goal of not ceding further ground, and ideally of establishing a new and vibrant base of L1 (first language) French speakers in the new enlarged Francophonie.

The task is not trivial. Of the scientific journals indexed in Scopus, 80% are English-language, which leaves not much room for French, German, Spanish and Russian, not to mention Chinese. In second language education world-wide outside Anglophone countries, English is overwhelmingly the first choice. And in commerce, tourism and international geopolitics, English is the language first chosen after the homeland language, even for use among speakers neither of whom has English as a first language. The advantages of learning English are so evident, and by such a wide margin, that nothing short of an elaborate and well targeted policy of French language promotion will have much chance of success.

The President has some ammunition, primarily leveraging activities and institutions already in place. Institutions like Agence France Presse. He also has an intriguing new role for the socio-topology of French. Rather than abandoning the field for English to be the default go-to language for speakers of other languages, he proposes to anchor French as a key player and promoter of international plurilingualism. Rather than promoting only or primarily French in the domain of Francophonie, as has been the dominant theme in the past, French is presented instead as a partner language for other languages. This would happen in two main ways. One would be for France to promote and support the production of quality dictionaries in the many languages with which it comes into contact. This would help to promote and validate the status and corpus definition of the languages with which French comes into contact in the Francophonie, and potentially elsewhere. The other would be to promote the production of bilingual dictionaries with French as one of the paired languages. French thus becomes not only an anchor for the 'other' language, but also the portal for speakers of that other language to access the international world where French already has a substantial position, reputation and networks:

> *La Francophonie doit faire droit aux autres langues, en particulier aux autres langues européennes mais à toutes les langues que la mondialisation fragilise ou isole.*

> Francophonie must valorise other languages, especially other European languages but also all languages which globalisation weakens or isolates.

The profile of French in this conception is far from the centralised prescriptive tradition. It is outwardly oriented, engaged, active and proactive, a language of interchange:

> *La Francophonie doit pouvoir toucher ces nouveaux publics, aller vers ceux qui ne viennent pas à nous [...].*

> Francophonie must be able to reach these new audiences, to reach out to those who do not come to us [...].

Language in education planning

The President is strategic and determined on language in education policy. As Robert Kaplan and Richard Baldauf and many others have argued, an effective language in education policy needs advocacy top-down and bottom-up, in addition to organisation, motivation, support, superior pedagogy, and resourcing.[28] Here the President is right on target. He speaks warmly and persuasively of the standing, dignity and contribution of language teachers, and of the central importance of training a cadre of quality teachers. He speaks with warmth of the core value of places like libraries. He points language pedagogy squarely at technology and the potential of MOOCs (Massive Open Online Courses, in French *CLOM = Cours en Ligne, Ouverts et Massifs*). He announces the unification of the Institut Français and the Alliances Françaises, and the creation of a Laboratoire de la Francophonie at Villers-Cotterêts, roughly between Reims and Paris and home of the 1539 *Ordonnance*, which also happened to be the domicile of the writer Alexandre Dumas. That is indeed putting one's decentralising money where one's mouth is. He places student numbers and teaching institutions on the table as policy lines with expansion targets often exceeding double. He ramps up the hours of study and access for students to French language instruction, both outside and in France. Quality language learning costs, and he has no hesitation in underwriting what it takes to achieve these goals, including access to libraries as places for the deeper assimilation and learning of French, its culture and its ways of thinking.

And he has some less conventional, and striking, policy proposals. The education of young women stands out as being something which is sorely neglected in many parts of the world, and he sees French as a language of emancipation and socialisation, on the one hand for immigrants and refugees in France itself, but also in the countries where French, as a first or second language, can be a vehicle of new learning.

If the ESL (English as a Second Language) industry is driven buyer-side by response to demand, the FLE (Français langue étrangère = French as a foreign language) industry is at least partly underpinned by the attraction of quality provision. The international network of Alliances Françaises, unlike anything except the British Council for English, are renowned for quality pedagogy. Their core funding comes from France. This soft diplomacy works (as the Chinese Confucius Institutes are discovering), and the French are exceedingly good at it.

Corpus and status: Centricity
We can pull these various threads together by contrasting the profiles, along a number of specific diagnostic factors, of the pre-Macron profile – one could almost say 'ideology' – of French

and that of English. This analysis is simplified to a degree, and deliberately uses a number of metaphors which are more heuristic than determinative. But its justification is that it aims to capture some of the key shifts which President Macron's address to the Académie is aiming to promote.

As we have seen, some languages like Japanese and Russian have a single agreed prestige form with official status, and are labelled monocentric – they have a single 'centre' which serves as the reference point for the prestige variant and for guidance on accepted or recommended usage.[29] Other languages like English are pluricentric, with multiple norms – British, American, Canadian, Australian, New Zealand and so on. Chinese, German and Spanish are also manifestly pluricentric. French is commonly seen as an *'exemple assez peu controversé d'une langue monocentrique'* (hardly controversial example of a monocentric language).[30] It has a reasonably transparent expression of a top-down, normative language based in a single nation-state, and with a strong tradition of 'bon usage'.[31] The dissemination of norms is centrifugal from educated normative French French. And the Académie projects and enforces prescriptive and proscriptive norms. The underlying ideology of language is purifying and managing. Diglossia – the coexistence of two languages, or two varieties of the same language, throughout a speech community – is seen in terms of variation *from* the norm, and French presents as overall self-contained and, at least insofar as the Académie is able to achieve this goal, homogeneous. And France is the only country where French is the sole official language.

In contrast, English has a far more distributed model. It is the single or co-national language in multiple countries, and the differentiation into Commonwealth vs American provides a fundamental bifurcation of norms which has no parallel in French. Diglossia in English is endemic, to the point where a journal can bear the title *World Englishes*; it is not yet feasible to consider the existence of *langues françaises* (French languages). And while it is still possible to consider metaphors of French in terms of core and edges, English is characterised by multiple overlapping grey areas and an unruly creativity which is largely not controlled. There is, for example, no direct French equivalent of urbandictionary.com, an un-moderated, and sometimes immoderate, online collecting place for English neologisms and new phrases and meanings. English is permeable, and as Bragge noted, that is part of its ethos and historical strength. It is defined in a more bottom-up fashion, and its norms are inductively set by usage and consensus. In contrast, French still preserves elements of top-down elegant authority.

Nonetheless, the growing norms of French in Quebec,[32] Louisiana, Haiti and French West Africa,[33] as well as New Caledonia,[34] show that French does not wholly fit into the binary opposition between monocentric and pluricentric. There is a clear sense in which French is more than simply monocentric, though it is also incontrovertibly less pluricentric than English. There are emerging standards outside France, less in the written language but certainly in the many spoken variants of French. And it is this pluricentric, distributed – and dare one say English? – model which M. Macron is advocating for the onward path of French.

Envoi

The Académie française has always been a top-down, directive institution. So it was appropriate and consistent for the President, who is also the President of the Académie, to address them in a similar vein, not that he actually used the phrase 'top-down' on that occasion. However, on 29 March 2018, only nine days after his address to the Académie française, M. Macron was addressing the Collège de France on the subject of artificial intelligence. During this presentation, and in a later tweet, he used a phrase which evoked barely-suppressed bruxism among the purists:

La démocratie est le système le plus bottom up de la terre.

Democracy is the most bottom-up system in the world.

Bottom up? Maybe the French President had been reading Bragge's 2003 book on English, and was exploring, in a French context, the evolutionary advantages which follow when a language becomes adept at absorption.

On Diplomacy

The management of relations between kingdoms or states is probably as old as civilisation itself. The earliest records are the Amarna letters written on clay tablets exchanged between the kings of ancient Egypt and the sovereigns of neighbouring kingdoms such as Babylon and Assyria during the fourteenth century BC. Even further back, during the Bronze Age, according to the Homeric epics, precious gifts were exchanged between rulers as a sign of friendship, a form of diplomatic practice with overtones of trade. It was therefore not the French who gave us diplomacy as such.

They certainly gave us the word, however, along with much of the language used to designate the agents and practices involved in the negotiation of international relations. The eighteenth-century French word 'diplomatique' (1721), which gave rise – during the French Revolutionary period, interestingly enough – to 'diplomatie' (1791) and then 'diplomate' (1792), was derived from the ancient Greek word *diplōma*, meaning 'folded paper', itself a derivative of *diplóos*, meaning 'double'. In the eighteenth century, folding a document in two and sealing it was a means of ensuring its contents remained secret. Sovereign rulers had developed the habit of providing their emissaries with such folded documents as a sign of their official privilege.

The position of power which France forged for itself during the early modern period, from the late Renaissance through to the Enlightenment and beyond, ensured that French thrived as the international language of diplomacy. The strict rules governing its syntax also meant that the French language was ideally suited to diplomatic discourse, with its requirement for precision. In more recent times, English has no doubt supplanted French as the world's lingua franca, but French remains an important international language and it has left a lasting legacy with respect to the language of diplomacy. No self-respecting embassy could do without a *chef de mission*, a *chargé d'affaires* or several *attachés*. A period of *rapprochement* between two countries might lead to a *détente* in their relations, and, in the best of scenarios, to an *entente cordiale*. Such developments are the subject of reports compiled by a *rapporteur* and announced via a *communiqué*. And then there are the many other terms that define the workings of the diplomatic world – from 'embassy' and 'ambassador' to 'conspiracy' and 'espionage' – that have all been anglicised from the French.

The language, of course, serves to reflect an essential cultural and political reality – that of the negotiation of international relations. This often means that diplomats, whose task it is to implement their country's foreign policy, devote much of their time to the portfolios of trade and conflict resolution. Those two areas have certainly been prominent in the relationship between France and Australia during the course of the twentieth century and up to the present. The historical list of international bilateral treaties between the two countries confirms this. Many of the earliest treaties concerned the extradition of fugitive criminals, but issues relating to war and peace – such as the question of war graves in France at the end of World War 1 – soon became a regular subject of negotiated agreement, as did trade.

The treaties dating from the nineteenth century, before Australia became a sovereign nation, were established between France and the British Empire, and thus extended to Australia by virtue of its status as a Dominion of that empire. But even after Australia's Federation on 1 January 1901, bilateral treaties with France continued for some time to be mediated by Great Britain. It was only in 1937 that

Australia signed a bilateral treaty with France in its own name – the 1937 Commercial Agreement. This suggests that Australia's foreign policy as a young nation was principally determined by London, and this seems in many respects to have been the case. But that does not mean that Australian leaders and officials left relations with France entirely in the hands of their British counterparts. On the contrary, as Colin Nettelbeck demonstrates, the Australian government was particularly active in engaging with France in the aftermath of the First World War, the sacrifice of so many Australians serving as a solid basis for the establishment of bilateral relations. The following essay offers a detailed analysis of that direct engagement with the French on the part of Australian representatives. In so doing, it presents a persuasive case for reassessing the role of France in Australia's growth to diplomatic and political independence.

JWS

2

Colin Nettelbeck

France and the French in Australia's growth to nationhood: 1914–1945

Preamble

Any reference in current times to the French-Australian relationship inevitably conjures up the now defunct Joint Strategic Partnership Agreement signed between the two countries in 2012 and reaffirmed in March 2017, before it was controversially abandoned in September 2021 in favour of the trilateral security pact between Australia, the United Kingdom and the United States, known as AUKUS. The French-Australian partnership agreement included the following statement:

> As friends and partners, together they address increasing global challenges, such as terrorism, transnational, serious and organised crime proliferation, and climate change. The two countries work together closely in order to foster innovative, sustainable and balanced growth.[1]

One key expression of the partnership was, of course, the submarine contract, which the French Ministry of Defence hailed as the beginning of a long, actual marriage between France and Australia.[2]

Submarines, as it turns out, are a good metaphor of things that exist beneath the surface, and it is to some of those things that I want to turn my attention here. The submarine contract and its subsequent demise are just one of the manifestations of a relationship that goes back a long time – almost to the time of European settlement of Australia. More precisely, though, I want to argue that France and the French have played a quite specific role in Australia's growth to nationhood. The period I have chosen is one that reveals the relationship's complexities: from the military alliance of World War I to the appointment of Australia's first ambassador to France in 1945, the tension between attempts to forge closer bonds, on the one hand, and frequently resurgent distrust and conflict, on the other hand, was crucial to Australia's self-definition and self-positioning in a geopolitical world that was anything but stable.[3]

Introduction

At 10.45 pm on Thursday 16 October 1941, a 31-year-old South Australian lance-corporal died in the 1st Australian General Hospital in Gaza, Palestine. His right leg had just been amputated high in the thigh, too late to stop the septicaemia, in the pre-penicillin era. Over the previous three-and-a-half months, a stubborn infection kept attacking the knee he had injured when he stumbled in rocky terrain during a campaign that neither he nor anyone else in the Australian army had any idea they were to be involved in. This was the Lebanon-Syria campaign, quite suddenly and unexpectedly ordered by Winston Churchill in response to his fears that the French Government in Vichy was preparing to open use of its airfields in Syria to German aviation. This was a short campaign, that ran for just five weeks from 12 June. It has largely been forgotten, and the few historians who have studied it in detail consider it to have been unnecessary, and indeed a costly distraction, an example of one of Churchill's less glorious decisions.[4]

I have chosen this episode to begin my reflection on the ways in which Australia and Australians have interacted with France and the French in Australia's development because it exemplifies two significant points. Firstly, it shows how strongly dependent on

Mother Britain Australia's military and political stances and actions still were. We know that, from Federation in 1901 until the Second World War, Australia's foreign policy was almost totally defined by Britain, and ongoing Australian diplomatic representation abroad existed only in Britain, the US and Canada. The second point follows from the first, namely that by no choice of their own, Australian soldiers (along with their fellow Commonwealth citizens from India) found themselves involved in killing and being killed by French soldiers, direct descendants of the very people with and for whom their own fathers and uncles had fought only a generation earlier. What Richard James calls an 'unlikely enemy' for Britain was even more unlikely for Australia. True, in 1941, Australia was far from shedding its own obsession with being British, but it had for some time been demonstrating fractious signs of its own distinctiveness, a process in which – as I hope to demonstrate – the role of France and the French was of far more importance than historians have commonly recognised.

In a general way, as Alexis Bergantz masterfully demonstrated in his 2015 PhD thesis, until the First World War, European Australians to a large extent simply inherited and continued historic British ambivalences towards the French: they were 'inheritors of a deeply entangled and complex cross-Channel relationship':[5]

> From food to fashion, high art to sexual degeneracy, and conflicting ideas and ideals of masculinity and femininity, Frenchness played an important part in what it meant to be civilised in the antipodes.[6]

And indeed, French impact on Australia's development is hardly unexpected. France, after all, at least until the Second World War, was universally recognised by friends and enemies alike as a beacon of civilisation and invention, and as a great military power. Whether in Britain, Spain, Italy, Germany, Russia, Japan, Thailand, the United States or Argentina, mastery of the French language and knowledge of its literature and thought were considered fundamental to a good education. The French Age of Enlightenment and the ensuing Revolution were universal reference points, and French was the language of diplomacy throughout the world until World War II. For much of the nineteenth century, Australian booksellers did a brisk trade in French language texts of all kinds, and we are all aware of the dozens of Australian artists – men and women such as John Peter Russell and Evelyn Chapman – who from the late nineteenth century on, made the long journey to Paris or other parts of France, to learn and refine their skills, often returning home to integrate their work into the Australian ethos.[7]

From another angle, most of us are probably aware, too, of various French people who, through their activities in Australia, have influenced the ways in which our culture has developed. A 2015 book edited by Éric Berti and Ivan Barko, called *French Lives in Australia*, contains a couple of dozen essays on explorers, diplomats, writers, artists, musicians, teachers, religious figures and so on, who are good examples of this kind of individual or institutional influence.[8] And as the editors point out, many more such stories could be told. This is a task currently being addressed by the Institute for the Study of French-Australian Relations (ISFAR) under the French-Australian Dictionary of Biography project. Here is a list of twenty more names:

Jacques Arago	Juliette Henry
Antoine Bruni d'Entrecasteaux	Charles Lancial
Joseph Chaleyer	Roger Laufer
Oscar Comettant	Charles-Alexandre Lesueur
Louis Coutance	Mirka Mora
Antoine Denat	Henri Rochefort
Irma Dreyfus	Jean Rosemberg
Charles Duret	Louis Sentis
Rose Freycinet	Marius Sestier
Henri Gilbert	Jean Trémoulet

Each of these people, at one time or another, has made a notable contribution (though not always a positive one) to Australian life. Readers might like to see how many of the twenty they can identify.

One area of French-Australian interaction where historical study has boomed is the French voyages of discovery of the eighteenth and nineteenth centuries. Since the pioneering work of Ernest Scott in the early twentieth century, there has been a steady flow of writing on this topic, notably by Adelaide scholars Jean Fornasiero and John West-Sooby. There are some complicated historical questions associated with many of those voyages. What did the French really contribute to the cartography of the Australian coastline? Were their intentions as purely scientific as some claim, or were there secret ideas – or at the least, latent desires – for settlement, colonisation and even invasion? One of the interesting aspects of such questions, beyond the indelible suspicion of Gallic perfidy that Australians have inherited from the British, is the irrational wondering, and even yearning, that is often expressed by otherwise quite sane Australians when they affirm that 'we' might have been French.[9] Then they ponder what it might have been like. It is, of course, obvious that, had Australia been settled by the French in the wake of Saint Aloüarn's 1772 claim in the west, or successfully conquered and permanently held thanks to some François Péron-inspired invasion of New South Wales, there would have been no 'we' and no 'what if' question.[10] On the other hand, I am inclined to ask if there is not, underlying this fanciful and speculative dreaming, another question – something like: 'What if we could be something different from what we are, something that is other than what the British origins of our nation have given us?' Now this question, in the context of the multiethnic and multicultural Australia of the post-World War II era, would be anachronistic and even just plain silly, were it not for my contention that one of the crucial elements in Australia's dramatic evolution is precisely the perspective offered by Australia's engagement with France and the French. My response to those who wonder what it would be like if Australia had been French is that it *is* much more shaped by contact with France than most people realise, and more than some others would care to know.

* * *

In what follows, I need to alert readers that this is work in progress, without any claim to being definitive. I am trying to bring light to an area I see as having suffered from historical neglect. I shall be using a time framework that encompasses three phases: the First World War and its aftermath, the inter-war period, and the Second World War and its aftermath. For reasons that will hopefully become clear, there will be more emphasis on the first period. Within the timeframe, I shall draw on four principal topic areas: military, civilian, economic and political.

The First World War and its aftermath
That France and the French entered so powerfully into the Australian consciousness in World War 1 was a result of the scale and intensity of the contact. This was the case most obviously for the military, but it was also the case for Australia's civilian population, and for the nation's wartime political leader, William Morris Hughes. That multi-level, multi-faceted contact led to a serious attempt, before the war ended, to create a large-scale direct bilateral economic relationship between the two nations. It is true that Australia went to war in 1914 as a British dominion under the aegis of the Entente Cordiale signed between Britain and France in 1904, but it is equally true that Australian soldiers always identified themselves as distinctively Australian and did so more and more vigorously as the war proceeded. And this determination to be recognised as Australian was just as much marked in relation to the French as it was in relation to the British.

That said, the first level of engagement, militarily, was as allies, and the Australians, for most of the war, and not seldom to the frustration of the troops, were under British command and were usually perceived by their French counterparts as generic 'English'. This was particularly true in relation to the ill-conceived, ill-fated and disastrously failed Dardanelles campaign. Australians generally are unaware that, when our troops landed at Gallipoli on 25 April 1915, the French had already been in the vicinity for a month. Ultimately, France would lose more dead and wounded than Australia, but what both nations had in common, without knowing it at that stage, was that they were both engaged on that front because of a bad British decision (driven by one Winston Churchill). The Australians, being under British command, had no choice in the matter; the French, fearful of ulterior British motives in respect to the Middle East as a whole, also felt they had no choice but to be there. Both France and Australia were victims of the same British fiasco.

The really substantial contact began from March 1916, when the Australian army was sent to the Western Front. Over the next two-and-a-half years, more than 295,000 young men and over 2,000 young women nurses voluntarily served in the theatre of war, at a time when the population of Australia was under five million. Of the men, over 60% (178,000) would be casualties and more than a quarter of that number killed (46,000).[11] I do not want to talk about that carnage, which left chasms of grief among so many families across the whole country and which remains a source of bitter and contested reflection in the nation's identity narrative even today. Rather, I want to insist on the considerable amount of evidence that, as this massive contingent of Australians got to know France and its people, a wave of veritable francophilia emerged. We find expressions of this love for France as a country and for the French as a people in soldiers' and nurses' diaries, in their letters home, in texts they wrote for trench journals, in post-war reflections on their experience, in the work of war artists, even in musical compositions. I shall give a couple of examples here.

The first is an extract from E.J. Rule's *Jacka's Mob* (1933). Edgar John Rule saw his share of brutality and gore, having fought at Gallipoli before moving to France, where he rose to the rank of sergeant, serving under the legendary Albert Jacka, Australia's first Victoria Cross recipient. Rule himself was wounded in action, and his accounts of military conflict do not mince words about the horror of the experience. And yet, we also find this highly romanticised, almost idyllic description of his journey from Marseille to the front:

> I have often wondered why it was that this trip through France left *an impression on our men's minds that was never erased* – a memory which men fondled to themselves, certain that no greater joy awaited them in the years to come. It was the month of June, and everything was radiant. Perhaps we were suffering the reaction from our experiences in the desert. For sixty hours we forgot that we were on a deadly mission [...].
>
> Mansions nestling in the folds of the hills, and old castles perched on crags, overlooked the verdant valleys, while the beautiful River Rhône was never out of the picture in the early stages of the journey. *The farms were the envy of us all.* Everything was so peaceful that the existence of a state of war was almost incredible. *At the main French cities, maidens handed out refreshments, chatting and laughing the while. Few understood them, but what did it matter. Eyes were sufficient.*[12]

There is much to be said about this text. Rule is clearly testifying that the joy of discovering France in 1916 was not just his own impression but a phenomenon shared by many. And there is plenty of other evidence that he was right. He also emphasises the physical beauty of southern France, but he especially notes the farms, and here we can remember that many of his fellow soldiers would have been from rural areas, with experience of much harsher landscapes. Admiration for the French care of the land is a fairly common reaction from Australian soldiers. It deepened their understanding of why the French were so vigorous in their defence of their territory; it also intensified their distress at the destruction of so much farmland by the war. And then, at the end, there is the sense of open-hearted welcome from French people.

At the other end of the Australians' sojourn in France, in early 1919, when those who were still left were waiting for ships to take them home, we find a text which I have elsewhere described as a 'landmark document in French-Australian friendship'.[13] This is the little magazine called The "Dernière Heure", published by Australian soldiers in Rouen.

Cover of The "Dernière Heure" (1919)
[NLA, Bib ID 507396]

Its literary editor, James R.W. Taylor (future London editor for the *Sydney Morning Herald* and hence a voice of some resonance and influence) was both an ardent promoter of Australian specificity and a total Francophile. When he evokes France, he does not just wax lyrical, he gushes:

> What can explain that love for France which fills the heart of the average Australian? Is it the fact that he is merely fascinated by the natural loveliness of the most beautiful country in the World? Is it because he has helped to defend her village and homes? Or is it because so many mates must lie forever under the shadow and protection of the tri-colour? No, it is scarcely an affection springing from such sources. It is more spontaneous, more natural, perhaps. One would say, rather, that it was the direct result of an intense admiration for a people who have endured the cruellest suffering imaginable with a fortitude of iron.[14]

We can note that, like Rule, Taylor thinks that he is speaking not just for himself, but for Australians in general. While editorial selection undoubtedly plays some part in it, there are many elements in *The 'Dernière Heure'* that support his view. Here are a couple of other examples, one an excerpt from an anonymous piece of doggerel, the other a piece by a French woman, illustrated by the magazine's artistic editor, Cyril Leyshon White.

> We left the old spot with regret.
> 'Twas home away from home
> And never will the boys forget
> When far across the foam
> The many friends they left behind
> In that old Norman town,
> Who to the Aussies were most kind,
> And never turned them down.[15]

'Au pays du soleil' ('In the land of the sun'), by Madame Georgy Pilar.
Artist: Cyril Leyshon White.
The "Dernière Heure", p. 30 [NLA, Bib ID 507396]

The woman in the picture is throwing a bouquet of mimosa to the Australian soldiers on behalf of a 'grateful France' ('la France reconnaissante').

This positive discovery of France and the French by Australia's soldiers – and one could adduce similar responses from a great

First page of a letter from Dr Helen Sexton to
Lady Helen Munro-Ferguson, dated 11 August 1915
[Australian Red Cross Archives, University of Melbourne]

many nurses as well – had more than its equivalent in the civilian population back in Australia. It is worth dwelling here on the general phenomenon of seemingly spontaneous generosity displayed by the Australian population in relation to suffering abroad. At the beginning of the war, fundraising activities sprang up everywhere for Belgium. But this was quickly overtaken by much larger efforts for France. In July 1915, while the Gallipoli campaign was still in its early stages, and nine months before the Australian soldiers landed in France, three Melbourne women, together with the two daughters of one of them, with the support of the French authorities, established at their own expense a 21-bed hospital for wounded French soldiers in Auteuil, in Paris. Their leader and medical officer was the formidable Dr Helen Sexton (1862–1950), the first female medical graduate from the University of Melbourne.

On 11 August 1915, Dr Sexton wrote a letter to Lady Helen Munro-Ferguson, President of the Australian Branch of the British Red Cross, describing what she and her friends had achieved. In the letter, she identifies her work as being partly in the cause of raising French opinion about 'the English', but the letterhead – 'HÔPITAL AUSTRALIEN DE PARIS' – unambiguously marks the Australian nature of the enterprise. She grumbles about French red tape, but pays tribute to the French soldiers and to the care they get from their own medical officers.[16]

Even earlier than Helen Sexton's remarkable adventure, back in Australia, two French women – Augustine Soubeiran (1858–1933) and Charlotte Crivelli (1863–1958) – had undertaken fundraising activities that, over the course of the war, would result in around twenty-eight million dollars, in today's terms, being raised from civilian Australia for the French war effort. Anyone wishing to know more about these amazing women will find detailed essays on them in the book *French Lives in Australia*, mentioned earlier.[17] Let us simply note here a few points about each of them. Soubeiran was a prominent member of Sydney's French community, and one of the founding principals of Kambala school, in Rose Bay. From late 1914, she was a driving force behind the French-Australian League of Help which, with the active support of the New South Wales State Premier, William Holman, gathered huge amounts of goods and money for France. Crivelli was a Melbourne resident, the wife of the city's most eminent French doctor. Like Soubeiran, she was a central figure in the French community, and was exceedingly well connected in the Melbourne establishment, always able to count on the support of leading figures from the political, business and legal worlds. While Soubeiran's activities were largely limited to New South Wales, Crivelli, who had four sons fighting in the war, managed to extend hers to Tasmania, Western Australia, South Australia and Queensland. There is no doubt that these women were both masterful fundraisers, well organised, brilliant handlers of publicity and propaganda, and endowed with seemingly inexhaustible energy. But it remains a fact, and for me an astonishing one, that the success of their initiatives depended on the sustained willingness of the Australian public – urban and rural, school children and adults, working-class people and the bourgeoisie – to put their concerns for the French on a footing comparable to their *sollicitude* for their own brothers, fathers, uncles and cousins, who, as the war advanced, were dying and being wounded in ever greater numbers. Melanie Oppenheimer, in her work on the Australian Red Cross, has underscored the harnessing of Australian civilian generosity for Australian troops under the leadership of Lady Helen Munro-Ferguson;[18] but the efforts of Soubeiran and Crivelli for French soldiers, widows and orphans, in goods and money, come to at least a third as much of what the Australian Red Cross raised during the war, and perhaps as much as half.[19]

One can ascribe the motivation for such generosity to Australian civil desire to support the country and people for whom their own soldiers were fighting – the nation's army may have left home to fight in the name of King and Empire, but the experience of the Western Front brought a quite different focus. In the press, in school papers and in the speeches from political leaders, France and the French were constantly portrayed as Jim Taylor presented them: courageous, long-suffering victims of brutal aggression, determined defenders of all that was good against horrendous evil.

But francophilia was also a political force, and even a political strategy. We have already noted the overt francophilia of the

New South Wales Premier William Holman. That other William, Prime Minister Billy Hughes, was no less forthright in his praise of the French. Hughes, somewhat to the discomfort of the British and many of his fellow Australian politicians, had not been slow, after his election to the Prime Ministerial role in 1915, to adopt a distinctively and aggressively Australian discourse in relation to foreign affairs. He was convinced that the scope of Australia's participation in the war had earned the fledgling nation the right to a place in international decision-making for the future of the world. He talked himself onto the world stage in 1916, for the Paris Economic Conference, and again after the Armistice, for the Versailles Peace Conference. Here is one of Hughes's statements from the 1916 visit:

> The spectacle of France in this great crisis is at once glorious and inspiring. The indomitable spirit of the people has filled me with admiration. I have seen women, old men, and children efficiently doing the work at home while menfolk are fighting. I have tendered them, on behalf of the Commonwealth and of Australian soldiers, the right hand of friendship, and have declared we will fight side by side until the invaders of France have been driven off.[20]

If we suspect that Hughes's constant buttering up of the French had ulterior motives, we would be right, from at least two different perspectives. Firstly, he wanted French help in making gains for Australia in the post-war settlement of accounts: he wanted Australia to receive significant reparations for its costs, he wanted Australia to be given the mandate to govern Germany's former colonial possessions in the Pacific, and he did not want the United States to dictate the terms of the Peace or the constitution of the League of Nations; he even wanted France to cede its place in the New Hebrides. Secondly, Hughes was attempting to use the French as leverage to give Australia a stronger voice *within* the British Empire. Hughes was a supporter of the Empire through and through, but his conception of what it meant did not include unchallenged centralised control from London. Developing closer relations directly with France was for him a way of making this point.

But self-interest does not preclude a genuine admiration, on Hughes's part, for French culture and achievement. At the Lyon Fair in 1919, he began a lasting friendship with the Mayor (and future French Prime Minister and President) Édouard Herriot, by delivering a stirring speech, in French, in which he extolled the future of Australian direct trade with France. He returned to France in 1921 to visit the Somme, at a time when the mediocre results of his earlier diplomacy were well established, but this did not prevent him from continuing to voice his enthusiasm for French achievements and seeking stronger direct relations. Here is the newspaper report on the speech he gave at Amiens:

> [He said] that France was a great country, equally great in peace. Civilisation would have groped in darkness but for this nation, with her gorgeous record in arts, sciences, and literature. The very name of France [is] a synonym for valour.
>
> 'If Australia is to hold what she has, and achieve more,' said Mr. Hughes, 'she must have friends. Where would she find them, except among those who faced with her the greatest trial to which humanity has been exposed since the beginning of the world. [...] We are a nation of but yesterday, like a flower opening in the morning [...], but we have proved ourselves fit to stand beside even France. The future of civilisation is likely to be fostered and nourished through the influence of the British Empire and France.'[21]

Hughes's desires were not, alas, to be fulfilled, though for a time it looked as if they may be. Military and civilian sentiment, together with political determination, facilitated the French government's agreement to the Australian request for a large-scale Economic Mission to be sent to Australia. It was an expensive commitment, and the visit, conducted by a strong team of specialists under the titular headship of the venerable General Pau, lasted almost six months, from 10 September 1918 to 1 March 1919. As Robert Aldrich has pointed out, the goals of the Mission included military and political dimensions, as well as economic ones.[22] The French wanted a continuation of Australia's contribution to the war effort and hoped for assistance in reconstruction; they also wanted to discuss the future of their role in the Pacific, especially in the New Hebrides. Economically, they were interested in displacing Germany as an Australian trade partner, and in redressing a balance of trade that was grossly in Australia's favour, largely because of French purchases of Australian wool.

The political and popular reception of the Mission as it toured Australia was nothing short of spectacular: it had the grandeur of a royal visit, and in many ways a broader reach, in that the Mission travelled extremely widely and received, from the authorities and from its own research, huge amounts of information. The reports of the Mission contained many recommendations and aspirations, very few of which, at least in the short term, amounted to anything. The presence of the Mission continued to foster the goodwill of the Australian public towards France: Australian support for the war effort, both military and civilian, continued to flow strongly. The Australian Branch of the French Red Cross conspicuously presented General Pau with a cheque for £100,000 (the equivalent of several million dollars today), and it is more than plausible that the momentum created by the Mission played into the post-Armistice enthusiasm in Australia for supporting French reconstruction, including the adoption by Australian cities of the French towns of Poilcourt (Sydney), Dernancourt (Adelaide) and Villers-Bretonneux (Melbourne). But although strong French participation in Australia's wool trade resumed after the war, Australia, fixated as it was on protectionist economic and ethnic policies and on its dependency on Britain, was in truth simply not ready to develop independent relations with France, or with any other country outside the Empire and the US. Only in 1936, after a nasty period of tariff wars, did Australia and France finally sign a bilateral trade agreement. In the intervening period, France was not much more, from an Australian governmental policy perspective, than one of the three reliable and significant customers for the nation's 'sheep's back' economy – the others being Britain and Japan.

The Inter-War Period
If Hughes's dream of a grand post-war economic partnership between Australia and France failed to materialise, it was partly because of the extraordinary global instability that so quickly turned the post-war period into an inter-war one. There is no space here to analyse that situation in detail, but we can mention just a few of the elements at work, such as the failure to create a viable League of Nations, the rapid rise of conflicting totalitarian ideologies (communism and fascism) and their struggles with liberal and religious thought, American isolationism, which proved contagious, the Great Depression, and the gradual fracturing of the grand empires. This was a period when France began to lose its Great Power status internationally and when its internal conflicts brought it to the brink of civil war. And Australia had its own share in this generalised disarray: our great Australian historian, Stuart Macintyre, portrays, beyond the extreme miseries of the Depression, a country riven by strikes and class tensions, limited by its dependence on primary industry, and lacking any dynamic national leadership.

Against this rather gloomy background, there were, however, two strands of Australian connection with France that mark a certain continuity in the French impact on Australia's growing nationhood. Both share political and people-to-people elements: one is the establishment of an Australian trade office in Paris; the other concerns the Australian construction (both literal and figurative) of its war memory in Picardy.

The appointment of a trade agent was one of the few recommendations of the Pau Mission that came to something. It takes us to the story of Australia's forgotten man in Paris, Clive Harold Voss (1888–1959), who held the position from 1919 to 1940, and then returned to a position in the newly created Australian Legation in France in 1945 until his retirement a few years later. Voss deserves a greater place in our history. His career spanned eleven Australian prime ministers and governments of many political persuasions, many of whom tried to get rid of him, and by virtue of the length of his time in Paris as well as of his actual activities, he was responsible for establishing the idea of a distinct Australian official representation in France as a *norm*. Appointed by Billy Hughes, for over twenty years he did everything he could, as a one-man-plus-typist show, to keep alive the Hughes vision that deeper links with France would benefit Australia's development as an economy and as a nation. Voss was constantly assailed by his London colleagues as being insufficiently experienced or competent to take on any serious responsibilities of negotiation or representation. Initially, they certainly had a case, because Voss, who had left his job as a lowly accountant in a suburban Sydney bank before the war in order to go to France to learn how to fly planes, was not much more than an adventurer. He did serve in the British army transport division, but he had no political or serious economic training or knowledge. Over time, however, he developed a quite sophisticated understanding of French ways of doing business, and generated useful advice to Australian government and business people alike. Beyond that, he acquired a reputation for providing a courteous and insightful welcome to the many hundreds of Australian visitors who began to flock to France again after the war had ended. He was a kind of informal de facto ambassador, and was widely recognised as such by the French authorities.

* * *

Let us now turn to the construction of Australian war memory. The opening of the $100 million John Monash Centre in Villers-Bretonneux in April 2018 can be seen as the latest – and perhaps the final – Australian government gesture in the monumentalising process of setting in concrete the official version of the nation's role – achievements and losses – on the Western Front in World War I. This is a process that began in the immediate post-war years with the adoption of Villers-Bretonneux by Melbourne. Romain Fathi, in his brilliant PhD thesis, published in book form by Cambridge University Press in 2019, compellingly demonstrates the complexities, the misunderstandings, the ambiguities of motive and the Australian will to self-aggrandisement present in the process, as well as the sometimes long historical breaks in the relationship between Australia and the little town that purportedly 'never forgets' it.[23] What I want to emphasise here is rather the phenomenon that Bruce Scates and other historians have drawn attention to, namely the very large numbers of Australian civilians who, as soon after the war as they could, and more and more regularly during the inter-war period, made the long and painful journey to France in order to visit the graves of loved ones killed in the war, and to see with their own eyes the places where the battles had taken place. Muriel Farr, the Adelaide journalist and activist, who reported very thoroughly on her own pilgrimage in 1922, testifies that there were as many as 400 people a month visiting the Australian graves and the surrounding area during the summers. Over time, in this way, through tens of thousands of Australian families, France became inscribed in the collective consciousness as a site of loss, a place of indelible memory, and a stimulus for profound questioning about what it meant to be Australian. I shall not suggest that there is any comfortable resolution to that questioning; I do claim, however, that, whatever position one takes in relation to Australia's and Australians' self-definition, the evidence of a significant French role is overwhelming.

The Second World War

One can, and must, constantly come back to the question: 'but *which* France?' For as we have already seen, the answer to that question can vary according to time and perspective. And it is an issue that became especially acute with the advent of the Second World War. At the start, it seemed like business as usual. On 3 June 1940, Australia's prime minister, Robert Menzies, cabled an encouraging message to his French counterpart, Paul Reynaud:

> This is the hour of danger for all of us who love freedom and who believe that the well-being of the individual is the chief purpose of Government. Australia has watched with sympathy and pride, the struggle of the French people to resist a barbarous invader whose plans must be overthrown if France is to be free and if the democratic world is to survive.
>
> Our people are stirred. Our young men are everywhere flocking to the colours. All that we have we pledge to victory. Your own inspiring leadership, the valour of your soldiers, the fortitude of your people – these things lit by the burning spirit of France will stir the world and lead to victory.[24]

We can note, in passing, the would-be diplomatic touch of paying homage to Reynaud's policies of economic liberalism, and the over-stretch of truth in the 'young men [...] everywhere flocking to the colours' (voluntary enlistment was in fact very slow); but the image of French valour and fortitude is very much the classic one formulated during the First World War.

Within three weeks of Menzies' cable, France had signed an armistice with Germany, and its democratic institutions had handed over power to a dictator in the form of Marshall Pétain. On 18 June, a renegade colonel named Charles de Gaulle made a speech on the BBC in which he announced the existence of a France that had not been defeated and that would continue the war. How did Australia react? Our National Archives show that, in relation to metropolitan France and what quickly became known as the 'Vichy' government, Canberra still depended heavily on Britain for information and direction. We have already seen that, in early to mid 1941, this dependency would mean, in Syria and Lebanon, a costly war between Australians and French. Closer to home, however, a rather different picture emerged, ambiguous in so far as Australia recognised the validity of the Pétain government, even while it demonstrated a pronounced bias towards de Gaulle's 'Free French' movement.

Margaret Barrett, in her article on 'Jean Trémoulet, the Unloved French Consul-General', offers penetrating insight into the carefully maintained ambivalence of the Australian authorities in their dealings with the colourful and passion-filled tensions between the anti-British, pro-Nazi and totally vile Trémoulet, and the de Gaulle-leaning Sydney French community.[25] In relation to New Caledonia, Australia actually intervened: first, in August 1940, by sending an official representative to study the mood of the local population; and then, in September, when it was determined that the general sentiment was pro-gaullist, by providing contingent support to install a 'Free French' governor, Henri Sautot.[26] The envoy, Bertram Ballard, can be considered as Australia's first diplomatic appointment to a non-English speaking country. As with Clive Voss before him, the first point of reference in an independent Australian reaching out beyond the anglosphere was French. In May 1941, shortly before Prime Minister Menzies visited New Caledonia, Australia saw the arrival of the first contingent of what would become the French Bataillon du Pacifique, a unit that would later see distinguished service in the Middle East. But before it went, it was trained, armed and clothed by Australia.

As the end of the Second World War approached, a much stronger will to independent decision-making emerged as post-war settlement matters began to preoccupy the formulators of Australian policy.

The failure of Britain to provide adequate defence for Australia against the Japanese had led to a greater orientation towards the United States, but the shedding of one master did not, in the minds of Australian leaders, mean a simple shift of fealty to another master, at least at that time. Contrary to the US and in considerable conflict with Britain, Australia pushed for both the early recognition of de Gaulle's Provisional Government as the legitimate government of France, and for the maintenance of the integrity of the French Empire, particularly in Indo-China. The reasons for this lay in both a continuing fear of Asian southward expansion, and a perceived need to counterbalance American ambitions and influence. As we now know, that situation did not last, but it demonstrates, once more, how pursuit of ongoing friendship with France was a key factor in Australia's self-positioning as an independent player in the changing geopolitical world.

At the opening of the 'Australia in Peace and War' exhibition in Paris in June 1945, there were interesting differences among the speeches given by the various dignitaries. The British Ambassador to France, Alfred Duff Cooper, extolled the British Commonwealth as a model for a new and better world, and distanced himself from the continuing war in Asia; the French Foreign Minister, Georges Bidault, spoke of France's 'immortal gratitude to Australia' and of his country's willingness to fight for Australia in the antipodes should that be required; Stanley Bruce, Australian High Commissioner in London, felt at ease in advising France to leave its recent messy internecine conflicts – what he called its 'black page' – behind, and to concentrate on its own better qualities. For me, this cameo threesome is a nice symbol of how, over the 1914 to 1945 period, Australia's growth to greater independence involved a certain distancing from Britain, and a deepening relationship with France.

This process reached a form of climax with the appointment of the first Australian Ambassador to France. Peter Edwards, in his history of Australian diplomacy, remarks:

In 1901 Australia was a colonial federation with no right to conduct her own foreign policy. By 1949 she had passed through the ambiguities of Dominion status to become a fully independent actor in world politics.[27]

Edwards refers to the appointment of William Hodgson as Australian Minister/Ambassador to Paris as an aspect of the 'crucial breakthrough' in Australia's move towards international autonomy.[28] Hodgson, a Gallipoli veteran, a speaker of French and German, and previously secretary and permanent head of the Department of External Affairs (since 1939), presented his credentials to Charles de Gaulle in December 1945. He reported back home in the following terms:

> I expressed my gratification at my appointment to Paris as the first Australian Minister. I went on to say that there were very considerable mutual interests between France and Australia and no points of difference. France and Australia had a long tradition of friendship, cemented by a common comradeship in arms during two great wars, and my objective was to maintain and extend, in a true spirit of cooperation, the happy relations which existed.
>
> Our mission here is now officially in being, and I think it fitting to report that there is a gratifying degree of goodwill towards us on the part of the French government and of French officials.[29]

Hodgsons's appointment was mirrored by corresponding appointments by France in Canberra: first the Minister representing de Gaulle's provisional government from March 1945 (Pierre Augé), and then a full Ambassador, from 1949 (Gabriel Padovani). One must say, though, that the diplomatic reciprocity was a long time in coming: the French, after all, had had consular representation in Australia for over a hundred years previously. Hodgson's assertions about 'mutual interests' and a 'long tradition of friendship' were no doubt valid enough; on the other hand, his claim that there were 'no points of difference' was at the least premature. As the Cold War developed and new conflicts occurred, including Korea, France's progressive and often bitterly fought losses of its colonial empire, the Vietnam war, the French nuclear testing programme in the Pacific, and Australian expressions of support for New Caledonian independence, relations between Australia and France were often less 'happy' than Hodgson suggested, sometimes even seriously strained. Even then, however, even when the French connections were in their most negative light, the French dimension of Australia's opening to the world beyond the British Commonwealth and the anglosphere remained significant.

Will France continue to be important to Australia's self-positioning in the world? I have no crystal ball for making predictions. At present, in strict economic terms, neither country is a major trading partner of the other, though here again, the interweavings are strong and complex. The balance of trade now, as distinct from during the 'sheep's back' era, is strongly in France's favour. On the strategic and political levels, we have expressions of a dynamic partnership (notwithstanding the collapse of the submarine deal); in many other domains, from sophisticated biomedical research or university and school exchange programmes to art and archival projects, or cinema, sport and tourism, there is a great deal of activity, and it seems to be increasing. In his somewhat mystical final and posthumous work, *Citadelle*, Antoine de Saint-Exupéry coined the aphorism: 'Your task is not to foresee the future, but to enable it.'[30] I think that quite nicely sums up the attitudes and intentions that Australia and France, and Australians and the French, have reached at this stage of their relationship with each other.

On Art

France's rich artistic heritage is undoubtedly one of the country's main attractions as a tourist destination. People from all over the world journey to the country in great numbers with the express purpose of visiting some of its many museums, galleries and architectural treasures. The fact that so much of this artistic heritage has been protected and preserved suggests that the French themselves likewise value it highly. A survey conducted in 2001 by *Beaux Arts Magazine* would seem to bear this out. In it, 67% of people agreed that art is 'something universal and essential for humanity' and that society does not afford it sufficient recognition. On the other hand, the same survey found that 51% of respondents never visit an art exhibition. While this conversely means that around half the population *is* in the habit of frequenting art exhibitions, it would clearly be fanciful to imagine that every French citizen routinely spends time at a gallery in thoughtful contemplation of a canonical painting or of a provocative piece of sculpture.

Nevertheless, the sheer number of museums and galleries in France can be taken as a measure of the country's long-standing commitment to the visual and plastic arts. In a very real sense, these institutions and the quality of their holdings are a reflection of the level of public and private investment that art has historically enjoyed in France, and from which it continues to benefit today. As a result, from Lille's Palais des Beaux-Arts in the north to Montpellier's Musée Fabre or Marseille's spectacular MuCEM (Musée des civilisations de l'Europe et de la Méditerranée) in the south, there is no shortage of options for art lovers – locals and overseas visitors alike.

The vibrancy of these regional institutions owes much to the policy of cultural decentralisation adopted by governments as far back as the 1950s and 60s. For all that, however, Paris remains the cultural capital of France. The city boasts a dizzying array of galleries and museums, chief among which is of course the Louvre, symbolically located in the very heart of Paris. With almost 73,000 square metres of exhibition space and around 550,000 works of art, the Louvre is one of the 'big three' art museums of the world, along with the Hermitage Museum in Saint Petersburg and the National Museum of China in Beijing. It is also the most highly frequented, with nine to ten million visitors annually (in pre-COVID times). The Louvre's collection is so rich that it has had no problem catering for the creation of two 'sister' museums: the Louvre-Lens (2012), designed with the aim of revitalising France's northern mining basin, and the Louvre Abu Dhabi (2017), flagged as the first universal museum of the Arab world and a noteworthy expression of French soft power.

In terms of art galleries, there is of course much more to Paris than the Louvre. The city houses museums devoted to all periods and styles of art, from the mediaeval (the Cluny Museum) to the modern and contemporary (the Pompidou Centre), from the decorative arts (the Musée des Arts décoratifs), to the history of Paris itself (the Musée Carnavalet). One of the most popular is the Musée d'Orsay, whose collection, covering the years 1848–1914, features the largest number of impressionist and post-impressionist works in the world.

The period extending from the mid nineteenth century to the First World War and beyond was particularly rich in artistic developments, as illustrated by the rapid succession of -isms it spawned: realism, impressionism (with its 'neo' and 'post' variations), symbolism, fauvism, cubism, dadaism, surrealism ... Most of these originated in France or had their locus there. As Christopher Allen reminds us, Paris was then an artistic Mecca, attracting artists from all over Europe and the rest of the world, including many who made the long journey from Australia. What the French gave these artists was a vibrant crucible of creativity and inspiration. It should also be remembered, however, that the visiting artists responded in kind: the artistic scene in Paris and elsewhere in France during that time might still somehow seem quintessentially French, but it was also a very multicultural affair.

JWS

3

Christopher Allen

Some Australian artists in France: 1890–1930s

When the first colony was founded in Sydney in 1788, Rome was still the centre of advanced training in painting and sculpture, as it had been, with a few interruptions, for 400 years. It would retain this role for at least another half century: the most important artist in Australia in the 1860s and 70s, Eugene von Guérard (1811–1901), a German born in Vienna, had spent formative years in Rome and Naples before coming to the new southern land. But since von Guérard's time in Italy, the epicentre of modern culture had moved north, and even at the height of his success, he was being displaced in the favour of the colonial audience by Abram Louis Buvelot, who was as widely travelled as von Guérard was, but lacked his classical grounding.[1]

By the time of Federation, Paris had long asserted itself as what Walter Benjamin would later call the capital of the nineteenth century. The city's ascendancy had its roots in the century of Louis XIV, and it had become the principal European marketplace for new ideas in the Enlightenment, but it was especially after the dramas of the Napoleonic period, during the rebuilding of the July Monarchy (1830–1848) and notably in the course of the Second Empire (1852–1870), when the city itself was rebuilt on a colossal scale by Baron Haussmann, that Paris began to attract writers and artists from around Europe.

In the last decades of the nineteenth century, after the Franco-Prussian War of 1870–1871, and the first decades of the twentieth, until the Nazi occupation – during the prosperous but politically unimpressive age of the Third Republic – Paris was home to almost every important movement of modernism, from Impressionism to Surrealism, as well as offering the widest range of both academic and modern art teaching. The city's cultural depth and cosmopolitan sophistication, as well as its intellectual and sexual tolerance, made it particularly attractive to nonconformists of every kind, and a place where they could mingle with other like-minded people. This was especially true for those who came from smaller countries, regional cities or the comparatively strait-laced colonial societies of America and Australia.

Australian and American artists did not, however, have quite the same relationship to the new art arising in Paris. American society was much wealthier than Australian, for one thing; it was eager buying by American collectors that enriched Monet from the mid-1880s and allowed him to purchase and develop his property at Giverny. This collecting activity also meant that American artists could be directly influenced by French Impressionism from this time onwards. The much greater proximity of America to Europe, finally, made it much easier for young American painters to visit or move to Paris in order to study there and assimilate the currents of modern art.

All these factors sound like advantages, but their real effect was that American Impressionist painting grew into a pale imitation of the French style, without much significance within world history, and what is worse with little obvious connection to the American culture of its own time. The pictures of John Henry Twachtman or Julian Alden Weir, for example, are very pleasant, but entirely derivative. The most famous of the Americans, Childe Hassam, directly imitates Monet's *Rue Montorgueil* (1878) in his *Rainy Day, Fifth Avenue* (1916), and Gustave Caillebotte's *Paris, A Rainy Day* (1877) in *A Rainy Day in Boston* (1885).

The Australian experience at the end of the nineteenth century was very different. We were much further away, we had to work everything out for ourselves, and as a result the art of Tom Roberts (1856–1931) and Arthur Streeton (1867–1943) is more original but also more vitally connected to the history and culture of its land of origin than anything made in America. Streeton, born in the colonies, did not go to Europe until after he had fully developed as a painter. Roberts, born in England but raised in Melbourne, had spent vital years studying in London and Paris from 1881 to 1884 where his academic training enabled him to paint the figure with confidence; but among the moderns, it was the realism of Jules Bastien-Lepage that impressed him, tempered by the orientalising aestheticism of James McNeill Whistler.

Roberts returned to Australia in 1885, and it was in the next few years that he developed the remarkable vision of the Heidelberg School, in collaboration with Arthur Streeton, Charles Conder (1868–1909), Frederick McCubbin (1855–1917) and others. The new group held Australia's first programmatic art exhibition in Melbourne in 1889, the *9 by 5 Impression Exhibition*. The movement continued to evolve until the middle of the 1890s. Then Streeton went to England in 1897, and Roberts followed in 1903 to undertake his enormous painting commemorating the opening of the first Federal Parliament in Melbourne on 9 May 1901; Australian art was left in the hands of secondary figures in the years up to the Great War, while our two greatest painters found themselves relatively becalmed in a much bigger ocean.

The independence of Australian artistic development between 1885 and 1895 in particular can be further illuminated by contrary examples from our own art history. Emanuel Phillips Fox (1865–1915), born to an eminent legal family in Melbourne, travelled to Paris in 1886 and enrolled at the Académie Julian, where he did very well, and then at the École des Beaux-Arts, which had been the Académie royale from its foundation in 1648 until the French

Revolution, and remained the peak institution for art teaching in Paris. His teachers there were the virtuoso late academic realists William Bouguereau (1825–1905) and Jean-Léon Gérôme (1824–1904). Phillips Fox's greatest influence, however, was Impressionism, and when he returned to Melbourne in 1891, it was an entirely French style that he brought back with him. The years of his absence from Australia had been precisely the crucial formative period of a new artistic movement; he had missed this experience, and his art for the rest of his life would continue to be a footnote to French Impressionism.

John Peter Russell (1858–1930), who has only recently been the subject of a monographic exhibition at the Art Gallery of New South Wales, is another interesting case. Unlike Roberts, he was born and raised in Australia, in a prosperous engineering family. After his father's death in 1879 he became financially independent and decided to devote himself to art. He had met Roberts in London and the two of them, together with a third friend, the American Dr Will Mahoney, travelled through Spain in 1883. Russell settled in France, eventually building a large house at Belle-Île in Brittany (1888), known locally as *Le Château anglais*; there he lived with his wife Marianna Mattiocco, a former artist's model with whom he had seven sons and a daughter.

Russell, who was wealthy and urbane, was remarkably well connected. He became friends with Vincent van Gogh, who was then an unknown, eccentric Dutch art student in Paris, and painted what Vincent considered the best portrait ever made of him. He was a close friend of Rodin, who modelled his wife's head on several occasions. He even knew Matisse later. But Russell's most fateful acquaintance was with Claude Monet, whom he met painting at Belle-Île in 1886. Monet allowed him, unusually, to watch him paint, and Russell was bewitched. What had been for Monet the work of one summer became for Russell almost a lifelong style, like a trap that he could not escape.

Roberts and Russell kept up a correspondence for some years, and Russell kept telling his friend about French Impressionism. Some have thought that Roberts' lack of interest in this news from the front-line of modernism betrayed a limited artistic curiosity, but the truth is that he was at work at another front-line, dealing with the nature and environment, the flora, light and history of Australia. He did not need to hear about someone else's formal or stylistic experiments. Poor Russell, in contrast – like later Australians chasing Cubism – pursued the new style but had nothing really to say. His art had no incidence on the history of painting in his own country, and when he came home after the war, still only in his fifties, he lived in obscurity at Watsons Bay for the last decade of his life.

Another painter who made a life in France and had little influence in Australia, although he fared much better with posterity than Russell, was Rupert Bunny (1864–1947). Bunny was in London and then Paris before Roberts returned to Australia, and developed there as part of the local art scene, and in complete disconnection from the emerging art environment of Australia. His work is initially in a late academic style, eventually incorporating a more informal modern realism to produce his most distinctive mature work, largely images of women waiting for something to happen, suffused with a discreet eroticism and often modelled on his beautiful French wife Jeanne Morel. His masterpiece in this manner is probably *The Sun Bath* (c. 1913) in Bendigo. He also painted fine portraits, including of Dame Nellie Melba (c. 1902) and of Percy Grainger (1904).

Unlike Russell, Bunny enjoyed a reputation in Australia, which he visited in 1911. After the war, he experimented with modernist styles and was inspired by the Ballets Russes. Following his wife's death in 1933, he returned to Australia, where he lived in relatively modest circumstances, although the National Gallery of Victoria gave him a retrospective in 1946 – the first for a living Australian artist – a year before his death.

Younger than Russell but sadly short-lived, Hugh Ramsay (1877–1906) was born in Scotland and came to Australia as an infant. He studied at the NGV school in Melbourne from 1894 and then in 1900 sailed to Europe, where he studied in Paris at the Académie Colarossi. There are several fine self-portraits standing at the easel from this period. In 1902, however, ill with tuberculosis, he was forced to return to Australia, where he died in 1906, looked after by his sisters, the subject of one his most striking paintings, *The Sisters* (1904), in the Art Gallery of New South Wales.

George Lambert (1873–1930) sailed to Europe on the same ship as Hugh Ramsay and the two became friends. Lambert, born in Russia, had been a star pupil of Julian Ashton's art school (originally called the Sydney Art School) and in 1901 he had won the first New South Wales Travelling Scholarship to Europe. He too studied in London and then in Paris, at the Académie Colarossi and also at the Académie Delécluse, eventually settling down in Chelsea and becoming part of what was then an important group of Australian artists resident in London.

Lambert had been touched in passing by the influence of the Heidelberg School as a young student. However, like Ramsay he was more drawn to the modern tonalist style that ultimately went back to seventeenth-century Spain, but had been revived, especially by Édouard Manet, as a kind of alternative classical tradition, because the mainstream of Italian and French classicism had been monopolised by the Academy – that is, by the École des Beaux-Arts in Paris, the Royal Academy in London, and the other similar institutions in the great capitals of Europe.

Lambert's *La Blanchisseuse* (1901), a portrait of his young wife Amy, their infant son Maurice, and a stout washerwoman, is a Parisian painting in the neo-Spanish tonalist style, all browns, blacks and creamy whites. Of all these expatriates, Lambert was the one to enjoy most success in Australia; following a period as a war painter in Palestine, he returned to Australia as an eminent modern artist, completing war-related commissions in both painting and sculpture until his premature death in 1930.

Most of the artists I have mentioned so far sought out Paris either as the centre of modern art or, indeed perhaps even more commonly, as the place to study the traditional skills of painting at an advanced level – hence the curious fact that so many modernist artists were the pupils of academic masters. But artists and others also chose to live in Paris, as already suggested, because of its generally tolerant social attitudes. This was, for example, the period in which Degas or Toulouse-Lautrec could explore the social underworld of brothels and dance clubs, and in which Montmartre was a pleasure district outside the jurisdiction of the city of Paris, as Yoshiwara was in Edo, the old name for Tokyo.

Manet drew attention – critically, but without moralistic judgement – to what the French called the *demi-monde*: a parallel world of casual prostitution, mistresses and kept women that provided young bourgeois men with girlfriends at a time when respectable girls were still expected to be virgins at marriage. Baudelaire had written about prostitutes and also lesbians, and in fact the first edition of *Les Fleurs du mal* (1857) was banned because of several poems that were deemed obscene. Gustave Courbet too had painted scenes of lesbians, although Baudelaire would have found them banal because they lacked the element of deliberate moral transgression that appealed to him in sapphic relationships.

There was in fact a coterie of rich and fashionable lesbians in Paris around the turn of the century, including the glamorous couple of Natalie Clifford Barney (1876–1972) and Renée Vivien (1877–1909). Barney was a brilliant and beautiful heiress and author from Ohio who fortuitously met Oscar Wilde when she was a little girl and later attended a French boarding school. At 23 she had formed a relationship with the famous courtesan Liane de Pougy, whose later book about their affair, *Idylle sapphique* (1901), became a bestseller.

In 1899 she met a beautiful English poetess who, like Barney, wrote in French and who went under the French pen name Renée Vivien. Their relationship was a stormy one, and Vivien had a self-destructive streak, given to alcohol, drugs and extremes of sado-masochism; her life later inspired Colette's novel *Le Pur et l'impur* (1932). This lesbian world in Paris, of which the most famous members were expatriates, continued between the wars, when Gertrude Stein lived there with her companion Alice B. Toklas, and when Brassaï took several famous photographs of the lesbian bar Le Monocle and of some of its regulars (one of whom, incidentally, Violette Morris, was a former female weightlifting champion who became a Nazi spy, betrayed important military secrets to the Germans, and was a collaborator during the Occupation; during the liberation of France in 1944, Resistance agents ambushed and shot her on a country road).

When we look back at Australian women artists of the first half of the twentieth century, they seem to have been mostly of lesbian or very ambivalent sexual orientation – few were married and fewer still had children – and were generally born into upper middle-class families, which allowed them to pursue an independent life. One of these was Janet Cumbrae Stewart (1883–1960), who studied at the National Gallery School in Melbourne and exhibited successfully both here and overseas before moving to France in 1922. From this period is a handsome portrait of Jessie Traill, also an upper-class and highly cultivated lesbian and one of the finest etchers in the history of Australian art (Melbourne, NGV).

Cumbrae Stewart spent the next seventeen years living in France and Italy – returning to Australia on the outbreak of World War II – with a Miss Argemore ffarington Bellairs, known to her friends as 'Bill'. In contrast to the implicit masculinity of Bill, Janet Cumbrae Stewart represents herself in a touching self-portrait at about the age of 28 as girlishly youthful, feminine and vulnerable, glancing to her right with a wistful expression (1911; National Library of

Australia). There is also a sensitive portrait of a handsome, if rather mannish woman which one would like to think represents Bill, although it remains unidentified. Another portrait in the NGV is of Mary Cockburn Mercer, also a painter and the daughter of a wealthy family, who led an adventurous life in Europe with both male and female lovers, including Cumbrae Stewart.

Otherwise, Cumbrae Stewart's work is almost entirely devoted to lovingly sensuous and yearning pastels of the female nude: *The Model Disrobing* (1917), from the Art Gallery of New South Wales collection, is typical, contrasting the creamy skin of the girl with the deep black of the background. The sensuality of these images is so plangent, and the way that they seem to trespass on the privacy of their models – as though the artist were imagining herself touching and caressing them – is so inescapable, that they would be considered disturbingly indiscreet as the work of a male painter. These pictures have circulated in private collections and a few have ended up in museums, but as an artist Cumbrae Stewart was very minor and had no impact on art in Australia; she was brought back to notice in Rodney James' exhibition *Janet Cumbrae Stewart: The Perfect Touch* at Mornington Peninsula Regional Gallery in 2003.

Agnes Goodsir (1864–1939) was almost twenty years older than Cumbrae Stewart, and is altogether a more substantial figure, although she too had been almost completely forgotten before she became the object of a small monographic exhibition: Karen Quinlan's *In a Picture Land over the Sea: Agnes Goodsir, 1864–1939* at the Bendigo Art Gallery – which owns one her most intriguing pictures – in 1998.

Agnes Goodsir was born in Portland, in Victoria, and studied painting at the Bendigo School of Mines, which is not as incongruous as it must sound to a contemporary reader, for this was just the name given, in a mining centre, to what would elsewhere have been called a School of Arts or a Mechanics' Institute: in the Victorian period, when universities were confined to the highly educated and taught only a limited range of academic subjects, much teaching that we would now regard as tertiary or advanced and technical secondary was provided by these special schools. In Sydney, for example, the National Art School grew out of classes initially provided at the Sydney Mechanics' School of Arts.

In 1899 Goodsir left for Paris, where she attended the Académie Colarossi, the Académie Julian and the Académie Delécluse. From 1912 onwards she moved between Paris and London, but around 1921 or a couple of years later she settled permanently in Paris, living at 18, rue de l'Odéon from then until her death in 1939 – incidentally making Goodsir the only artist we have discussed to die as well as live in Paris. Sylvia Beach's famous English bookshop Shakespeare and Company relocated to 12, rue de l'Odéon in 1922 (it closed under the Occupation in 1941; the present bookshop in rue de la Bûcherie was opened in 1951 by George Whitman and revived the name as a tribute to Sylvia Beach). It was from here too that Beach first published James Joyce's *Ulysses*, also in 1922.[2]

One of Goodsir's most impressive early works is *La Femme de ménage* (1905), which adopts the same neo-Spanish tonalist palette discussed earlier, but with a distinct influence of Whistler in the compositional angle as well as the subtle play of tones. Her work was well received and hung at the Salon, the Royal Academy, the Salon des Indépendants, the Société Nationale des Beaux-Arts and elsewhere. Presumably most of these pictures were portraits, and she is known to have painted Bertrand Russell, Count Leo L. Tolstoy (Tolstoy's son, 1869–1945),[3] Ellen Terry (the picture was stolen from the Savoy Theatre in London) and, during her visit to Australia in 1927, Banjo Paterson (State Library of New South Wales). It is said that she was commissioned to paint Benito Mussolini's portrait while in Rome on the way back to Paris, although this may not have come to fruition.[4]

If she did complete the Mussolini commission, Agnes Goodsir would not have been the only Australian to execute his portrait.

Another expatriate lesbian, Dora Ohlfsen (1869–1948), who was born in Ballarat but spent most of her life in Europe, first in Germany studying music, then in Russia and finally in Rome as a sculptor and a fine medallist, most certainly did so. In 1925–1926 she produced a war memorial at Formia titled *Sacrifice*, which is still standing today, and in 1926 she executed a portrait of Mussolini, presumably as a medal, which apparently met with the Duce's approval.

Because of the disappearance of so much of Goodsir's public work as a portraitist, what we know of her œuvre is largely confined to the private part, and to works that remained in her own collection at her death. Most of that consists of portraits of her companion Rachel Dunn (1886–1950), known as Cherry.[5] Rachel, who was American – and who may have been a concert pianist in her youth[6] – had been the wife of Goodsir's close friend Bernard Roelvink, but left him for Goodsir, reverting to her maiden name after her divorce, though retaining the married title: Mrs Rachel Dunn.

It is thanks to Cherry that we have much of what survives of Goodsir's work, for after the latter's death in 1939, it was she who sent a considerable number of paintings back to Australia.[7] So it is fitting that the most intriguing of the extant paintings should be portraits of Cherry, starting with the compelling *Girl with Cigarette* (1925) in the Bendigo Art Gallery and *La Parisienne* (c. 1924) in the National Gallery of Australia. In both of these pictures Cherry, who appears rather timid and submissive in a head and shoulders portrait dated a few years later, has been transformed: in the earlier portrait, into a stylish flapper and a sexually ambivalent *femme fatale*; in the Bendigo picture into a poised young woman who looks directly at the viewer while smoking a cigarette, then still chic and for women an assertion of independence.

A decade later, in the 1933 *Chinese Skirt* (Art Gallery of New South Wales), Cherry appears in a different guise again, this time as the embodiment of a quiet inner life, reading a book and surrounded by ceramics, shelves of bound volumes, and a full-length mirror which hints at hidden recesses of intimacy. But these were also the years in which Goodsir's health declined and in which Cherry increasingly became her nurse.

Goodsir made her will in October 1938 and died on 11 August 1939, only weeks before the German invasion of Poland and the consequent declaration of war. Cherry wrote to her family and among other things spoke of sending around 40 pictures to Australia for safekeeping. After the war, in 1947, she sent several more to Daryl Lindsay, including *The Letter* (1926; National Gallery of Victoria). We do not know much more about Cherry's later life except that she continued to live at 18, rue de l'Odéon until her death in 1950, and was buried in the same grave as Goodsir at Bagneux Cemetery.[8]

These streets in Paris are full of history in a way that we can scarcely imagine in Australia, where the oldest extant buildings are barely two centuries old. The Latin Quarter alone is full of plaques commemorating colossal figures of the past: many years ago I stayed in the adjacent rue Monsieur-le-Prince almost opposite where Blaise Pascal himself had lived in the seventeenth century. Countless interesting but lesser individuals are inevitably forgotten, falling away like the leaf litter of an ancient forest.

Expatriation has always been a conundrum for Australian artists. London and Paris, and later New York, might offer a more exciting and stimulating cultural environment, and a more tolerant one for unconventional ways of life. You might even make a respectable living and enjoy the regard of professional colleagues; but you were unlikely to become a dominant figure on that metropolitan stage, and meanwhile your chance of becoming a leading artist in the much smaller and more provincial scene at home was diminishing with every year spent abroad.

Of all the great expatriates, Lambert had the most successful repatriation, for although he had made his reputation in Britain, rather than Australia, he had become renaturalised, as it were, as a war artist, and returned with great national commissions to complete. Streeton had a successful re-entry too, but he had already established his status in Australia before departing for a rather lacklustre time in Europe – though he too had been given a shot in the arm by his appointment as a war artist (during which, among other things, he had discovered a wonderful talent for watercolour). Bunny had done reasonably well – at least he had the belated recognition of a retrospective – though life in Melbourne must have seemed drab after his *belle époque* years in Paris. And poor Russell returned to almost complete obscurity.

These difficulties may have been partly due to narrow-mindedness, provincialism and even envy, but we also have to recognise, as I observed at the outset, that a provincial outpost can sometimes offer opportunities that are not found in the metropolis. Our Heidelberg painters are more interesting than the American Impressionists because they are less derivative, less vacuously formalist, and more responsive to the social and cultural realities of their own world. There was after all some justice in the way that Russell was ignored, because he had nothing to say to Australia. As for Agnes Goodsir, there was no reason why she should not have been considered a significant Australian portrait painter, except that she had so little presence here. And there was perhaps another obstacle: even though the Archibald Prize is the single biggest art event on the Australian art calendar, it has little to do with serious art and no Australian painter has ever achieved the highest status or reputation as a portraitist. But that is *une autre histoire*.

Bibliography and further reading

Allen, Christopher, *Art in Australia from Colonization to Postmodernism*, London: Thames & Hudson, 1997.

Allen, Christopher (ed.), *A Companion to Australian Art*, Boston: Wiley Blackwell, 2021.

Goddard, Angela, *Art, Love and Life: Ethel Carrick and E. Phillips Fox*, Brisbane: Queensland Art Gallery, 2011.

Anna Gray, *George Lambert: Heroes and Icons*, Canberra: National Gallery, 2007.

James, Rodney, *Janet Cumbrae Stewart: the Perfect Touch*, Mornington: Mornington Peninsula Regional Gallery, 2003 (exhibition: 27 May – 13 July 2003).

Motion, Andrew, *The Lamberts*, London: Chatto and Windus, 1986.

Quinlan, Karen, *In a Picture Land over the Sea: Agnes Goodsir, 1864–1939*, Bendigo: Bendigo Art Gallery, 1998.

Tunnicliffe, Wayne, *John Peter Russell: Australia's French Impressionist*, Sydney: Art Gallery of New South Wales, 2018.

On Literature

In the summer of 1941, the French writer and artist Jean Bruller compiled a short novel that would soon make him famous. In February 1942, under the pseudonym Vercors, *Le Silence de la mer* (*The Silence of the Sea*) was secretly published in German-occupied Paris and quickly became a symbol of French resistance against the invader. A copy reached London, where the leader of the Free French forces, General Charles de Gaulle, ordered it to be reprinted and widely distributed. Very quickly, the novella acquired cult status. One of the reprints ended up in the hands of film director, Jean-Pierre Melville, who would later adapt the story for the screen (1947). The novella's initial publication also marked the birth of the (then clandestine) publishing house *Les Éditions de Minuit*, which Bruller co-founded with Pierre de Lescure and which is still in operation today.

The publication history outlined above attests to the power of literature, particularly in troubled times. Appropriately enough, the story itself of *Le Silence de la mer* includes a lengthy passage emphasising the importance of books. The plot, such as it is, is simple. In a small village in occupied France, an elderly man and his niece are obliged to provide lodgings for a German officer. The officer in question is something of a dreamer who believes the war is necessary to bring about the fusion – or 'marriage' – of France and Germany, whose complementary strengths make them ideal partners in his vision of a new and revitalised Europe. Each evening, he comes down to the drawing room to share his thoughts on this subject with his hosts, who remain steadfastly silent – a noble form of resistance which eventually becomes a strait-jacket preventing them from expressing any human sentiments towards their strangely endearing 'guest'. During one of the officer's monologues, he muses on the literary heritage of various countries. When you think of England, he says, Shakespeare instantly comes to mind. For Italy it is Dante; for Spain, Cervantes; for Germany, Goethe. But in the case of France, what writer's name is immediately conjured – Molière, Racine, Hugo, Voltaire, Rabelais, someone else? There are too many candidates. It is impossible to choose.

The many French writers mentioned in this monologue have long enjoyed canonical status, though such a list might seem a little outdated these days. During the second half of the twentieth century, as scholars began to challenge traditional understandings of the (Western) canon, our literary horizons steadily widened beyond the 'classics' to include texts by a much broader range of authors. Nevertheless, even if our German officer were to update his list, his basic message would remain essentially the same: over the centuries France has produced a steady stream of writers responsible for countless memorable works. And in a society where the writer is still highly respected – sometimes to the point of veneration – that stream shows no signs of drying up.

In France perhaps more than elsewhere, the idealised image of the writer as an inspired genius touched by grace and cloistered in creative solitude still has wide currency. As demonstrated by Paul Bénichou in *Le Sacre de l'écrivain* (*The Consecration of the Writer*, 1973), this view of the writer originated in France during the second half of the eighteenth century and gathered strength in the wake of the French Revolution, finally becoming entrenched in the 1820s and beyond thanks to the Romantics. The persistence of this mythologised idea of the writer is no doubt one of the main reasons why French universities have been so reluctant to embrace courses in creative writing. How is it possible to teach someone how to be a genius? (Paradoxically, no such qualms prevent the teaching in France of technical skills in music, dance and painting ...) This resistance to creative writing courses is even more curious given the 'democratisation' of writing that modern technologies have facilitated. Be that as it may, writers continue to enjoy a revered status in France and are still the object of adulation at public events such as writers' festivals, though France is admittedly not alone in that respect.

If the French have given us a rich trove of literary works to enjoy, they have also provided the world with a new and original suite of analytical tools for interpreting them. For better or for worse, depending on your point of view, French Theory, at the heart of which is the notion of deconstruction, has transformed our intellectual landscape. The names of some of its leading lights, such as Jacques Derrida, Michel Foucault and Julia Kristeva, now have universal currency. Ironically, at least as far as literary criticism is concerned, the take-up of postmodernist approaches by scholars has been much more common in the Anglo-Saxon world – notably in the United States – than in France itself. So much so that the French now refer to this collective set of ideas using English terminology – 'la French Theory'.

JWS

4

Brian Castro

Languephile

My father's first wife was French. She died of tuberculosis at the age of 22 after playing tennis in the snow in the French Concession in Shanghai. There is an old photo of her in a flapper frock, looking very cool during the opening of the *Cercle Sportif* in 1926.

Having re-married – my mother was both Chinese and English – my father took to preserving French culture by reading *Les Trois mousquetaires* to me at bedtime. Thank goodness he broke into English in summary of each chapter, otherwise I was wondering what three mosquitoes had to do with the story and was waiting for the punch-line which never came. He would also rattle off the titles of books he never read: *La Condition humaine*, which he translated to me as *A Storm in Shanghai*; *Le Lotus bleu* by Hergé in the Tintin series which I dug out of my school library. My father said that was a spy story and that Shanghai was full of spies.

It was this translating and interpreting back and forth to myself and to my parents which made life for me much like a spy's; more interestingly for a child-observer, one could mistranslate to tailor one's childhood wishes. One could ignore; one could invent. It also helped me understand that my father's trade was tied up in business across languages. He was full of language. Sometimes he came home drunk, speaking in Hindi. He was what was known as a *compradore* in Portuguese, a purchaser or trader between cultures and nations.

He was also a *matador* of what he detected as bull. His favourite phrase was *American baloney*.

So what 1 grew up with was not Francophilia so much as *languephile* ... the progeny of a love of a language fostered by a multicultural background within a multilingual society. Because 1 was brought up by *amahs*, my first language could correctly be said to be Cantonese. My grandmother was from Liverpool, so English was my second language and the *lingua franca* in the family. My father mainly spoke Portuguese with the odd smattering of French, as the two languages are actually not that far apart. Needless to say, there was never any intimacy expressed, and this may have driven me into writing.

In Australia, my initial interest at university was in confessional literature, based on Julian Green's diaries (which were not entirely published in English, so that forced me to read them in French). 1 began with these diaries as an imaginary thesis in the French Department at Sydney University. Little did 1 know, but 1 was directed to Corneille, Racine and Molière. 1 avoided them and read my way into Gide and Proust, not for their predilections but for their language. This was the surest way to not being admitted into the Honours stream. 1 specialised in American Literature instead, and spent a large part of my time listening to what was happening in Paris on my short-wave radio. The year was 1968. My father wrote me long letters on the terrible state of the world.

Diaries and letters are literary productions as much as any novel, and 1 think this was the beginning of my interest in the epistolary and diaristic form, in semi-autobiographical work spiced with fiction, a *métissage* which resulted in *Shanghai Dancing* and many of my other novels which contained letters, diaries, photographs and melancholic objects from which 1 extracted a secret life. When my father died 1 found amongst his belongings an intricately carved mango seed. From this 1 spun another strand of story about mango traders. It was only recently that through Ancestry DNA 1 discovered my father's grandmother was Polynesian, born on the island of Espiritu Santo, which now forms part of the archipelago of Vanuatu and which was successively colonised by the Portuguese, the French and the British. Fiction invents ancestry which proves to be true most of the time. There's something in DNA which directs the spirit. It was my *Saint-Esprit*.

In 1976 I went to Paris on the back of a scholarship as an *assistant en langues* at Aulnay-sous-Bois, in the industrial north of Paris. While I was teaching there I attended a public lecture by someone called Roland Barthes at the Collège de France. They were heady times. People still remembered the '68 revolution. Barthes spoke about affect and semiology and I detected something of a hidden autobiographical nature in his use of language, in his seemingly dispassionate *regard sémiologique*. The confessional was never far away.

Back in the north of Paris, the tough edge of language without theory reigned. My nineteenth-century French, learned in the old way of *explications de texte* and intensive literary reading, seemed out of place, though I refashioned it with the local argot. I was quaintly respected by the students, as though some resonance of Balzac roamed the vicinity, striving for a richer vocabulary. I toyed with the idea of wearing a dressing gown and a cravat to my classes in honour of Honoré. My headmaster, who was so near-sighted he was almost blind, insisted I drive him around in my 2CV and was impressed by my employment of the subjunctive mood.

One night, on a trip to Amsterdam and probably under the influence of hashish, I had a dream in which Raymond Queneau came to me and spoke in the same way he spoke in reality to Marguerite Duras. He said: 'Do nothing but write.' And so, I did. I did nothing for the next three years except write. I lived precariously, but there is nothing more true than when you have nothing left to lose, you begin to write.

My first book, *Birds of Passage – Les Oiseaux de passage*, was translated by Xavier Pons. My publicity visit to Toulouse and Paris was exciting and hectic. I met Marguerite Duras in a Parisian bookshop through a manoeuvre by my publisher ... pass yourself off, he said, make like *un type vietnamien*. Marguerite was quite inebriated, but terribly chatty. I had, as my guest to the launch of my book, the daughter of Maurice Merleau-Ponty, Marianne Merleau-Ponty. Again, there was some strange connection with her dead father, a philosopher who was interested in China and in language as the core of culture. I was interviewed on Radio-France Culture, and was reviewed in *Le Monde*.

When I returned to Australia it had become an alien place, or more disappointingly, no-one knew what I had written. One journalist referred to my book as *Birds of Paradise*. After that, it was often found in the Wildlife category.

I published other books but I was always destined, I believed, to be better known post-humously. *D'outre-tombe*. Even though I kept returning to Paris, both physically and imaginatively, it was always going to be an unattainable goal to live there. Besides, there were too many literary fathers to kill.

My latest book, *Blindness and Rage, a Phantasmagoria: A Novel in 34 Cantos*, was a kind of eulogy for my love affair with France. There had been too much written, both theoretically and creatively, about the monumental intellectual and literary influence of the French and I wanted to tell a story about someone fleeing from it. As Hans Gumbrecht has indicated, since the beginning of the 1990s, no new theory of literature has posed a real intellectual or institutional challenge.

Writers were also exhausting the field. Take, for example, Enrique Vila-Matas' *Montano's Malady* ... in which the protagonist is a writer like Woody Allen, so obsessed with French culture he finds it impossible to distinguish between real life and fiction. And there is his *Never Any End To Paris*, in which a novelist rents Marguerite Duras' apartment and spends every night with writers, intellectuals and eccentrics. Irony has finally reached the stage of parody. There was certainly no *Bibliothèque de la Pléiade* awaiting me in Australia.

In *Blindness and Rage* I named my protagonist Lucien Gracq after Julien Gracq, whose real name was Louis Poirier and who took his pseudonym from Stendhal's hero and the Roman Gracchi. When he died, no-one knew who he was and then they found out he had refused the Prix Goncourt when it was offered to him ... yes, there is no mistaking this writer whom I greatly admired for his devastatingly frank assessment of literary prizes and cheap journalism and the so-called 'reading' that people claim they do when the new and passing parade of literary *ingénues* are processed every year. Indeed, Gracq's *La Littérature à l'estomac* can be read in two ways: firstly, the consumption of culture is fundamentally crude and transient ... like the tea-trolley going past laden with cakes; and secondly, do people have the stomach for real literature anymore, for form and prosody and 'atmosphere' or what the Germans call *Stimmung*? In other words, are we cutting off our tongues to spite our language and our emotions in the brush with transient fame and larger contracts? Thus, my protagonist gives up his job, rents a flat in Paris next door to the now deceased Georges Perec, and conjures up the dead in order to exorcise them. Which is indeed what I did, renting a flat two doors down from Georges Perec's former apartment on the rue Linné near the Jardin des Plantes.

Another writer whom I admire is Chateaubriand.

In her introduction to the latest edition of his *Mémoires d'outre-tombe*, Anka Muhlstein writes:

[Chateaubriand] turns to archaic French in the pages on his childhood in the medieval atmosphere of Brittany; he grows technical in his description of Atlantic navigation; he produces sumptuous lyrical poetry when he evokes Niagara Falls or the melancholy of Roman ruins. He has a taste for the rare word and a passion for precision. He was himself very conscious of his gift for shifting from a classical register to boldly romantic forms of expression rendered in a language so free that to men of the previous generations it appeared barbarous. His extravagance was, he claimed, always tempered by his ability to 'respect the ear.'[1]

Indeed, he is a fellow *languephiliste*.

Chateaubriand is of course my namesake. On formal occasions in France I am always introduced as *Monsieur Castrobrian*. Etymologically 'Castro' is a Roman camp from which the word 'château' or 'castle' is derived. Thus I have found another forebear, whom I will have to kill in time. This haunted exile, the adventurer of the imagination and the solitary writer who claimed his mother 'inflicted' life on him on the day of his birth, is someone I want to know better.

So, in a couple of years, since there is never any end to Paris, my partner and I hope to spend three months of the year in Nantes or in Calvados, and I will read into my retirement the *Mémoires* by Chateaubriand, retrieving everything that I have lost, especially the tongue that has been cut out of me by the tyranny of distance. It will be a recrudescence. *Un regain.*

Indeed, as Duras said, 'I am worn out with desire to write'.[2]

* * *

5

Françoise Grauby

The polos of Michel Foucault (and other tales of French literary life)

Observing the hustle and bustle of French literary life from a distance is both entertaining and instructive. The *persona* of the French writer, for example, is quite fascinating and an object of study in itself. It lends itself to caricatures and criticisms, one of the best being of course 'The Writer on Holiday' in Roland Barthes's *Mythologies*, in which he talks about the 'essence' of the author that produces books like the tree produces fruit: 'one is a writer as Louis XIV was king, even on the commode'.[1]

One is invariably struck, when looking at French culture, by the overwhelming presence of the past and the degree to which French society turns to its past to legitimise and justify the present. The posture of the writer has been eloquently incarnated by Voltaire, Zola or Sartre and the French tradition has helped shape, on an international scale, the writer's role: 'More open, less "Byzantine" than in days past, French literary culture today would nevertheless soon make Balzac or Hugo, perhaps even Voltaire, feel quite at home'.[2] The idealised image of the writer as creative genius inherited from the nineteenth century remains extraordinarily tenacious. This is evidenced by the veneration which authors continue to inspire: from Victor Hugo to Michel Houellebecq, thanks to media exposure, the writer continues to stage the activity of 'being a writer' for the public.

The reasons are, of course, historical. The writer and literature have traditionally been invested with high symbolic value in France. There was indeed a transfer of elitist and aristocratic qualities into the realm of literature after the Revolution. The institutional presence of the Académie, the continued concentration of literary institutions in Paris and the education system fortified literary identity. They also dictated to the writer to cultivate the regime of singularity, which highlights the unique personality, marginality or originality of the writer, and to abide by the myth of an activity purified of all material attachment.

The opposition between art and money is the fundamental law governing the functioning of literature and art in French society. By the nineteenth century, the authors of serial novels, such as Balzac and Dumas, who were paid by the line and multiplied the dialogues and descriptions to improve their remuneration, were considered as 'mercenaries'. The logic of art needed to deny the logic of the market and present 'literary value [as] a symbolic, not a practical value'.[3] The metaphor of prostitution was used to describe those who 'sell their pen'.

This rather rough binary situation remains fairly unchallenged in more recent times. Even though creative writing workshops flourish in every area of French culture nowadays, in particular at universities (there are now eight degree programs in France), the idea that one can *learn to write* still raises skepticism in France, especially among writers (even if some, like François Bon, conduct writing workshops). These programs do offer dynamic platforms for critical reflection on contemporary culture and society. Nevertheless, the social and symbolic image of the writer remains attached to the romantic ideology of the 'uncreated creator',[4] to use Bourdieu's expression. The idea that literature is the expression of inspired beings is still prevalent – despite what Barthes, Ricardou and the emancipatory writing of the 60s and 70s did to literature.

Literary prizes still flourish today as a century ago (new prizes are indeed being established as we write). Works are still subject to public debate – for instance, the delayed publication of Louis-Ferdinand Céline's anti-Semitic pamphlets, out of print since 1945, recently sparked many heated debates about literary censorship and ethics. Much conviction gets invested in discussions about works or artists that really stir public opinion. Elected presidents continue to reward and revere writers (as evidenced by the national tribute to the late Jean d'Ormesson). Undoubtedly, in a transfer of values from the literary to the civic domain, quoting literary authors increases a politician's authority. The ultimate consecration remains a seat at the Académie française or the honour of a street in Paris and a place in the Pantheon. Supported, legitimated and promoted by a broad spectrum of formal and informal institutions, the French literary world is often represented as central to the nation's identity.

* * *

And yet, there are undeniable changes. The image of the writer as marginal yet also superior, the prophetic dimension of the writer, so anchored in France, are competing with a view that is increasingly influenced by a more pragmatic (and less sacred) representation of writing. It is still unusual for writers to talk about their creative processes, that remain as mysterious and elusive today as they were in the past (indeed quite a few prefer to take refuge in romantic topos), but when the young writer Leïla Slimani, Goncourt laureate in 2016, admitted to having passed through a writing workshop organised by her publisher, Gallimard, registration requests increased sharply.

The desacralisation of the creative gesture is increasingly underway in schools and university programs thanks to the inclusion of contemporary literature in the curriculum. Experimentations in language and narration reflect on the fabrication of the conditions that produce the great writer, which have been developed over two centuries and on 'the image of a single author, reclusive in his office-workshop [...] speaking *in absentia* to a massified and anonymous public'.[5] The 'Authorial Posture' that allows an author to mark his or her position in the literary field is becoming an area of study in its own right. It aptly reminds us that every 50 years or so, some tables are turned and what was recognised as the 'canon' disappears from the stage. In *French Poets and Novelists* (1884),[6] Henry James devotes a chapter to Flaubert and to Charles de Bernard. Who was Charles de Bernard? A disciple of Balzac, author of many novels of which posterity has not remembered the names.

The works of the young artist Clémentine Mélois, bridging the gap between underground and high culture, provide a playful example of such revitalisation. She hijacks the covers of the classics from European literature – *Moby Dick* by Herman Melville becomes *Maudit Bic* (*Accursed Biro*); *War and Peace/Guerre et Paix* by Leo Tolstoy becomes *Père et Gay* (*Father and Gay*).[7] Even the philosopher Michel Foucault and his polos become iconic objects of a pseudo Autumn/Winter Collection.[8] The overwhelming masculine concept of creative genius is also being challenged by these representations.

In the current transition from the traditional regime of text, when printing prevailed, to a digital regime which is constantly evolving, one must wonder also whether new forms of authorship will compete with the old ones. There is room for imagining other worlds.

Meanwhile, back in Australia, some of these images still persist because the school and university programs continue to focus on the traditional symbolic representations of the French literary field. Indeed, students in French often *expect* confirmation of what they believe to be 'l'exception française' – whether it is the cult of the Great Writer, the classics of literature, the French Academy or literary awards, which constitute, according to Sylvie Ducas, 'with the Tour de France, the Michelin Guide and Beaujolais Nouveau, what is called a "French exception"'.[9] It is not easy to dispense with references inherited from literary traditions that are all the more vivid because they are closely linked to a collective imagination that has, among other things, transmuted artists into national objects (in the 1970s, writers accounted for five of the seven individuals on French bank notes in circulation: Hugo, Voltaire, Racine, Corneille and Pascal). This is amplified, of course, by the aura of the literary milieu: its literary walks, its museums and writers' houses, its rituals, as illustrated by popular literary tours and excursions.[10]

Given this long history, any writer will try to position him or herself with respect to literary tradition. All aspiring authors legitimise their writing by reference to great ancestors from which they borrow beliefs, motifs, forms and postures. Piling up ancestors to demonstrate one's true literary affiliation precedes any literary venture because of the persistent influence of venerable literary icons like Flaubert and Proust. Flaubert, agonising over every phrase, raising the linguistic consciousness of French literary culture to a cult, forms a major reference in 'les Lettres françaises'. When interviewed, some contemporary writers will refer to him simply as 'the Boss'.[11] The writer Pierre Michon talks about writing *'in Flaubert'*.[12] And Barthes notes 'the flaubertisation of writing', insisting that Flaubert, '(grinding away at his sentences at Croisset)', popularised 'an image of the writer as a craftsman who shuts himself away in some legendary place, like a workman operating at home, and who roughs out, cuts, polishes and sets his form exactly as a jeweller extracts art from his material'.[13] His dedication to art still greatly influences how we approach literature. Besides establishing an author's singularity, granting him or her the ethos of a craftsman, through the topos of the *poeta faber*, is a sign of literary quality.

Going against the grain of stock cultural ideas may come with its own militant agenda and values. In *Words*, Jean-Paul Sartre's autobiography of his early years, the child Poulou wants to become a writer. His natural habitat is a sixth-floor Paris apartment with a view over the roofs where he breathed the 'rarefied air of belles-lettres'.[14] He says that 'without this fundamental illusion', without his 'symbolic sixth-floor' vantage point, he knew he would have never written a line. Ironically, *Words* reaffirms the very rights of literary myths that it tries to debunk and reasserts the mandate of the writer.

This ambivalence is also observed in several contemporary authors who testify to the difficulty of having to face these overwhelming models. While the myth of the great writer is no longer incarnated by anyone, it does continue to deeply nourish the imagination of critics and writers themselves. Pierre Michon, in *Small Lives*, deconstructs the religion of literature as an absolute in which he can no longer believe but for which he remains nostalgic: 'I was the lonely illiterate at the foot of an Olympus where all the others, Great Writers and Difficult Readers, read and wrote while playing on uneven pages'.[15] All contemporary writers have to work *with* or *from* this illegitimacy.

This simultaneous denial and affirmation of the rights and power of literature is quite representative of the current ambiguities and struggles, as it attests to the difficulty of burying the past. Sartre realised that he had to write against the believer who remains hidden but definitely present. Nostalgia for the old regime? 'No doubt one may be nostalgic for this "sacred", but it would be a mistake to reclaim it because the meaning of literature – its sense, its direction – has been to undo the sacralisations', comments Dominique Viard.[16]

I began by mentioning how peculiar consecrating institutions and mediations of the French literary field may appear when viewed from another vantage point. There is more. From a distance, one can also creatively reflect on *how* and *why* the rites and practices of a rather small community can still dictate and influence our approach to literature. Indeed, it is essential to take a step back to open a space in which distance, criticism and creation work together to reframe the configurations of literature.

Further reading

Bertiau, Christophe and Chanel de Halleux (eds), *Autopsie de l'échec littéraire, Contextes*, nº 27, 2020.

Grauby, Françoise, *Le Roman de la création, Écrire entre mythes et pratiques*, Amsterdam, New York, Rodopi/Brill, 2015.

Grauby, Françoise, 'The "Ready-Made-Writer" in a Selection of Contemporary Francophone Literary Advice Manuals', in A. Masschelein and D. De Geest (eds), *Writing Manuals for the Masses: The Rise of the Literary Advice from Quill to Keyboard*, New York: Palgrave (New Directions in Book History), 2021, pp. 199–216.

Mélois, Clémentine, *Les Six Fonctions du langage (roman-photo)*, Paris: Le Seuil, 2021.

* * *

6

Stephen Muecke

'French Theory', anyone?

You ask me what the French ever did for Australia, and I can answer without any doubt. They gave us revolutionary thought, which can come in handy from time to time. You know what happened in 1788 at Port Jackson, and then a year later, in Paris. It is easy to imagine what those chain-gang convicts building Sydney must have thought when they got the news of the French Revolution. They would have looked at the red-coats with a little more menace – once they understood what 'revolution' meant. To understand that, you do need a little theory.

I had very little theory when, as a 17-year-old visiting Paris, I witnessed the 1968 attempt at replicating the famous events of French revolutionary history. Thousands of students and hundreds of CRS riot police were converging in waves on the Place St Michel, in the mist of smoke and tear gas; I ran for a Metro entrance, only to be caught with a truncheon blow to the back of the head. *Matraque* was a word I would never forget.

This late 60s baby-boomer generation was asserting its presence, but there was also an intellectual revolution fomenting: structuralism. It seemed to change everything in the Humanities and Social Sciences, and the students of '68 were already protesting against it with slogans on the walls: 'Les structures ne descendent pas dans la rues' ('Structures don't go down into the streets'). From the 1950s through to the 1980s, when it was 'deconstructed' by post-structuralism, structuralism, which started as a philosophy and a method in linguistics, swept through anthropology, sociology, psychology and psychoanalysis, literary studies, history, economics. It was a revolution in thought that highlighted a theory that 'surface' phenomena were underpinned by 'deep structures' organised 'like a language', and it went to every corner of the academic and intellectual world. In Melbourne, in 1973, you could read about Althusser and the theoretical cell of the Communist Party of Australia in the party's monthly, *Australian Left Review*. French structuralist Marxism was being imported and debated.

In less militant ways, structuralism made other modes of thought possible. General and Comparative Literature was introduced by my father, Doug Muecke, to Monash University in the late 60s. It was a reaction to more narrow nationalist agendas in the teaching of literature. Lévi-Strauss' structuralist analysis of myth found human universals, and when coupled with comparative folkloristics, suddenly there were tools for asserting that the art of James Joyce or Baudelaire was rooted in more universal 'structures' than their own national literary contexts. Later, structuralist theory and method also paved the way for Cultural Studies, and that is in fact what eventually succeeded my father's Centre for General and Comparative Literature at Monash.

Cultural Studies was born in the UK, but was strongly influenced by the French theory. The French post-68 intellectuals who became identified with post-structuralism (Foucault, Derrida, Kristeva, Deleuze and Guattari ...) were seen by some as having too much influence in the UK, and the debate spilled over into the popular press once the more conservative bastions of Oxford and Cambridge were being threatened. 'Have they caught the Cambridge structuralist yet?' one cartoonist joked after Colin McCabe was refused promotion at Cambridge.

The momentum that was structuralist thought continued with all the corrections of post-structuralism, in terms of 'gender', 'power', 'desire' and so on, and while the revolution had dissipated by the turn of the century, the effects still remain in university teaching. Fifty years of continual export of ideas from France, starting, perhaps, with the propensity for revolutionary thought in the first place, but reinforced and maintained by a strong, centralised system of education and administration that was founded and alimented, no doubt, by the French imperial economy, but was also needed to maintain that empire. There is a contradiction, of course, between the solidity of the institutions making up the Republic and the flexibility that must inform the freedom of revolutionary thought.

The intellectual gifts that French thought offers Australia, and the world, have today entered a new phase with the current crisis of climate change, which once again changes everything. If we are to survive it, we will have to change the way we do science, economics, social sciences, history, politics and even art. Bruno Latour, in his 2018 book, *Down to Earth: Politics in the New Climatic Regime*, announces that 'the present ecological mutation has organized the whole political landscape for the last thirty years.'

'French theory', bold and revolutionary thinking, is what France thankfully keeps doing. Vive la révolution!

On Music

In movies, the sound of the accordion has become a short-hand means for signalling that the action is about to unfold in France, or more specifically Paris. It is now a cinematographic cliché, used by directors from all over the world, including France itself. In a sense, the sound of the accordion is the audio equivalent of the panning shot of the Eiffel Tower or the zinc roofs of Paris. It is impossible to think of films like *Amélie* and *Ratatouille* without hearing it in our mind's ear.

This use of music is a highly effective device, but there is of course much more to France's musical heritage than the accordion and the *bal musette*. From the tenth-century Gregorian organum – a plainchant melody with one or more additional voices for harmonic effect – to the electronic dance music of David Guetta, via the compositions of the French Romantics, the Paris jazz scene and the tradition of the 'chanson française', the French have a long history of engagement with music in all its forms. Indeed, according to surveys, listening to music (or playing it) is their favourite cultural activity and the one they say they could least do without.

Recognising this, in 1982, Jack Lang, the Minister for Culture in François Mitterrand's government, inaugurated a musical event that is now a fixture on the French cultural calendar. Every year, on 21 June, music is played and celebrated throughout France and even overseas in places as far away as Australia (thanks to the Alliance Française network) under the banner of the 'Fête de la musique'. While the name of Jack Lang will forever be associated with this annual event, the idea itself is said to have come from an American by the name of Joel Cohen. While working as a producer for Radio France in 1976, he came up with the idea of organising a special all-night musical programme on radio station France Musique to celebrate the summer and winter solstices, on 21 June and 21 December. These were to be called the 'Saturnales de la musique', the Saturnalia being an ancient Roman festival in honour of the god Saturn. The composer Maurice Fleuret, at the time Director of Music and Dance in the Ministry of Culture, is then understood to have mentioned this to Jack Lang. As the saying goes, the rest is history.

The first Fête de la musique was a gloriously chaotic affair, with predominantly amateur musicians popping up spontaneously to play well into the night on street corners and in gardens, squares and train stations all over France. Today, there is a greater level of organisation, and the programme of events includes ticketed and open-air concerts showcasing music by symphony orchestras as well as the current stars of pop music. But at its heart it remains a people's festival. In villages throughout the land, local musicians still play traditional dance tunes, recreating the festive atmosphere of the 'bal musette' – an informal kind of dance hosted in bars, restaurants and dance halls which first became popular in Paris in the 1880s, and where the 'musette' or bagpipe was quickly superseded by the accordion ...

At around the same time, something extraordinary was taking place in France on the classical music front. The period encompassing the late nineteenth and early twentieth century was a flourishing time for the arts generally in Paris. The city was bursting at the seams with painters, composers, dancers, writers and poets, all feeding off the creative energy generated by their collective efforts. From this great melting pot, some truly remarkable collaborative projects emerged, with arguably the most emblematic and influential being the one-act ballet *L'Après-midi d'un faune* (*Afternoon of a faun*), whose first performance at the Théâtre du Châtelet on 29 May 1912 completely stunned the Parisian audience. Created by Sergei Diaghilev's Ballets Russes – a company which famously visited Australia three times between 1936 and 1940 – this short ballet was choreographed by Vaslav Nijinsky, who also performed the lead role. It was set to a ten-minute symphonic poem composed in 1894 by Claude Debussy, who in turn drew his inspiration from an 1876 poem by Stéphane Mallarmé ('L'Après-midi d'un faune').

Debussy was not the only composer to find in the poems of the period a fertile source of ideas. Something of a revolution had taken place in French poetry following the publication in 1857 of Charles Baudelaire's *Les Fleurs du mal*, thanks not only to the modernity of the subject matter, but also to his non-traditional use of rhythms, among other innovations. The subsequent publication of his prose poems further broke the shackles of convention. This type of experimentation gave the poets who came after Baudelaire *carte blanche* to challenge the conventions of French verse and produce innovations of their own, including some original and creative uses of rhythm. In retrospect, it might seem only natural that this innovative poetry might catch the attention of composers, given the intimate and symbiotic relationship between verse and music. But, as Emily Kilpatrick demonstrates, it still required some original and creative solutions to translate this new poetry to music. The legacy is some of the most memorable compositions in the classical repertoire.

JWS

7

Emily Kilpatrick

'To the depths of the Unknown in search of the New!': How French composers accepted Baudelaire's 'Invitation au voyage'

Early in 1870, the twenty-four-year-old Gabriel Fauré was dismissed from his post as organist of the Basilica of Saint-Sauveur in Rennes. The *curé* had grown tired of his habit of smoking in the porch during the sermons, and when, one Sunday, he turned up for service still in the white tie and tails he had worn to a municipal ball the night before, matters came to a head. Discreetly sent packing, Fauré returned to Paris and took up a new post at Notre-Dame de Clignancourt. This did not last long either, as he was more interested in catching up on the operas and concerts he had missed out on in Rennes than attending services.

Few derelictions of ecclesiastical duty, however, could have left Western music so rich a legacy. Delighted to be back in Paris, Fauré was quick to form new friendships, meeting a clutch of brilliant and ambitious young composers who were – like himself – at turning points in their professional lives. If, in the spring of 1870, one had asked Fauré, Henri Duparc or Vincent d'Indy what their jobs were, Fauré would have replied that he was an organist. Duparc was on the cusp of becoming a lawyer; d'Indy, recently graduated, seemed destined for a career in the law or the military. Emmanuel Chabrier, meanwhile, was an official in the Ministry of the Interior (a post he would hold for another decade), with dreams of writing opera.

But the same question, posed a year or two later, would have elicited a different answer. By this time Duparc had failed his bar exams and had decided to pursue a musical career; Fauré had composed a clutch of extraordinary songs and made his way into some of the city's most adventurous artistic salons; and d'Indy had scrawled a resolution in his diary: 'From today onwards, I wish to devote myself entirely to Art, to Music, not merely as a simple amateur but as an *Artist*, I make this formal vow and will never retract it.'[1] What had happened? Friendships forged in the salons and concert halls in the last months of the Second Empire had been tested by the triple catastrophes of war, siege and civil war (1870–1871), and from the wreckage of the *année terrible* this group of young composers emerged, their priorities and aspirations tempered and honed by their experiences. By the mid-1870s, these composers would become, in d'Indy's words, 'a small, inseparable group';[2] in 1887, Fauré would write: 'In reality, the musicians who interest me most are my friends, d'Indy, Chabrier, Chausson, Duparc, etc. ... those, in short, who arrived at a time where it was more difficult than ever to be an original musician.'[3]

In February 1871, with the ink on the 'shameful' Treaty of Versailles barely dry, their association would crystallise in the formation of the Société nationale de musique. But perhaps the more interesting testament to the interactions and friendships of these young composers is that within the space of a few months, in the summer and autumn of 1870, Chabrier, Duparc and Fauré had all made song settings of the poetry of Charles Baudelaire. This seems on the face of it a curious coincidence. Not a single serious composer had then attempted to set Baudelaire's poems: why now should three of them turn to his words almost simultaneously?

Just as the *année terrible* is a great inflection point in French political and social history, so these Baudelaire settings mark a musical watershed, a point at which French composers began to reckon more boldly and more consciously not just with the structures and rules of poetry, nor how they could 'transpose' it (a verb Ravel liked) into music, but also with the debates that were swirling around its very nature and purpose. Across the third quarter of the nineteenth century, first Baudelaire, then Verlaine, Rimbaud and Mallarmé grappled with the nature of poetry itself – what it was, what it could achieve, where its limits lay – and where it intersected with the other arts: how closely could music and poetry be melded, and what facets of each art remained unreachable to the other?

In the last quarter of the century it was French music, shaken by the Wagnerian revolution, that had to grapple with fundamental questions of syntax and form, synthesis and purpose. It is no coincidence that we slide into the coda of Chabrier's *L'Invitation au voyage* via an obvious quotation from *Tristan und Isolde* (see **Ex. I**): Baudelaire, after all, had been one of Wagner's first and greatest prophets in France, and Chabrier was a passionate Wagnerian long before it was fashionable.

By the 1880s, however, *wagnérisme* had overwhelmed French musical discourse. In a letter of October 1885, Debussy ruminates about 'using' Wagner to get around some compositional corners: 'I find myself obliged to invent new forms. I could turn to Wagner, but I don't need to tell you how ridiculous it would be even to try; I could only adapt his way of running scenes together'.[4] Those composers who weathered the Wagnerian storm most effectively were those who were able to shape certain aspects of Wagner's musical language to serve their own ends, just as Debussy foreshadows here. Ravel was later to argue cogently that the limits of Wagner's possibilities for French musicians lay in an essential incompatibility between Germanic procedures and the French language.[5] If, in the early 1870s, French poetry, literature and the language itself were a way of rebuilding and reclaiming artistic impetus after the catastrophic end of the Second Empire, in the 1880s and 1890s poetry offered a way to buttress French musical thought against the incursions of *wagnérisme*.

Example 1. Emmanuel Chabrier, *L'Invitation au voyage* (1870), bars 143–146; quotation of Wagner's *Tristan und Isolde* (Prelude to Act 1) shown boxed.

Rigorously schooled in aesthetics, philosophy and literature as well as music, the French composers of the Third Republic well understood the 'rules' of French poetry, and their musico-literary explorations were founded in a depth of knowledge both theoretical and applied. The vocal outputs of Fauré, Debussy and Ravel all include settings of their own, very capable, texts, as well as of the poetry of their friends.[6] (Fauré sometimes wrote to friends in comic quatrains; Debussy in turn peppered his letters with quotations from poetry.[7]) In the 1860s, Chabrier's circle of friends included the writers and poets Villiers de l'Isle-Adam, Catulle Mendès, Jean Richepin and Paul Verlaine, as well as many lesser lights; Chabrier also attended the salons of the Goncourt brothers, Leconte de Lisle and the Marquis de Ricard. In the early 1870s, Duparc and d'Indy lived in the same apartment building, with the Parnassian poet Robert de Bonnières a fellow resident and friend, whose salons attracted (among others) Anatole France, Paul Bourget and Mallarmé, as well as Saint-Saëns. Twenty years later, Debussy would be a regular guest at Mallarmé's famous *mardis*.

In the period from 1870 to the First World War and beyond, poetry reached beyond song to infuse French music in every genre, from Debussy's orchestral reimagining of Mallarmé's *L'Après-midi d'un faune* (a work with the same number of bars as the poem has lines) to Ravel's use of a poetic verse form to mould the scherzo of his 1914 Piano Trio (as we shall see), via the harmonic and textural overspill of Fauré's Verlaine *mélodies* in his piano music of the 1890s. Song, in turn, became a kind of compositional crucible, a proving ground for larger ventures: Ravel made this explicit when he described his 1907 songs *Histoires naturelles* as 'preliminary sketches' for his opera *L'Heure espagnole*.[8] In French poetry and literature, composers found new ways to approach musical structure and syntax, harmony, melodic gesture and rhythm. This chapter explores these *correspondances* (to borrow Baudelaire's term), tracing some of the dialogues that French literature engendered within and across composers' œuvres. And if we had to isolate a single point at which French music took on this spirit of cross-disciplinary adventure, it would be June 1870, when, as the political storm clouds gathered, Emmanuel Chabrier accepted Baudelaire's 'Invitation au voyage'.

Correspondances: Music and poetry at the crossroads

Chabrier set 'L'Invitation au voyage' for voice, piano and bassoon,[9] with the appellation 'scène lyrique': too big for a *mélodie*, not quite an aria, this sweepingly beautiful account remains one of the most extraordinary vocal works in the French repertoire. Its startling dissonances and chromatic sequences of sevenths have no precedent (if anything, they anticipate Bruckner a decade later), while its added-ninth harmonies, major/minor interchange and the upwards resolution of the sharpened fourth degree all introduce gestures that were to become fingerprints of Chabrier's later harmonic language. (We will return to Chabrier's setting below.) A few months after Chabrier made that setting, Duparc – serving in the *Gardes mobiles* during the Siege of Paris – also composed an *Invitation au voyage*. And over the course of the *année terrible*, Fauré made at least one, and probably three Baudelaire settings: *Hymne*, *La Rançon* and *Chant d'automne*.[10] Why did these three composers all begin to set Baudelaire essentially simultaneously? Their new friendship was founded in a passionate shared love of music as well as poetry, and they were consciously determined to forge new paths. The fruits of their creative exchange are obvious: Fauré's *Hymne* shows the unmistakable imprint of two of Duparc's op. 2 songs, published in 1869; reciprocally, the chromatically rising middle section of *Hymne* reappears at the beginning of Duparc's *Extase* of 1874 (see **Ex. 2**).

In the 1850s, Baudelaire, angered and disheartened first by the 1851 *coup d'État* and then by his own 1857 trial, had lost confidence in what Lawrence Porter terms 'the power of his message to reach and influence an audience'.[11] This crisis found some expression in his collection of prose poems, *Le Spleen de Paris*, also known as *Petits*

Example 2. Correspondences between Fauré and Duparc songs, 1869–1874

a. Henri Duparc, *Sérénade* (op. 2/4, 1869), bars 1–2

b. Henri Duparc, *Chanson triste* (op. 2/1, 1869), bars 28–29

c. Gabriel Fauré, *Hymne* (c. 1870), bars 1–2

d. Gabriel Fauré, *Hymne*, bars (12)–16

e. Gabriel Fauré, *Hymne*, bars 37–41

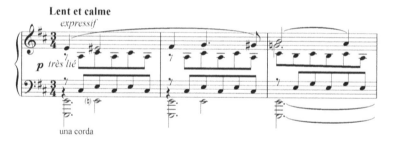

f. Henri Duparc, *Extase* (1874), bars 1–3

poèmes en prose. In this new, exploratory medium, he was no longer bound by the strictures of rhyme and metre. This collection appeared in print for the first time in 1869 (though many of its component prose poems had been separately published during Baudelaire's lifetime), as the fourth volume in the posthumous *Œuvres complètes de Charles Baudelaire.* In electing to set Baudelaire's poetry in 1870,

Fauré, Duparc and Chabrier were undoubtedly responding in part to the eighteenth *petit poème*, a prose commentary on 'L'Invitation au voyage'. There, Baudelaire entreats: 'A musician [Weber] has written *L'Invitation à la valse*; where is he who will compose *L'Invitation au voyage*?'[12]

Perhaps our composers also took some inspiration from the words with which Baudelaire closed *Les Fleurs du mal* (in the 1861 edition), concluding the poem 'Le Voyage': 'Plonger au fond du gouffre, Enfer ou Ciel, qu'importe? / Au fond de l'Inconnu pour trouver du nouveau!' ('To dive into the depths of the abyss, Heaven or Hell, what does it matter? / To the depths of the Unknown in search of the new!').[13] Fauré's third and final Baudelaire text, 'Chant d'automne', employs similar imagery and language. David Evans writes that this poem is one of several in which, through imagery of the autumn and the setting sun, the poet imagines, 'with the death of the previous poetics, the advent of the new'.[14] A song of departure, it offers like 'Le Voyage' an invitation to a voyage into the unknown (both poems use the verb *plonger*), with imagery of sunsets, and a conclusion that brings death near. (The final part of 'Le Voyage' begins, 'O Mort, vieux capitaine, il est temps! levons l'ancre!' ['O Death, old captain, it is time! Raise the anchor!'].)

Fauré's setting of 'Chant d'automne' omits Baudelaire's second, sixth and seventh quatrains, thus excising the final shift to the imperative voice ('Et pourtant, aimez-moi ...' ['And yet, love me ...']), and the evocation of the impatient tomb. By closing his song instead with the image of the autumn sun setting over the sea, Fauré perhaps aligns his reading of the poem more closely with 'Le Voyage'. His *Chant d'automne*, seemingly composed in the wake of the *année terrible*, looks beyond mortality to a redemptive hope for the future.[15] In the creation of these first Baudelaire *mélodies*, then, Chabrier, Duparc and Fauré were placing themselves in the vanguard of French musical and literary discourse: in an act of conscious artistic convergence – for it could not have been simple coincidence – they responded to the circuitous dialogues around the fusion and communicative power of the arts by simply taking the questioning, exploratory language of Baudelaire and setting it to music.[16]

A language 'not designed for poetry'[17]

The flexible emphases of the French language confounded Richard Strauss, who in 1907 wrote despairingly to Romain Rolland that on a single page of *Pelléas et Mélisande* Debussy emphasised variously

> CheVEUX, CHEveux, DES cheveux. For heaven's sake, I ask you, of these three ways there can really only be *one* which is right![18]

In response, Rolland explained:

> the great difficulty with our language is that for a very large number of words, accentuation is variable – never arbitrary, but in accordance with logical or psychological reasons. When you say to me: '... Of these 3 (cheveux) *only one can be right'*, what you say is doubtless true of German, but not of French.[19]

French poetry is syllabic rather than accentual, its forms governed not by the regular metres of English poetry but by patterns of fixed line length – the twelve-syllable alexandrine, the octosyllable, the decasyllable. Degrees of rhyme are meticulously classified, and patterns of masculine and feminine line-ends attended to; but within and across lines, accentuation is flexible, a poet's genius often revealed in the complexity of their rhythmic play. An obvious challenge when setting such malleable lines of poetry to metred music is that stresses are typically corralled into regular patterns (Debussy was one of the first composers to break decisively with such regularity). The literal application of the expected musical emphases on strong beats can thus appear to distort poetic stresses. Fauré's early songs have been condemned as somewhat inept for precisely this reason.[20] Consider the seemingly unfortunate fashion in which the weak second syllable of the word *digne* falls on a downbeat in *S'il est un charmant gazon* (long published as *Rêve d'amour*) (see **Exx. 3a – b**), or even the first bar of Fauré's first published song, *Le Papillon et la fleur*, in which the weak syllable *-vre* falls on the half-bar (see **Ex. 3c**).

Example 3. Hemiola rhythms in early Fauré songs

a. *S'il est un charmant gazon* (*Rêve d'amour*), first editions (Choudens), 1875–1879

b. *S'il est un charmant gazon* (*Rêve d'amour*), revised medium-voice edition (Hamelle), 1890

c. *Le Papillon et la fleur* (1861, published 1869), bars 10–13

Although Fauré did revise several songs to eliminate potentially unidiomatic syllabification, such instances often point to a more sophisticated grasp of the interplay of poetic and musical rhythm, one that foregrounds cross-rhythms and hemiola; his revisions in turn sometimes acknowledge that performers failed to grasp this rhythmic play. For example, in **Ex. 3a** above, if we consider the last two bars as falling into three two-beat groups (like a bar of 3/2 rather than the two three-beat bars suggested by the 3/4 time signature), the poetic emphases immediately fall into place ('<u>Bat</u> pour un <u>digne</u> des<u>sein</u>'). The apparent failure of performers to recognise this probably led him to revise the underlay in a later edition as a guard against misaccentuation (**Ex. 3b**), but if the resulting hiatus across the barline avoids the obvious pitfall, it has a cost in the loss of the rhythmic vigour of the original. In similar fashion, hearing the first two bars of the vocal entry in *Le Papillon et la fleur* as effective bars of 3/4 (above the piano's 6/8) makes sense of the poetic rhythms and establishes a pattern that pervades most of the song. Far from youthful *gaucherie*, the metric sophistication of this, the sixteen-year-old Fauré's earliest surviving work, sets a pattern that would continue across his entire compositional career, one that is rooted in the ambiguous and flexible stresses of French poetry.[21]

We see the same beguiling flexibility in the first vocal entry of Chabrier's *L'Invitation au voyage*, where the metre is deliberately, tantalisingly obscured (see **Ex. 4**). The first bars undermine the notated 6/4 with an effective 3/2 hemiola, while *sforzandi* on the fifth crotchets of bars 5 and 7 (the effective beat 3) and the rolled piano chords sounding on the second crotchet of bars 5–8 (with a rest on the first crotchet) conceal the downbeat. For the singer, the line demands a declamation that prioritises the natural and irregular inflections of the poetry above the hierarchy of the musical beat.

Catching these rhythms in performance relies on an appreciation of what singers and critics of the era referred to as *l'art de dire*: the art of declamation. Over and over again, we find composers emphasising speech rather than song: Mary Garden, the first Mélisande, recalled Debussy exhorting the cast of *Pelléas et Mélisande*, 'oubliez que vous êtes chanteurs!' ('Forget that you are singers!').[22] Jane Bathori, who premiered Ravel's *Histoires naturelles* (and others of his songs) explained of that set: 'If you try *speaking* the words, without singing but in time, you will understand straight away what Ravel wanted.'[23] Ravel made his intentions explicit on the

Example 4. Emmanuel Chabrier, *L'Invitation au voyage* (1870), bars 5–12

printed score of his opera *L'Heure espagnole*, explaining: 'Apart from the final Quintet, and, for the most part, the role of Gonzalve, who sings with an affected lyricism, [the performers should] *speak* rather than *sing* [*dire* plutôt que *chanter*]'. The mezzo Claire Croiza, who worked closely with Fauré in his later years, repeatedly emphasised that in singing French song one should first learn to recite the poetry: only thus can tempo and emphasis be determined.[24]

Contesting lyricism: Verlaine and Debussy

Baudelaire's *Le Spleen de Paris* carries a famous preface, in which Baudelaire sets out his ideal: 'Who among us has not dreamed, in his ambitious moments, of the miracle of a poetic prose, musical, without rhyme or rhythm, and sufficiently supple and striking as to shape itself around the lyrical movements of the soul, to the undulations of the imagination, to the somersaults of consciousness?'[25] These words were to resonate through French music for decades. We might sense Chabrier's response to them in the flexible declamation of his *L'Invitation*, and we hear a distant echo in Ravel's 1911 reflection on poetry and text-setting: 'It seems to me that, in dealing with things that are truly experienced and felt, free verse is preferable to regular verse', he writes, describing Jules Renard's prose poems, *Histoires naturelles*, as 'delicate, rhythmic, though rhythmic in a completely different way from classical verse'.[26] We hear Baudelaire again, quoted directly, in Debussy's October 1885 letter already cited above, in which the composer explains that his 'symphonic ode' *Zuleima* (his first *envoi* from Rome, never published and now lost) is 'not anything like the sort of music that I want to write, I want a music that will be sufficiently supple and striking to shape itself around the lyrical movements of the soul ...'[27] It was surely Baudelaire's preface, too, that offered a prompt for Debussy's *Proses lyriques* (1892–1893, published 1895), composed to his own texts. Here, Debussy's explicit rejection of *poésie* in favour of 'le miracle d'une prose poétique' ('the miracle of a poetic prose') may also have been something of a musical counterpart to the contradictory title that Paul Verlaine had appended to his 1874 collection of poems: *Romances sans paroles* (*Songs without words*).

As Baudelaire had wrestled with form and rhythm in the 1850s, across the 1860s Verlaine had begun to question the communicative power of words themselves. His troubled explorations culminated in the 1869 collection *Fêtes galantes*, which call on silence, wordplay, satire, and pure, wordless sound, lines of poetry vanishing in musical notes (the 'do, mi, sol, la, si' of 'Sur l'herbe'). The volume's concluding poem, 'Colloque sentimental', sees what Porter terms a 'failure of dialogue'[28] made dramatic and explicit, words of intimacy and love abruptly negated: 'Toujours vois-tu mon âme en rêve? – Non.' ('Do you still see my soul when you dream? – No.') Debussy was to choose 'Colloque sentimental' as the last of his 17 Verlaine settings, in 1904, using the stubbornly contrarian poem to turn the very impossibility of the language against itself. The vocal

Example 5. Claude Debussy, 'Colloque sentimental'
(*Fêtes galantes* II, 1904),
bars 4–8

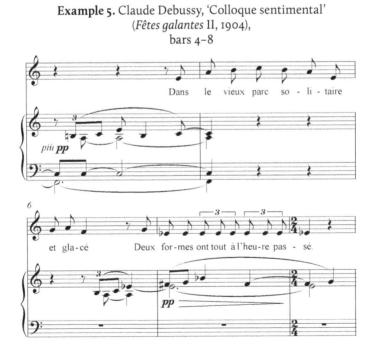

line is often hesitant, ungainly: the first line, for example, sees the two least important words, *le* and *et*, fall on the two downbeats (see **Ex. 5**) (there is little sense here of Fauréen hemiola). Just as the poem's attempts to take flight are grounded by the bleakly prosaic respondent, here deliberately 'awkward' text-setting equivalently conveys its grim nihilism.

If Verlaine's *Fêtes galantes* marked the apex of the poet's frustration with his craft, *Romances sans paroles*, at least by its title, abandons words altogether – instead, it looks explicitly to music (its title echoes Mendelssohn's *Lieder ohne Worte*). Its poems, however, represent a reassembling of poetic technique and purpose. For the most part, they leave the grotesques of the *Fêtes galantes* behind, with a fluid and virtuoso play of rhythm and rhyme creating the impression, as Porter observes, of replacing words 'without actually doing so'.[29] For all the significance of Baudelaire's words and ideas at that inflection point of 1870, it was Verlaine's poetry above all – and these two collections in particular – that shaped the *mélodie* of the 1880s and 1890s.

Among the most remarkable of the innumerable Verlaine *mélodies* are the young Debussy's early settings, the first of them composed when he was not yet 20 years old, at a time when no other serious composer had published a setting of Verlaine's poetry. Verlaine's turbulent personal life – in 1872 he had deserted his young wife and son for Arthur Rimbaud, and in 1873 he was imprisoned after wounding Rimbaud in a duel – had shadowed his reputation, and it was not until the later 1880s that his work began to receive more widespread acclaim. And yet in 1882 Debussy had begun setting Verlaine's words: 'Fantoches', 'En sourdine', 'Mandoline', 'Clair de lune', 'Pantomime'. These five songs, collectively titled *Fêtes galantes*, open the collection known as the *Recueil Vasnier*: a set of 13 songs that Debussy composed for his muse and mistress Marie Vasnier, presenting her with the manuscript volume on his departure for Rome in January 1885.[30]

The songs of the *Recueil Vasnier*, which were not then intended for publication,[31] are like nothing else in the French repertoire to that time, and very little since: they demand an agile coloratura, rare in a repertoire that typically preferences mid-range voices in order to privilege the delivery of poetic text above vocal display. The significant vocalising passages found in a number of the songs were plainly intended to reflect Mme Vasnier's virtuosity. It is interesting, however, that the most significant of these wordless vocalises are found in the five Verlaine settings, given the poetry's complex dialogues of text and subtext, its tension between form and content, and its overt and implicit juggling with poetry as sound.[32] 'Fantoches', 'Mandoline' and 'Pantomime' all feature extended vocalises: in 'Pantomime' this passage gives voice to the unspoken text foreshadowed in the poem's conclusion, which evokes the voices that Columbine hears 'in her heart': 'Colombine rêve, surprise / De sentir un cœur dans la brise / Et d'entendre en son cœur des voix' ('Columbine dreams, amazed / to sense a heart in the wind / and hear voices in her heart'). As the voice becomes a purely melodic instrument (Debussy's manuscript shows no text underlay at all), Verlaine's words literally dissolve in unfiltered sound. In 'Fantoches' and 'Pantomime' in particular, the vertiginous virtuosity of these passages heightens the inherent sense of menace in the poems. On the vocal tightrope, we hang above a poetic abyss (Baudelaire's *gouffre*, Mallarmé's *Néant*?).

In 1891 and 1892, Debussy revised 'Fantoches' and recomposed 'En sourdine' and 'Clair de lune' entirely; the three songs were published collectively in 1903 (as *Fêtes galantes*, vol. 1). In 'Fantoches', the most significant musical differences between the 1882 and 1891 versions lie in the setting of the last tercet, which sees the final extravagant vocalise cut down to a tauter conclusion, on a single, twice repeated 'la ...' Alongside this, Debussy revised the endings of the first two strophes, replacing a melisma on the final syllable of each verse with more repeated 'la's (see **Ex. 6**). More focused in musical terms, the choice of this syllable also seems to respond directly to the repeated 'la' sounds inherent in Verlaine's text: 'Scaramouche et Pulcinel*la* / Qu'un mauvais dessein rassem*bla* / Gesticulent, noirs sous *la* lune ('Scaramouche and Pulcinella / Drawn together by some evil scheme / Gesticulate, black beneath the moon').[33] Again, Debussy probes the borderlands between poetic syntax and musical sound, in ways that echo Verlaine's manipulations of that same liminal space.

Example 6. Claude Debussy, 'Fantoches' (*Fêtes galantes* I, 1891), bars 10–16

Interesting, in this context, is Debussy's choice *not* to set the two poems from *Fêtes galantes* in which Verlaine plays explicitly on musical pitches: 'Colombine' and 'Sur l'herbe'. Ravel, on the other hand, set 'Sur l'herbe' in 1907, his one published Verlaine setting. While he obediently sets the poet's solfeging to the equivalent pitches, more subtle is a fleeting quotation from Debussy's 'Clair de lune' – not either version of the song, this time, but the piano piece, the third movement of the *Suite bergamasque* (published in 1905).

This reminiscence, which occurs on the song's final words – 'Hé! Bonsoir la Lune!' – is so obvious as to suggest quotation marks, a fleeting dip into an E-flat ninth chord in which every note in the bar contradicts the four-sharp key signature (see **Ex. 7**).

Example 7.

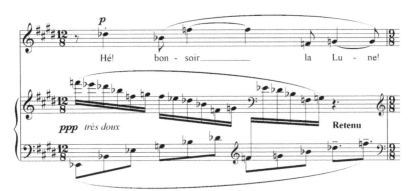

a. Debussy, 'Clair de lune' (*Suite bergamasque*, 1905), bars 29–30

b. Ravel, *Sur l'herbe* (1907), bar 21

An interesting dialogue emerges when we consider that by this time Ravel had fallen out with Debussy, a rift largely manufactured by others and one that distressed him greatly, as Romain Rolland recorded in his journal on 22 May 1907.[34] It was around the height of this tension that Ravel composed *Sur l'herbe*, whose manuscript is dated 6 June. The quotation of 'Clair de lune' is surely deliberate in its obviousness, an audible salute to the composer Ravel stood accused of mindlessly imitating. Although Ravel and Debussy had never been close, and would have little direct communication thereafter, their literary tastes overlapped significantly, notably in their shared love of Baudelaire and Mallarmé above all other French poets, and in their attraction to the darker side of Verlaine. (An awkward moment occurred a few years later, when both composers published a set of three Mallarmé settings and realised that they had chosen two of the same poems.) Ravel's decision to set (and publish) a *Fête galante* in 1907, in the wake of Debussy's two recently published collections of songs from the same volume, was therefore a charged one. His quotation of 'Clair de lune', in the context of this sardonic poem, must be ironic, but one wonders whether it might equally have served as a subtle olive branch, one composer reaching out to the other through their shared language of musical and poetic gesture.

Songs without words: Verlaine and Fauré

Fauré, like Debussy, made 17 Verlaine settings, all between 1887 and 1894. These songs coincide with a great stylistic leap in his instrumental music, which it is hard not to ascribe, at least in part, to the galvanising impetus of Verlaine's words. Fauré's letters and reflections reveal such eagerness about the poetry, its potential, and his own response to it, that the overflow from song into instrumental music seems natural. 'Verlaine is a marvellous poet to set', he wrote in 1911,[35] while his letters, at the time of composing the five 'Venetian' songs (op. 58) of 1891, bubble with excitement:

> I enclose ['Green'] herewith in fear and trembling! Have I adequately expressed this marvellous hymn of adoration! [*sic*] I don't know. [...] And if on first reading it doesn't please you, will you promise me not to lose heart and to read it again? It's a difficult one to interpret: slow-moving and agitated in expression, happy and sad, fervent and downcast! So many things in thirty bars! And you'll perhaps find I'm making a great fuss.[36]

The apex of Fauré's Verlaine years was the cycle *La Bonne Chanson* (completed early in 1894, on poems from Verlaine's 1870 collection), a work of such harmonic daring and pianistic complexity that it reportedly prompted his dear friend Saint-Saëns to exclaim: 'Fauré has gone completely mad!'[37] Hard on the heels of this great cycle, in 1894 Fauré composed three of his finest piano pieces: his Fourth Valse-Caprice, Fifth Barcarolle and Sixth Nocturne. Each of them reaches beyond what its predecessors in each genre had attempted, in terms of pianistic technique, and harmonic and structural daring. Each of them, too, shows remarkable overlaps with the musical content of the Verlaine settings, a closer encounter between piano music and song than anywhere else in Fauré's catalogue. Perhaps most obvious is the overflow from 'En sourdine' evident in both the Barcarolle and the Nocturne. 'En sourdine' is shown here not in its manuscript key of E-flat major, but the later high-voice transposition of F-sharp major, in which these textural and pianistic affinities are closest (see **Ex. 8**).[38]

Further correspondences abound. One can very easily play directly from 'C'est l'extase', the fifth of the 'Venetian' songs, into the opening of the Sixth Nocturne (in the same key), particularly across their shared rising arpeggio figures leading up to a singing line, while the Nocturne's minuet-like middle section (from bar 19) develops a figure first heard in 'Green' (and reprised in 'C'est l'extase'). (This melodic gesture returns in the development section of the first movement of Fauré's First Quintet, on which he was working at the same time.) The central tonal progression of the Nocturne, too, from the D-flat conclusion in bar 63 to the A major of bar 65, moving to C major in bar 66, has a direct parallel in the equivalent progression (D-flat – A – C) of 'Avant que tu ne t'en ailles', the sixth song of *La Bonne Chanson* (see **Ex. 9**).[39]

While the conclusion of the Fifth Barcarolle gestures directly to 'En sourdine', its opening, under the hand and gesturally, lies close to 'J'allais par des chemins perfides', the fourth song of *La Bonne Chanson*, both F-sharp minor movements characterised by their torturous chromaticism (see **Ex. 10**).

Example 8. Correspondences across Fauré's Fifth Barcarolle (op. 66, 1894), Sixth Nocturne (op. 63, 1894) and 'En sourdine' (*Cinq mélodies 'de Venise'*, op. 58, 1891)

a. 'En sourdine', bars 39–42

b. Fifth Barcarolle, bars 126–127

c. Sixth Nocturne, bar 69

Example 9. Correspondences between Fauré's Sixth Nocturne and 'Avant que tu ne t'en ailles' (*La Bonne Chanson*, op. 61, 1894)

a. 'Avant que tu ne t'en ailles', bars 6–10

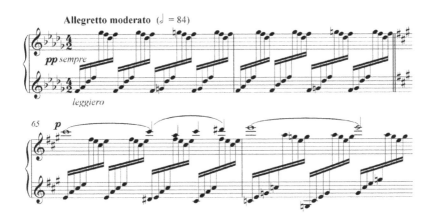

b. Sixth Nocturne, bars 63–66

Example 10. Correspondences between Fauré's Fifth Barcarolle and 'J'allais par des chemins perfides' (*La Bonne Chanson*)

a. 'J'allais par des chemins perfides', bars 1–4

b. Fifth Barcarolle, bars 1–2

The Fourth Valse-Caprice, meanwhile, is the only one of Fauré's instrumental works to make reference to his song *Lydia*, whose characteristic rising gesture in Lydian mode is threaded through *La Bonne Chanson* (most obviously in its third, fifth and eighth songs). Its appearance in bars 146–152 of the Valse-Caprice corresponds both texturally and structurally with bars 31–34 of the cycle's eighth song, 'N'est-ce pas?': a touching-down between musical paragraphs, both passages show similar voice-leading, with rising fourths between bass and treble across the sequence (see **Ex. 11**). The A-flat tonality of the Valse-Caprice also recalls the first song of *La Bonne Chanson*, 'Une Sainte dans son auréole', while the Valse-Caprice's four-part 'noodling' passages of bars 34–57 (and similar) closely recall that song's textures, inverting its characteristic descending figure with ascending ones.

Example 11. Correspondences between Fauré's Fourth Valse-Caprice and 'N'est-ce pas?' (*La Bonne Chanson*)

a. 'N'est-ce pas?', bars 31–35

b. Fourth Valse-Caprice, bars 146–153

A philosophy of composition: Maurice Ravel

In December 1894, Fauré returned to Verlaine's poetry for the last time, with the shattering *Prison*. Around the same time, the nineteen-year-old Ravel attempted a setting of the same poem ('Le ciel est, par-dessus le toit', from *Sagesse* of 1881), though he later abandoned it. However, around that time Ravel was developing another, and – for him – more potent literary passion. In October, his friend Ricardo Viñes recorded in his journal that he had visited the Ravel family to return some Baudelaire he had borrowed, 'and there I saw the six censored and forbidden extracts of *Les Fleurs du mal*; needless to say, they're the most beautiful. When Ravel has copied them out, from a copy that a friend has passed to him, he will lend them to me so that I can copy them myself.'[40] A year later, the pair were talking 'of literature and art, and [Ravel] said that the copy of *Gaspard de la nuit* that I'd bought in London was very rare'.[41]

Aloysius Bertrand's *Gaspard de la nuit* (posthumously published in 1842) is the only significant collection of French prose poetry before Baudelaire's *Spleen de Paris*, and Baudelaire's preface to his volume acknowledges his debt. It takes the form of a letter, addressed to the historian and *homme de lettres* Arsène Houssaye, and explains that it was 'the famous *Gaspard de la nuit* (a book known to you, to me, and to some of our friends; isn't that sufficient to call it famous?), which gave me the idea to try something similar ...'[42] It was undoubtedly Baudelaire, therefore, who had inspired the young Ravel and Viñes to seek out Bertrand, a connection that would blossom 14 years later, when Ravel composed a virtuosic piano triptych on three of Bertrand's prose poems (Viñes gave the premiere).

The published score of Ravel's *Gaspard de la nuit* prefaces each piece with the poem that inspired it, and the pieces trace the three narratives with vivid precision – we hear Ondine's sulking tear, Scarbo's scratching at the curtains, the spider spinning its macabre necklace. The pianist Vlado Perlemuter, who studied all Ravel's piano music with the composer, recalled him explaining that he had wanted to produce in *Gaspard* 'a caricature of Romanticism': 'but maybe it got the better of me ...'[43] But what structure did Ravel employ to sustain these 'caricatures', these extravagant, vividly pictorial musicalised poems? The underlying forms – concealed, sometimes distorted, but nevertheless discernible – are, as Roy Howat has shown, those of that most rational and intellectual of musical containers: the Classical sonata form.[44] In this ironic allusion, we sense the influence of a near-exact contemporary of Bertrand: Edgar Allan Poe. In his essay 'The Philosophy of Composition', Poe declared that the composition of his poem 'The Raven' 'proceeded step by step, to its completion, with the precision and rigid consequence of a mathematical problem'.[45] Ravel, in turn, claimed that 'The Philosophy of Composition' was 'The finest treatise on composition, in my opinion, and the one which in any case had the greatest influence upon me'.[46] It was certainly one that resonated perfectly with this son of a distinguished engineer and inventor. Elsewhere, he explained, 'Poe taught me that true art is a perfect balance between pure intellect and emotion.'[47]

If Classical forms underpin the wild prose poems of *Gaspard*, in his Piano Trio of 1914 Ravel turned his models on their head: the Trio's second movement (the effective scherzo) bears the heading 'Pantoum'. In this poetic form, the second and fourth lines of one strophe become the first and third lines of the next, creating an intricate dance in which partners are continually exchanged, antecedent and consequent lines changing places in each strophe. In his *Petit traité de poésie française*, Théodore de Banville set out the procedures of the pantoum, demonstrating that the poem is essentially formed of two separate ideas, which are developed in tandem and woven together.[48] One of Baudelaire's best-known pantoums is 'Harmonie du soir', a poem set by Debussy in 1889 (the second of his *Cinq poèmes de Charles Baudelaire*). 'Harmonie du soir' was also to provide the inspiration for the fourth of Debussy's piano Preludes of 1910 ('Les sons et les parfums tournent dans l'air du soir ...'), while a musical echo of the Prelude recurs in the piano piece 'Les soirs illuminés par l'ardeur du charbon' of 1917. Completing a pantoum-like pattern, this title is drawn in its turn from Baudelaire's poem 'Le Balcon' (the first of Debussy's *Cinq poèmes*) ...

Ravel never set a poetic pantoum, but his Trio echoes its interchange of contrasted material. Brian Newbould has shown how the premise of pantoum form – the alternate development of two themes that 'may be extricated and reassembled as separate, intelligible entities'[49] – maps precisely over Ravel's 'Pantoum'. Just as interesting, though, is the way in which related exchanges of antecedent and consequent gestures underpin other works. Howat has demonstrated the deployment of such exchanges in Ravel's piano suite *Le Tombeau de Couperin* (a work begun around the same time, though completed three years later), for example.[50] If we look back again to *Gaspard*, of 1908, we realise that the poems that Ravel chose make a feature of the repetition and reassembling of ideas and syntax: the repeated 'Que de fois ...' ('How many times ...') of 'Scarbo', the 'Serait-ce ...' ('Could it be ...') of 'Le Gibet'. Ravel liked the discipline of repetition, the way it compelled him to find originality in startling ways. We hear this, *par excellence*, in *Boléro* (1928), but also in, for example, the unrelenting B-flat bell of 'Le Gibet'. 'This bell', the composer told the young pianist Henriette Faure, 'does not dominate, it *is*, it tolls unwearyingly.' He linked it, appropriately, to Edgar Allan Poe's grim raven, with its ceaseless refrain of 'Nevermore.'[51] In 'The Philosophy of Composition', Poe explains how he constructed 'The Raven': 'I determined to produce continuously novel effects by the variation of the application of the refrain', he writes, 'the refrain itself remaining for the most part, unvaried.'[52] The variation of the *application* of the refrain: this remains one of the most effective summations of Ravel's compositional practice. He brings us back and back again to the same place, but on each arrival it looks and sounds a little different.

Shortly before he undertook his Trio, Ravel made three settings of Stéphane Mallarmé's poetry.[53] The third of his chosen poems, 'Surgi de la croupe et du bond' ('Risen from the crupper and the leap'), is Mallarmé at his most opaque, and Ravel's setting similarly represents his most abstruse musical creation, his furthest flight from tonality. What drew Ravel to what he himself described as 'the strangest, if not the most hermetic of [Mallarmé's] sonnets'?[54] One reading of this difficult poem centres around its play of symmetries and inversions. The vase's rounded shape is suggestive of plenitude and promise, but this is denied: it remains empty, holding neither water nor the flower towards which it aspires. The tercets, in particular, emphasise words connected with death, and thus nothingness: *veuvage, agonise, funèbres, expirer, tenèbres* ('widowhood', 'is dying', 'funereal', 'expire/breathe out', 'darkness').[55] Against this emptiness, however, Mallarmé reveals the perfect symmetry of the object itself, reflected through the metaphor of two mouths or meeting lips and the final allusion to the rose, an ancient symbol of fulfilment and perfection.

Ravel's setting of this sonnet is the only clear ternary structure of his three Mallarmé settings. The verb *s'interrompt* ('stops short') that ends the first A section (and poetic quatrain) effectively places the B section (bars 9–18) as an interruption, in conceptual as well as harmonic terms. However, the ternary form instead mirrors the poem's delineation of symmetry, through the physical form of the vase. This is reinforced through the very appearance of Ravel's score: the outer sections, with their upward arpeggio figures and sinuous melodic lines, visually suggest the leaping form of the vase and the curves of its mouth. The corresponding blankness in the staves of the central passage (which begin to fill as the strings take over from the piano after the *volta*, from bar 16) is visually evocative of the empty belly of the vase, just as the aural effect, of bell-like piano chimes resonating in near-silence (the strings sound *pianissimo* chords in harmonics), contrasts with the more linear movement of the outer sections. Given Mallarmé's own preoccupation with

Example 12. Maurice Ravel, 'Surgi de la croupe et du bond'
(*Trois Poèmes de Stéphane Mallarmé*, 1914), bars 22–24

the visual appearance of his poetry on the page, and the suggestive possibilities or symbolism inherent in the shapes of individual letters, words, lines, and strophes, it is hard not to view Ravel's setting as responding to this visual patterning in his own medium.[56]

Emptiness and completion are echoed, too, in the opposition of the pitches C and F-sharp: a tritone apart, these pitches represent an exact division of the octave, and respectively the 'emptiest' and 'fullest' key signatures, sitting at diametrically opposite points on the 'circle of fifths' that defines Western musical tonalities. This opposition is threaded through all three of Ravel's Mallarmé settings, but it is foregrounded in the third. The opening pedal C gives way to F-sharp (via C-sharp) in bar 8, marking the 'interruption', while in the final bar of the song, the piano returns to the bass C of the opening as the voice sings that key word *rose* on F-sharp. For the space of one quaver beat we hear the tritone – emptiness and fulfilment – unadorned (see **Ex. 12**).

The French composers of the pre-World War 1 generation, then, gave the twentieth century the tools for bringing the arts together, for translating or 'transposing' one art form into another. These were the precise, studied tools of orchestration, musical form, harmony and text-setting: not just an expressive language, but a rigorously intellectual one. In a 1933 article, Ravel acknowledged that 'for me there are not several arts, but one alone: music, painting and literature differ only in their means of expression. [...] As for me, I was certainly born a musician, but [...] I realise that I read professionally, as if I were a writer. The same is true of painting; I look at a painting not as an amateur, but as a painter.'[57] Claude Monet would have appreciated this. That great pioneer, an artist of searing, scientific discipline, reflected in his turn that he 'should be regarded by posterity [...] as a contemporary of Stéphane Mallarmé and Claude Debussy. Like them, and like Baudelaire, I say there are points at which the arts meet.'[58]

Further reading

Abbott, Helen, *Between Baudelaire and Mallarmé: Voice, Conversation and Music*, Farnham: Ashgate, 2009.

Howat, Roy, *The Art of French Piano Music: Debussy, Ravel, Fauré, Chabrier*, London and New Haven: Yale University Press, 2009.

Kilpatrick, Emily, *French Art Song: History of a New Music, 1870–1914*, Rochester, NY: University of Rochester Press (Eastman Studies in Music), 2022.

Langham Smith, Richard, and Caroline Potter (eds), *French Music Since Berlioz*, Aldershot: Ashgate, 2006.

On Cinema

Commercial cinema as we know it today was born on 28 December 1895 in the Salon indien of the Grand Café on the boulevard des Capucines in Paris, not far from the place de l'Opéra. On that day, 33 people paid for the privilege of watching the projection on a screen of ten short films – or 'animated photographic views', as they were dubbed by Louis Lumière, the engineer from Lyon who had made them using a machine called the 'Cinématographe' that he and fellow engineer Jules Carpentier had invented. Louis and his older brother Auguste had organised this public screening, the first time moving pictures were presented to a paying audience. If the Lumière brothers were disappointed by the initial turn-out, they very quickly had reason to smile: news of this novel form of entertainment spread like wildfire through the city and, over the weeks and months that followed, Parisians queued in growing numbers along the boulevard des Capucines and around the corner into the rue de Caumartin, awaiting their turn to experience this new phenomenon. This was quite literally a 'block-buster' of a show.

Louis Lumière's new-fangled machine made it possible for the viewing of moving pictures to become a publicly shared experience, thereby earning him and his brother Auguste a well-deserved place in history. It should be noted, however, that the Lumière brothers never laid claim to having invented cinema as such. That honour, it is generally acknowledged, belongs to Thomas Edison and his collaborator William Kennedy Dickson, who first produced moving photographic images, or a 'motion picture', four years before the

Lumière brothers. The short sequence of about ten seconds showing Dickson dipping his hat – the *Dickson Greeting* – was filmed in Edison's Black Maria studio in West Orange, New Jersey, on 20 May 1891. Using a machine called the Kinetoscope, it was presented to a gathering of around 150 activists of the Federation of Women's Clubs, to great acclaim. Edison's Kinetoscope had one major drawback, however: it only allowed viewing by one person at a time, or two at the most.

Meanwhile, back in Paris, the photographer and science teacher Émile Reynaud had been working on a device that would project rapid sequences of drawings onto a screen, making them appear animated. On 28 October 1892, using his 'Théâtre optique', he presented the first animated 'cartoon' at the Musée Grévin, Paris's wax museum. A piano was played to accompany the projection, using an original composition by Gaston Paulin.

There was clearly a frenzy of activity taking place during this period in different parts of the world, all of which was leading to the development of cinema as we know it today. It is worth remembering, however, that the various innovations outlined above did not emerge from a void. They were in a sense the culmination or crystallisation of a series of earlier inventions dating back to flipped picture books, magic lanterns and various other optical gadgets, not to mention photography itself. Like all origin stories, that of cinema is more complex than it might first appear.

What we can say with more certainty, however, is that the conception of cinema as an art form originated in France, where it is referred to as 'le septième art' (the seventh art). This puts cinema on an equivalent footing to architecture, sculpture, music and literature. Given this status, it is no surprise that French directors came to earn recognition as *auteurs*. As Phil Powrie points out, however, the world of French cinema is not confined to high-brow arty films. French directors make films covering all styles and genres, and audiences in France enjoy a Hollywood-style blockbuster as much as people anywhere. The French are naturally heavily invested in their own home-grown cinema, and many in the industry there have reservations and concerns about the influence and dominance of Hollywood. But that does not mean that everyone in France is hostile to American cinema. Indeed, the country's highest accolade, the Légion d'honneur, has been awarded numerous times to American actors and directors, from Robert Redford and Shirley McLaine to Jerry Lewis and Sylvester Stallone. Contrary to the myth, there is nothing snobbish about France's love of cinema.

JWS

8

Phil Powrie

(Re(viewing) French cinema

Given that film took off in France in 1895, it is obvious that where the cinema is concerned the French have done rather a lot for us. And as if that were not enough, the concept of film as a 'seventh art' originates in France in the 1920s with Riccioto Canudo, legitimising what might otherwise have been seen as no more than a sophisticated fairground attraction. Even more than that, in the 1950s the Young Turks of the New Wave argued that the film director was no less important to a film than a novelist might be for a novel, and they extended what Riccioto Canudo had started with the idea of film as a seventh art by elevating certain directors, some, like Alfred Hitchcock, the directors of mainstream Hollywood films, to the status of *auteurs*.

If you are a traditional cinephile, French cinema is therefore synonymous with high art. It has great artists and movements, like literature or painting. Your attention will be focused on the two Golden Ages: the Poetic Realism of the 1930s or the New Wave of the early 1960s. You might grudgingly admit that a handful of later films, even if you do not like them – for example the squeaky cleanness of *Le Fabuleux Destin d'Amélie Poulain/Amélie* (Jean-Pierre Jeunet, 2001) or the saccharine sweetness of *Les Choristes/The Chorus* (Christophe Barratier, 2004) – are important markers of social change, and particularly of the fondness for nostalgia. Given that you are a firm believer in the pre-eminence of the *auteur*, you will also admire a slew of mavericks and quirky individuals, for example Robert Bresson or Jean-Pierre Melville. And last but not least, you will perhaps grudgingly admit that none of this would work without the celebrity culture surrounding charismatic stars, such as Jean Gabin, Catherine Deneuve, Alain Delon, Gérard Depardieu, Juliette Binoche amongst others.

In this chapter, paradoxically, I want both to extend the idea of French cinema as one of the world's great art cinemas, as well as challenge the accepted history of French cinema as the inevitable genealogy of usually individual (white) male genius, supported by whiter than white stars. The history of French cinema, no less than the history of cinema *tout court* is also the history of popular cinema. In the case of French cinema it is in addition the history of an institution that has allowed more women and ethnic-minority directors (in this case Maghrebi) to make films than any other country.

Our question is: 'what have the French done for us?' The self-evident answer where cinema is concerned is that the French gave us film and turned it into an art. I will, however, add a number of key points. In the friendly competition between Hollywood and French cinema, the French have known how to borrow from Hollywood and to Gallicise different film genres in what we could call, borrowing the term from electronica music and the luxury goods industry, the 'French touch'. To art, the feminisation of the industry and Gallicisation, we can add that the French cinema has developed in recent years a strong star system for ethnic-minority actors, and, finally, has managed to export what is often seen as unexportable: film comedies. What these comedies have done for us in their touching displays of disavowed self-examination is to lay bare social tensions in a multicultural society that politically denies its multiculturalism. From turning a fairground attraction into high art, to maintaining fairground attractions that make you laugh while making you think, the French have therefore done a lot for us.

Before embarking on these issues, I would like to offer some basic background so as to demonstrate why French cinema is important beyond the borders of the Hexagon.[1] The French industry releases between 250 and 300 films every year. While this is clearly nowhere near the massive volume of the Hollywood, Indian, Chinese or Nollywood industries, nonetheless France is the European leader in terms of the number of films produced each year (Table 1). In 1994 the French argued that films should be a 'cultural exception' in the complex negotiations of the World Trade Organization's General Agreement on Tariffs and Trade (GATT), much to the dismay of the Americans, who saw this as a protectionist measure. It allowed the French to continue to provide State support for the cinema industry through subsidies from taxes on cinema ticket sales (the *avance sur recettes*). This has to a large extent allowed French cinema to maintain a high volume of films annually, and has correlatively also enabled the development of a high number of first-time films, particularly by women directors, something I shall return to. The GATT round relating to the cinema industry was of course not the first time that the industries in France and the USA had been in tension, as we shall see.

Table 1. Largest number of films produced and revenue globally (2015–2016).

Country	No. of Films	Revenue US$ bn
India	1,986	2.4
Nigeria	997	Not known
USA	791	10.3
China	686	8.9
France	300	1.5
UK	298	1.7
Spain	255	0.7
Germany	226	1.2
Italy	185	0.7

Source: UNESCO Institute for Statistics (number of films) and Statista (revenue).

French films regularly win international awards. In the case of the Oscars, for example, a French film has won the Best Foreign Language Film 12 times, a record second only to that of Italian films (14 Oscars). The following films won Academy Awards and remain well known by cinephiles: *Mon oncle/My Uncle* (Jacques Tati, 1958), *Un homme et une femme/A Man and a Woman* (Claude Lelouch, 1966), famous for its haunting signature tune, the surreal satire *Le Charme discret de la bourgeoisie/The Discreet Charm of the Bourgeoisie* (Luis Buñuel, 1972), *La Nuit américaine/Day for Night* (François Truffaut, 1973) and *Indochine* (Régis Wargnier, 1992). Of course, some films won Oscars and are now forgotten, such as *Les Dimanches de Ville d'Avray/Sundays and Cybele* (Serge Bourguignon, 1962) or *La Vie devant soi/Madame Rosa* (Moshé Misrahi, 1977); while others were nominated but failed to win despite now being seen as critical in the history of French cinema, such as *Les Parapluies de Cherbourg/The Umbrellas of Cherbourg* (Jacques Demy, 1964), *Lacombe, Lucien* (Louis Malle, 1974), *37°2 le matin/Betty Blue* (Jean-Jacques Beineix, 1986), *Cyrano de Bergerac* (Jean-Paul Rappeneau, 1990) and *Le Fabuleux Destin d'Amélie Poulain*. Sometimes the BAFTAs have given Best Foreign Film to French films when the Oscars did not, such as in the case of *La Nuit américaine* and *Ridicule* (Patrice Leconte, 1996); indeed, in the 2000s Jacques Audiard won the top award twice, for *De battre mon cœur s'est arrêté/The Beat That My Heart Skipped* (2005) and *Un prophète/A Prophet* (2009).

Celebrity culture plays a large part in the visibility of French cinema, not just in France but also in the USA. Many French actors have worked for Hollywood, such as Léa Seydoux and Sophie Marceau, who have both starred in James Bond films; or the status of French stars is sufficiently strong that their films do well when distributed abroad, such as the films of Gérard Depardieu, Catherine Deneuve and Juliette Binoche.

Certain genres, such as heritage films, which in France are seen as mainstream, can pass elsewhere as art-house films; and indeed in some cases they have been adopted by other media, such as in the case of the well-known Stella Artois 'Reassuringly Expensive' TV campaign in the UK, whose advertisements were initially based on one of the first French heritage films, *Jean de Florette* (Claude Berri, 1986). The advertisements nearly all used the Verdi theme from *Jean de Florette* and the rustic French setting of the film; moreover, two of them were pastiches of films by other heritage films: 'Returning Hero' (1999) pastiches *La Vie et rien d'autre/Life and Nothing But* (Bertrand Tavernier, 1989) and 'The Good Doctor' (2002) pastiches *Le Hussard sur le toit/The Horseman on the Roof* (Jean-Paul Rappeneau,1995). This last ad won the top advertising award in the 2002 Cannes Lions International Festival of Creativity. Astonishingly, the dialogue for these advertisements broadcast on UK TV was entirely in French without subtitles, demonstrating the extent to which the heritage genre *à la française* was part of the 1990s zeitgeist.[2]

The French touch
French cinema matters, then, because it carries with it, rightly or wrongly, a mark of quality, of high art, and more particularly a mark of European quality in the face of Hollywood domination of the English-speaking market. But as I commented above, the intercultural exchange between French cinema and Hollywood goes back well beyond the 1994 GATT negotiations.

Cinema may have originated in France with the realist shorts of the Lumière brothers or the fantastical and often surreal shorts of Georges Méliès, but it quickly became a global phenomenon, as demonstrated not least in the USA where the French firm Pathé had studios, turning out some ten films a week. A new development occurred in 1908 with the creation of the Société du Film d'Art. The purpose of this organisation was to lift film out of its popular origins in fairground entertainment, and to give it cultural respectability. These films, often historical epics, as was the case with the first one, *L'Assassinat du duc de Guise/The Assassination of the Duc de Guise* (André Calmettes, 1908), are the forerunners of the *tradition de qualité* of the 1950s, much despised by the Young Turks of the New Wave, and the heritage film of the 1980s and 1990s. This early expansion of the French cinema marks a high point. Pathé had built their own filmstock factories, so were no longer dependent on American filmstock; French films accounted for something like 60% of the world market. But two events were critical in upsetting the balance of power between the French and US industries: the first was the Great War with its disruption to supplies, and the second the coming of sound. The latter in particular meant that Pathé's dominance of the world market collapsed due to the linguistic specificity of sound cinema.

For a few short years in the early 1930s, film companies made 'multi-language' films: the same film was made in the same studios in different languages. This expensive and complex practice was soon abandoned. But the French in particular began to adopt Hollywood genres, such as the ubiquitous film musical, which Hollywood had inherited from the French and Viennese stage operetta tradition; indeed, the quintessential screen Frenchman of the time, Maurice Chevalier, went from the French music-hall to star in a series of Hollywood film musicals with Jeanette McDonald. The interplay between the two cinemas carried on with the adoption by Hollywood of many of the stylistic features of 1930s Poetic Realism in the film noir of the 1940s and 1950s; filmmakers then re-adopted some of the features in Hollywood-style police thrillers, for example Jean-Pierre Melville during the 1960s. Perhaps the most successful recent example of this interplay is Luc Besson, whose early films, such as *Subway* (1986) or the action thriller *Nikita* (1990), adopted Hollywood styles – the opening car-chase in the first film, for example, or the shoot-out in the Train bleu restaurant in the second – while introducing a particularly Gallic and often very quirky flavour. The interplay in the case of *Nikita* is even more complex, in that Hollywood then produced a remake, *Point of No Return* (John Badham, 1993), and the film inspired a Canadian-based TV series, *La Femme Nikita* (five seasons, 1997–2001) as well as an American TV series with CW (CBS/Warner, four seasons, 2010–2013). Besson turned to English-language films, of which *The Fifth Element* (1997) is the most intriguing, as it combines sci-fi with the *Die Hard* action films starring Bruce Willis. Gallic quirkiness is at its most evident in Jean-Paul Gaultier's costumes, not least Bruce Willis's trademark T-shirt, which from white in *Die Hard* (John McTiernan, 1988) becomes a vivid orange in *The Fifth Element* as he eliminates grotesque aliens (and Gary Oldman) instead of Alan Rickman's bad guys in *Die Hard* (we note sadly that the bad guys both for the Americans and for the French are British ...). Moreover, Besson's production company has produced a range of well-known English-language action thrillers, using French money and mostly French directors: the *Transporter* series starring Jason Statham and the even more popular (and lucrative) *Taken* series starring Liam Neeson: *The Transporter* (Corey Yuen, 2002), *Transporter 2* (Louis Leterrier, 2005), *Transporter 3* (Olivier Megaton, 2008), *Taken* (Pierre Morel, 2008), *Taken 2* (Olivier Megaton, 2012), *Taken 3* (Olivier Megaton, 2014), *The Transporter Refueled* (Camille Delamarre, 2015). These films may well be popular entertainment, but they have a crucial function for French cinema in that revenue returns to France to be invested in French cinema (see Table 2).[3]

Table 2. Revenue and spectator figures for the
Transporter and *Taken* film series produced by Luc Besson.
Sales from IMDB; spectator figures from CNC.

Title	Revenue	Spectators
The Transporter	$44 m	8 m
Transporter 2	$85.2 m	13 m
Transporter 3	$109 m	17 m
Taken	$226.8 m	30.2 m
Taken 2	$376.1 m	47.4 m
Taken 3	$326.5 m	44.4 m
The Transporter Refueled	$72.6 m	13 m

Women directors

One of the first and immensely prolific directors at the turn of the
nineteenth and twentieth centuries was Alice Guy-Blaché (1873–
1968), who worked for Gaumont and then set up her own company
in New York in 1910. But until the 1980s, women directors in French
cinema were few and far between, the most well known being
Germaine Dulac (1882–1942), active during the 1920s, Jacqueline
Audry (1908–1977), Marguerite Duras (1914–1996), better known as
a novelist, and Agnès Varda (1928–2019). The 1980s saw a gradual
increase with a new generation of women directors, such as Chantal
Akerman and Diane Kurys, the first at the more experimental end
of filmmaking, the second more mainstream; her lesbian World
War II romance *Coup de foudre/Entre nous* (1983) garnered 1.2 million
spectators. Coline Serreau was one of the first to obtain a more
significant success with the comedy *Trois hommes et un couffin/Three
Men and a Cradle* (1985; 10.3 million spectators), quickly remade in
the USA as *Three Men and a Baby* (Leonard Nimoy, 1987). In the
period 1996–1999 more than 50 women directors released feature
films;[4] in the 2000s the average number of films released by women
directors on an annual basis was 36,[5] corresponding to 18% of the
total number of films released (Table 3).

Table 3. Women's film-making in France 2000–2010 adapted from Carrie Tarr, 'Introduction: Women's Film-Making in France 2000–2010', *Studies in French Cinema*, vol. 12, no. 3, 2012, p. 191.

Year of release	Proportion of total production	%
2000	38:188	20.2
2001	25:199	12.6
2002	32:187	17.1
2003	33:195	16.9
2004	34:209	16.3
2005	31:196	15.8
2006	33:208	15.9
2007	51:216	23.6
2008	41:210	19.5
2009	48:223	21.5
2010	47:229	20.5
Totals	413:2260	18.3

Many women directors, particularly those who began their careers in the 1970s, have made and continue to make art-house films that are challenging, such as Catherine Breillat and Claire Denis, their work extended by the directors loosely linked to what has been called *le jeune cinéma* (Dominique Cabrera, Noémie Lvovsky, Laetitia Masson and Marion Vernoux).[6] But a far greater number work in comedy, some with significant success, such as Josiane Balasko, whose *Gazon maudit/French Twist* (1995) won a César award for Best Writing and had 4 million spectators in France as well as, unusually, 1.7 million beyond France, partly because it was one of the few French films to be distributed in a dubbed rather than subtitled version. Women directors have also increasingly favoured the genre of the rom-com, although, as was the case with Besson and the action thriller, tweaking the genre with the French touch.[7] Women directors have in addition been successful in heritage filmmaking, such as Anne Fontaine, whose *Coco avant Chanel/Coco*

Before Chanel (2009) obtained just over one million spectators, and Rose Bosch, whose World War II drama, *La Rafle/The Round Up* (2010), attracted 2.9 million, at a time when the heritage film was rarely managing on average more than 500,000 spectators. The *banlieue* film, epitomised by *La Haine/Hatred* (Matthieu Kassovitz, 1995), a very aggressively male genre, has, like the heritage film, also attracted women directors, one of the most notable being Céline Sciamma, whose *Bande de filles/Girlhood* (2014) explores what it means to be a girl in the outer suburbs of Paris.

The increase in the number of women directors is partly if not mainly due to the policy of France's major film school, the Fémis (Fondation Européenne pour les Métiers de l'Image et du Son), to support gender parity, particularly with regard to its directing strand. Some of the Fémis women working as directors include Emmanuelle Bercot and Marina de Van. The former is also known as an actress, indeed winning the Best Actress César in Maïwenn's exploration of a couple relationship *Mon roi/My King* (2015). Many women directors – more so than men – are also actresses; the most successful of these is Agnès Jaoui, whose *Le Goût des autres/The Taste of Others* (2000), in which she acts as well as being the director, had 3.8 million spectators. Two of her other films have had more than a million spectators. Other actress-directors include Maïwenn, Balasko, Valérie Donzelli, Mia Hansen-Løve, Valérie Lemercier, Sophie Marceau, among many others.

Of Tunisian origin, Jaoui is also a rare example of a female ethnic minority director, of which there have only been a handful in the 2000s. The best known after Jaoui is Yamina Benguigui, of Algerian origin, whose *Inch'Allah Dimanche* (2001) may only have achieved 181,000 spectators, but has been of considerable interest to academics for its exploration of an Algerian immigrant woman's experience of living in France.[8] In the same vein is Houda Benyamina, of Moroccan origin, whose *banlieue* film *Divines* (2016) acts as an important contrast with Sciamma's *Bande de filles*.[9] Finally,

Géraldine Nakache, of Algerian origin, both directs and acts in a female buddy film, *Tout ce qui brille/All that Glitters* (2010, co-directed with Hervé Mimran), alongside one of the major ethnic minority stars, Leïla Bekhti. Although not quite in the same league as *Le Goût des autres*, Nakache's film nonetheless had 1.4 million spectators, breaking through the one million spectator threshold, which is the barometer for successful films: 28 films by women directors broke through this threshold during 2000–2010, two women directors have done so three times (Jaoui and Danièle Thompson), and four have done so twice (Lisa Azuelos, Valérie Guignabodet, Alexandra Leclère and Coline Serreau).[10]

Ethnic minority directors and stars
Bekhti and Jaoui, the first in particular, have become stars in the French star system, which I define for the purposes of this chapter as actors who have performed in a large number and wide range of films, with high spectator numbers, extending beyond well-trodden genres, and who have won significant awards. Bekhti won the Most Promising Actress César for *Tout ce qui brille*, and has since extended her range across several genres, including dramas, biopics and police thrillers. Jaoui has won more awards, but they are mostly for her work as a director, the awards relating to her performances being in the Best Supporting Actress category.

Male ethnic minority actors are more numerous, and many of them can be considered stars if we accept the working definition I gave above. This is partly due to the increasing prominence of male ethnic minority directors, starting with the *beur* cinema of the 1980s and 1990s,[11] for example the early *banlieue* films, *Le Thé au harem d'Archimède/Tea in the Harem* (Mehdi Charef, 1985) and *Hexagone* (Malik Chibane, 1994), and what has been called the post-*beur* directors of the 2000s.[12] Maghrebi directors have since then become more prolific, with some making films in the USA and the UK. The major directors of Maghrebi origin are French-Algerian

Rachid Bouchareb and French-Tunisian Abdellatif Kechiche. The latter's early 2000s trilogy – *La Faute à Voltaire/Poetical Refugee* (2000), *L'Esquive/Games of Love and Chance* (2003) and *La Graine et le mulet/Couscous* (2007) – is of particular interest to academics for its exploration of immigrant issues.[13] The last two won Kechiche Best Director César awards, and his controversial lesbian romance *La Vie d'Adèle/Blue Is the Warmest Colour* (2013) was awarded the Palme d'Or at Cannes. Bouchareb's film on Maghrebi troops fighting for France in World War II, *Indigènes/Days of Glory* (2006), was very successful with 3.2 million spectators, and was unusually awarded a César Best Actor for its five main actors, four of whom are of Maghrebi origin and are very visible in French cinema (Jamel Debbouze, Samy Naceri, Roschdy Zem, Sami Bouajila).[14]

Maghrebi stars have undoubtedly been helped by the successes of prominent Maghrebi directors; but they are a major feature of contemporary French cinema, working for a wide range of directors, as the following list will make clear.

- The first major film of Sami Bouajila (b. 1966, French-Tunisian origin) was Karim Dridi's *Bye-Bye* (1995) but the film that made him a star was *Drôle de Félix/Adventures of Felix* (Olivier Ducastel and Jacques Martineau, 2000), a road movie in which he plays a gay man who travels the length of France and meets a range of unrelated people who are characterised as his 'family'.[15]

- Jamel Debbouze (b. 1975, French-Moroccan origin) is more of a TV star, hosting the *Jamel Comedy Club* on Canal+ since the mid-2000s. A familiar face in Astérix film comedies, he has starred in *Angel-A* (Luc Besson, 2005), in Bouchareb's ensemble film *Indigènes* and in Bouchareb's award-winning follow-up *Hors la loi/Outlaws* (2010).

- Gad Elmaleh (b. 1971, French-Moroccan-Canadian origin), like Debbouze, is a TV stand-up star, but has also acted in a wide range of films. He starred in the transvestite comedy *Chouchou*

(Merzak Allouache, 2003), which had 3.9 million spectators and for which he was awarded the Best Actor César, and alongside Audrey Tautou in *Hors de prix/Priceless* (Pierre Salvadori, 2006).

- Reda Kateb (b. 1977, French-Algerian origin) is not quite yet a star; he won the Best Supporting Actor César for his role in the medical drama *Hippocrate/Hippocrates: Diary of a French Doctor* (Thomas Lilti, 2014) but has since been very visible, notably in major biopics, such as *L'Astragale* (Brigitte Sy, 2015), the biography of Albertine Sarrazin (played by Leïla Bekhti), and then as the lead star in a biopic of Django Reinhardt, *Django* (Étienne Comar, 2017).
- Samy Naceri (French-Algerian origin) is best known for the Luc Besson-produced *Taxi* series.
- Tahar Rahim (b. 1981, French-Algerian origin) starred as a relative unknown in *Un prophète*, for which he received no less than seven Best Actor awards, including a César. The film also won the Cannes Jury Prize and attracted 1.3 million spectators. He had a major role in *Samba* (2014), the follow-up to Omar Sy and Olivier Nakache and Éric Toledano's follow-up to *Intouchables/Untouchable* (2011).
- Roschdy Zem (b. 1965, French-Moroccan origin) won the Best Actor César for *Mauvaise foi* (Roschdy Zem, 2006). The only Maghrebi actor to have moved into directing feature films, he directed the biopic of the Black clown *Chocolat* (2016), which starred Omar Sy and which was awarded Best Film by the French Press Association's Globes de cristal.

While this list of Maghrebi stars demonstrates the high visibility of ethnic stars, it is clear that there are fewer female Maghrebi stars. Apart from Leïla Bekhti, the only emerging Maghrebi female star is Hafzia Herzi, who acted in *La Graine et le mulet* and who is rapidly becoming well known in art-house films.

Whereas there is a substantial group of Maghrebi stars, French-African stars are fewer and further between. A rising female star is

Aïssa Maïga, of French–Senegalese–Malian origin, who won a Most Promising Actress for her role in the political Malian film *Bamako* (Abderrahmane Sissako, 2006), and who has been in a range of well-received comedies such as the rom-com *Prêt à tout/Anything for Alice* (Nicolas Cuche, 2014), the provincial doctor comedy *Bienvenue à Marly-Gaumont/The African Doctor* (Lucien Jean-Baptiste, 2016) and *Il a déjà tes yeux/He Even Has Your Eyes* (Lucien Jean-Baptiste, 2017), a comedy in which she is part of a French-African couple who adopt a white child. The only French-African star of any note, however, is Omar Sy, whose role in *Intouchables* as the carer from the *banlieue* for the tetraplegic played by François Cluzet won him the Best Actor César. *Intouchables* is one of the best-attended films of recent years, its 19.5 million spectators running a close second to the top-ranking film, *Bienvenue chez les Ch'tis/Welcome to the Sticks* (Dany Boon, 2008), with 20.5 million and starring two actors with ethnic minority origins, Dany Boon and Kad Merad, both of French-Algerian origin, and much more obviously stars than those mentioned above. These two comedies are the top two films of all time in France in terms of audience numbers. The third high-scoring comedy dealing with issues of racial tension is *Qu'est-ce qu'on a fait au Bon Dieu?/Serial (Bad) Weddings* (Philippe de Chauveron, 2014), which attracted 12.4 million spectators. In the final section, I shall consider what these very successful comedies tell us about the French.

The multiculturalist debate in popular comedies

All three of the films just mentioned take stereotypes – regional, class, ethnic – and use them to interrogate social attitudes in a society that has become multi-ethnic and multi-cultural. This is an issue for the French, whose Republican constitution does not allow for the expression of difference; hence the major political row concerning the use of the veil (either the *niqab* which covers half of the face or the *burka* which covers the whole of the face) for Muslim women.

In *Bienvenue chez les Ch'tis*, Philippe is a postmaster who works in the south of France and is posted to the land of the Ch'tis in the north. The locals play on his fear of a poverty-stricken mining region full of alcoholics and simpletons who speak an incomprehensible dialect, but he discovers that the stereotypes are false. They are replaced by what amount to idealised positive stereotypes, and Philippe and his family are eventually integrated into the community. In *Qu'est-ce qu'on a fait au Bon Dieu?*, a right-wing bourgeois couple have four daughters, three of whom, much to their dismay, are married to men from ethnic minorities: Rachid (French-Algerian), David (Sephardic Jew), Chao (French-Chinese). Laure, their unmarried daughter, brings 'Charles' back home as her fiancé; they are relieved that he sounds like a 'true' Frenchman (with echoes of Charles de Gaulle), but they are shocked when they meet him to discover that he is French-Ivoirian. His parents visit and turn out to be as racist as Laure's parents. Finally, in *Intouchables*, tetraplegic Philippe hires Driss, played by Omar Sy, to look after him, principally because he realises that Driss does not pity him.

All three films led to considerable debate in the media, but I want to focus on *Intouchables* because it has led to more academic work than the other two films.[16] The broad lines of the debate revolved around the opposition between racist stereotype and feel-good fantasy. One journalist laid out what he saw as the film's positives:[17] mutual support between the classes, in that the wealthy man finds a taste for life once more while the young man from the *banlieue* is no longer the victim of discrimination and gains access to the cultural capital that allows him to function socially. This is because Driss is amazed by Philippe's art collection and says naively that he could do the same as some of the more modern paintings. He proceeds to do so, and Philippe arranges a sale anonymously. A second positive point is one of social responsibility: Philippe suggests that the rich can care more about people than money. And then by not being the stereotypical *banlieue* kid who is into drugs and petty theft, Driss gives a positive image of youngsters from the projects and their values.

France's left-wing dailies were less impressed, and focused more on what one might call the 'opium of the people' argument. *Libération*, for example, commented that the film 'abolishes the mistrust between social classes, replacing it with a mixture of congeniality and cheekiness'.[18] American reviewers, with a very different view of racial issues, were scathing. Jay Weissberg in *Variety* wrote the following, saying that the film was the worst kind of Uncle Tomism:

> Driss is treated as nothing but a performing monkey (with all the racist associations of such a term), teaching the stuck-up white folk how to get 'down' by replacing Vivaldi with 'Boogie Wonderland' and showing off his moves on the dance floor. It's painful to see Sy, a joyfully charismatic performer, in a role barely removed from the jolly house slave of yore, entertaining the master while embodying all the usual stereotypes about class and race.[19]

Interestingly, this severe critique by an American motivated a shift in *Libération*'s position. The actress and writer Sylvie Granotier appears to have been commissioned to write a rebuttal a couple of months later, in which she emphasises the feel-good aspect: 'I don't like to be judged, me and seven million of my fellow spectators, stupid enough to confuse fairy-tales and reality. My taste for reality doesn't mean that I can't enjoy a fairy-tale'.[20]

These comedies undeniably process issues of multi-culturalism in a multi-ethnic society, working in all three cases to an idealised integration. They also give high visibility to ethnic minority actors, indeed turning one of them into one of France's major stars: Sy has gone on to make a range of high-profile films, in the USA as well as in France. But as is normal with comedies, they reinforce stereotypes as much as they destabilise them. All three are in the end 'bloke-ish': indeed, in two of them one of the major scenes of reconciliation and integration is focused on two drunk men discovering that they have more in common than they thought. The women, meanwhile, are relegated to the kitchen, or marginalised. In *Intouchables* as well, we have a tight focus on the friendship between Philippe and Driss, in which the women are presented in broad brush-strokes: the lesbian secretary, the frustrated housekeeper, the teenager daughter lacking in self-confidence. And to cap it all, the end of the film sees Driss walking away having sorted out Philippe's romantic life, sacrificing himself for his wealthy employer.

Conclusion

The French film industry is one of the most vibrant in the world, and it has done a wide range of things for us. It has made the European film industry both quantitatively and perhaps more obviously qualitatively able to compete with the hegemony of Hollywood. In so doing it has retained its quintessential Gallic flavour, what I have called its 'French touch', even when, and perhaps especially when playing Hollywood at its own game. Importantly, especially at a time when issues of equality loom large, it has brought us an impressive range of women and ethnic minority directors, as well as ethnic minority stars. And, finally, its comedies in particular have laid bare the essential debates that need to be had in a society that constitutionally prides itself on equality but finds it difficult to accept the logical consequences of a multi-ethnic and multi-cultural society.

Filmography

37°2 *le matin*, 1986, Jean-Jacques Beineix, France.
Angel-A, 2005, Luc Besson, France.
Assassinat du duc de Guise, L', 1908, André Calmettes, France.
Astragale, L', 2015, Brigitte Sy, France.
Bamako, 2006, Abderrahmane Sissako, Mali/USA/France.
Bande de filles, 2014, Céline Sciamma, France.
Bienvenue à Marly-Gaumont, 2016, Lucien Jean-Baptiste, France/Belgium.
Bienvenue chez les Ch'tis, 2008, Dany Boon, France.

Bye-Bye, 1995, Karim Dridi, France/Belgium/Switzerland.

Charme discret de la bourgeoisie, Le, 1972, Luis Buñuel, France.

Choristes, Les, 2004, Christophe Barratier, France/Switzerland/ Germany.

Chouchou, 2003, Merzak Allouache, France.

Coco avant Chanel, 2009, Anne Fontaine, France/Belgium

Coup de foudre, 1983, Diane Kurys, France.

Cyrano de Bergerac, 1990, Jean-Paul Rappeneau, France.

De battre mon cœur s'est arrêté, 2005, Jacques Audiard, France.

Die Hard, 1988, John McTiernan, USA.

Dimanches de Ville d'Avray, Les, 1962, Serge Bourguignon, France/ Austria.

Divines, 2016, Houda Benyamina, France/Qatar.

Django, 2017, Étienne Comar, France.

Drôle de Félix, 2000, Olivier Ducastel and Jacques Martineau, France.

Esquive, L', 2003, Abdellatif Kechiche, France.

Fabuleux Destin d'Amélie Poulain, Le, 2001, Jean-Pierre Jeunet, France/ Germany.

Faute à Voltaire, La, 2000, Abdellatif Kechiche, France.

Fifth Element, The, 1997, Luc Besson, France.

Gazon maudit, 1995, Josiane Balasko, France.

Goût des autres, Le, 2000, Agnès Jaoui, France.

Graine et le mulet, La, 2007, Abdellatif Kechiche, France.

Haine, La, 1995, Matthieu Kassovitz, France.

Hexagone, 1994, Malik Chibane, France.

Hippocrate, 2014, Thomas Lilti, France.

Hors de prix, 2006, Pierre Salvadori, France.

Hors la loi, 2010, Rachid Bouchareb, France/Algeria/Belgium/ Tunisia/Italy.

Hussard sur le toit, Le, 1995, Jean-Paul Rappeneau, France.

Il a déjà tes yeux, 2017, Lucien Jean-Baptiste, France/Belgium.

Inch'Allah Dimanche, 2001, Yamina Benguigui, France/Algeria.

Indigènes, 2006, Rachid Bouchareb, Algeria/France/Morocco/ Belgium.

Indochine, 1992, Régis Wargnier, France.

Intouchables, 2011, Olivier Nakache and Éric Toledano, France.

Jean de Florette, 1986, Claude Berri, Switzerland/France/Italy.

Just Like a Woman, 2012, Rachid Bouchareb, UK/USA/France.

Lacombe, Lucien, 1974, Louis Malle, France/Italy/West Germany.

London River, 2009, Rachid Bouchareb, UK/France/Algeria.

Mauvaise foi, 2006, Roschdy Zem, Belgium/France.

Mon oncle, 1958, Jacques Tati, France/Italy.

Mon roi, 2015, Maïwenn, France.

Nikita, 1990, Luc Besson, France/Italy.

Nuit américaine, La, 1973, François Truffaut, France/Italy.

Parapluies de Cherbourg, Les, 1964, Jacques Demy, France/West Germany.

Point of No Return, 1997, John Badham, USA.

Prêt à tout, 2014, Nicolas Cuche, France.

Qu'est-ce qu'on a fait au Bon Dieu?, 2014, Philippe de Chauveron, France.

Rafle, La, 2010, Rose Bosch, France/Germany/Hungary.

Ridicule, 1996, Patrice Leconte, France.

Samba, 2014, Olivier Nakache and Éric Toledano, France.

Subway, 1986, Luc Besson, France.

Taken, 2008, Pierre Morel, France/USA.

Taken 2, 2012, Olivier Megaton, France/USA.

Taken 3, 2014, Olivier Megaton, France/USA/Spain/UK/Germany.

Taxi, 1998, Gérard Pirès, France.

Taxi 2, 2000, Gérard Krawczyk, France.

Taxi 3, 2003, Gérard Krawczyk, France.

Taxi 4, 2007, Gérard Krawczyk, France.

Thé au harem d'Archimède, Le, 1985, Mehdi Charef, France.

Three Men and a Baby, 1987, Leonard Nimoy, USA.

Tout ce qui brille, 2010, Géraldine Nakache and Hervé Mimran, France.

Transporter, The, 2002, Corey Yuen, France/USA.

Transporter 2, 2005, Louis Leterrier, France/USA.

Transporter 3, 2008, Olivier Megaton, France/USA/Ukraine.

Transporter Refueled, The, 2015, Camille Delamarre, France/China/ Belgium.

Trois hommes et un couffin, 1985, Coline Serreau, France.

Two Men in Town, 2014, Rachid Bouchareb, France/Belgium/Algeria/ USA.

Un homme et une femme, 1966, Claude Lelouch, France.

Un prophète, 2009, Jacques Audiard, France/Italy.

Vie d'Adèle, La, 2013, Abdellatif Kechiche, France/Belgium/Spain.

Vie devant soi, La, 1977, Moshé Misrahi, France.

Vie et rien d'autre, La, 1989, Bertrand Tavernier, France.

On Books and Other Treasures

Anyone who has walked along the banks of the Seine in central Paris will be familiar with the sight of the 'bouquinistes' with their enticing displays of second-hand books, prints, posters and old postcards for sale. For the collector, the famous 'green boxes' offer the chance of finding a much sought-after and elusive book among the eclectic items on display. In days gone by, it was not unheard of for someone with the patience to sift carefully through them all to pick up a rare first edition or some other gem at a bargain price. Such a find would be highly unlikely now, though; even if the bouquinistes could still get their hands on rare treasures of that nature, they are too savvy to let them slip through their hands unnoticed.

The existence of the bouquinistes, who have occupied the banks of the Seine since the sixteenth century in one form or other, testifies to the enduring place of books in French culture and society. As far back as the thirteenth century, there was already a lively book trade in Paris involving copyists, binders, illuminists, parchment makers and dealers. The first printed book in France was produced in Paris in 1470 – a collection of letters in Latin (Gasparinus de Bergamo's *Epistolae*). Others books quickly followed, in Latin and in French. A century earlier, around 1369, King Charles V had transferred his 'librairie' to the Louvre Palace, thereby laying the foundations for today's national library. His collection included works of theology, law, literature and history, but was notable for its coverage of the sciences and for the number of works translated into vernacular language. On the king's death in 1380, the collection comprised around 1,200 bound manuscripts, which compared well to the 1,720 manuscripts listed in the 1340 inventory of the university library at the Sorbonne. When the 'bibliothèque du roi' (king's library) was opened to the public in 1692, it was home to over 10,000 items. In 1790, in the aftermath of the Revolution, it was re-named the Bibliothèque de la Nation. It became the Bibliothèque nationale in 1849 and acquired its current name, the Bibliothèque nationale de France, in 1994. It now houses over 40 million items and has the largest collection of mediaeval and modern manuscripts in the world.

Libraries and their collections are one measure of the value we place on books. Another is the care taken in producing them. In France, the publishing house Gallimard has a special collection – 'la Pléiade' – devoted to authors whose work is deemed worthy of the most serious scholarly treatment. The Pléiade books, in pocket format, are bound in leather with the spine stamped in gold. The use of bible paper adds to the aesthetic appeal and allows for the binding of a higher than usual number of pages (often over 1,000). This provides scope for the inclusion of an extensive introduction and copious notes compiled by leading experts – a hallmark of the collection. For an author, publication in the Pléiade is a consecration; it is rare for a living writer to be afforded that honour. These expensive and prestigious tomes are essential tools for scholars and prized possessions for collectors. Illustrating this latter point, it is said that an elderly woman visited the Gallimard bookshop in Paris one day and asked the salesman for what he understood as 'un maître de la Pléiade' (a master of the Pléiade). Keen to please, he asked if she had any particular master in mind: Flaubert, perhaps, or Balzac, or Proust ...? The woman then explained that she was in fact after 'un mètre de la Pléiade' – a metre's worth of Pléiade volumes – to feature on the bookshelves she had just had installed. An apocryphal anecdote? Perhaps. But it is also entirely plausible.

We can, of course, collect and treasure books for reasons other than their monetary or aesthetic value. When I was a student in Grenoble, in south-eastern France, I visited an antiquarian book-ship on the banks of the Isère river one day with a friend who was visiting from Paris. After longingly perusing the shelves, my eye settled on an old edition of Dante's *Divine Comedy* in French translation. It was not an especially prestigious book but its age and the context somehow made it desirable. As I was on a meagre scholarship, book purchases were always the subject of careful assessment. I therefore hesitated. To resolve the matter, I said to my friend that I would toss a coin: if it came up heads, I would buy the book; tails, I would leave it. She said that she would expect nothing less of someone who was writing a thesis on the topic of chance and destiny in the novels of Stendhal! The coin came down tails. I bought the book anyway. Forty years later, it still counts as a treasured item in my collection. Sometimes destiny needs a nudge.

As Véronique Duché shows us, Australia's public libraries have a surprising number of French treasures – books, manuscripts, maps and other artefacts – all of which are objectively much more valuable than my old copy of Dante. But value also rests in the eye of the beholder.

JWS

9

Véronique Duché

Treasured possessions in Australian rare book collections

Libraries today are diverse places with great popular appeal. The creation of permanent exhibition areas, including treasures galleries that draw on the libraries' own collections, has undoubtedly contributed to the formation of a new identity for the humble library. Such collections of 'treasures' contain not only books, as one would expect, but also manuscripts, maps or plans, photographs, videos, interviews (oral histories), objects and artwork. In this chapter we will examine the content of Australian treasures exhibitions, focusing on the French component of these showcases. We will begin with a review of treasures exhibitions over time to establish firstly the historical and theoretical background.

Art Treasures Exhibitions

Treasures in Australian libraries appear to be a rather recent phenomenon, having emerged in the late twentieth and early twenty-first century. According to Tim Bonyhady, however, 'Exhibitions of "treasures" have a long, though interrupted, history. They were first staged in the 1850s and 1860s, then again from the 1970s. In both periods the public response [was ...] immense, turning several exhibitions into blockbusters.'[1] The Manchester Arts treasures exhibition, as 'the first comprehensive exhibition ever held of art treasures from private collections in Great Britain',[2] formed the prototype for Australian events. Held between 5 May and 29 October 1857, 'it was organised by a committee of private citizens, whose aim was to correct the popular impression that the English had no taste for art, and to demonstrate that their collections equalled if not surpassed those of Continental Europe'.[3] The works of art contained in this pioneering exhibition were divided into nine sections, among them a very successful 'British portrait gallery'. The section devoted to 'Paintings by Ancient Masters' was particularly remarkable, with hundreds of masterpieces by famous painters such as Titian, Tintoretto, Rubens, Van Dyck, Rembrandt, Poussin, Watteau or Greuze.

Although the Manchester exhibition targeted a large audience, it also demonstrated a new approach to art as a science. As William Bürger writes in the preface of the French translation of the Manchester catalogue:

> The specificity of our time, in art, literature, science, as well as in social economy and industry, is generalisation, it is universality. [...] How can the universal history of art be told, if not by gathering facts, dates, peculiarities of all kinds, which help to understand the different epochs, the different countries, the different geniuses, and especially to seize the analogies and harmonies that connect them in a greater unity?[4]

The Manchester exhibition had a big impact on Australia. Newspapers from many states published extensive reviews,[5] and the idea of replicating the concept quickly took hold. It was Hobart – a city 'often at the forefront of colonial culture from the 1820s'[6] – that led the charge, opening its treasures exhibition (described as 'the first exhibition of Paintings and Statuary ever [...] held in Tasmania')[7] on 21 June 1858, just over a year after the Manchester event. A total of 359 works of art were showcased – too many, according to the *Hobart Town Daily Mercury* reviewer:

If we attempt to fix our attention exclusively upon any painting, we find that those which immediately surround it intrude themselves upon us, and mar the enjoyment which we should otherwise have experienced. This is a fault; but it is a fault inherent to all Exhibitions of this nature.[8]

Morton Allport, whose family was closely connected to the Allport Library and Museum of Fine arts, was a major organiser of this exhibition, and a member of the committee responsible for sending Tasmanian exhibits to the 1862 London International Exhibition.

A similar exhibition was then held in 1861 in Melbourne – Australia's cultural capital for most of the second half of the nineteenth century. According to the *Argus* reviewer, Melbourne's exhibition was 'the best that we have had the pleasure of witnessing in this colony'.[9] It was organised in order to bring together articles of produce and manufacturing so that worthy items could be selected for display at the London International Exhibition the following year. Among them was a painting by Nicolas Poussin, *The Birth of Bacchus, and the Death of Narcissus* (#29), whose authenticity was questioned at the time: 'We have heard it stated more than once that this is a copy, but on no better grounds, that we could learn, than that if it had been an "original" it would never have found its way out here.'[10]

Nevertheless, the next Melbourne exhibition, 'Works of Art, Ornamental and Decorative Art', held in the Great Hall of the State Library from March to June 1869, was a record-breaking event. It seemed that fostering a 'love of art' had fallen into the state's civic responsibility, as an antidote to 'barbarism'.[11] The Melbourne Public Library, Australia's first government-funded and operated library, had been charged with the mission of educating public taste and instructing the worker, and took the exhibition very seriously. According to Alison Inglis: 'Alongside art historical display principles, Melbourne's exhibition echoed Manchester in the priority given to public access.'[12] The organisers sought to make the art accessible for working men and women 'whose ordinary occupations would debar them from the enjoyment'.[13] And it worked! People flocked to see the 'art treasures': 'In all, over 5,000 people bought season tickets, while almost 55,000 paid for admission at the door'.[14]

Australian treasures

The size of the 1869 Melbourne event was unprecedented for an Australian art exhibition. According to Bonyhady:

> The 2,640 objects on display in Melbourne were even more diverse than those in Manchester. They included needle, feather and leather work, carvings in wood, metal and ivory, jewellery, coins, cameos, seals, arms and armour, ceramics, glass, lacquer and waxwork, writing, printing and bookbinding.

Plus '300 objects defying all these categories'![15]

Such an exhibition calls into question, however, the meaning of the word 'treasure'. Bonyhady states that at the 1869 Melbourne exhibition, 'only one object was on display because of its Australian historical significance'.[16] Furthermore, the vast majority of Old Masters and even some of the modern artworks on display were copies, not originals. According to Inglis, however:

> Their inclusion as art treasures should not be dismissed as an unfortunate consequence of colonial taste. Instead it reflected contemporary European collecting practices. Fine copies of Old Master works had long been valued by aristocratic connoisseurs. [...] For colonial collectors Old Master copies symbolised their desire to establish the values of civilised society in their new home.[17]

Indeed, the word 'treasure' is a broad term that encapsulates a range of subtly different meanings. It can refer to a set of valuable items (such as gold, silver, precious stones, etc.), painstakingly gathered and often carefully hidden from prying eyes.[18] It can also signify a set of works considered to be artistically valuable (such as archaeological objects, or paintings). It can be something held to be particularly beautiful, noble or precious (on an emotional, intellectual or moral level). Such 'tiny treasures' are significant objects which 'help us to remember things about the past'.[19] A treasure may even be a scholarly book, such as a dictionary, encyclopaedia or other monumental work that organises and disseminates vast swathes of human knowledge.[20] Finally, a treasure can refer to written accounts (literary, philosophical, scientific, etc.), the products of human thought, which constitute the essential intellectual resources and culture of a country, a community.

While it is unclear which definition of 'treasure' the nineteenth-century Australian exhibitions worked from and developed, the term soon fell into disuse, only to reappear a century later. It was indeed in the late 1970s that Australian cultural institutions returned to the language of treasures. Their migration back to libraries reaffirmed their importance, prompting Bonyhady to assert: 'What masterpieces are to galleries, treasures have become to libraries.'

But, as Robert Hughes writes in 1988, this aspect to the library is not self-evident:

> People are apt to think of libraries as caves and gullies that support the marginal fauna of public life – the book-worm, the academic, the 'pseudo-intellectual'. Nor have the libraries the glamour that goes with art museums and concert halls, because they are not associated with either conspicuous consumption or social display. All you can do in them is read and whisper, and not too much of the latter.[21]

As he added a few lines later, however, with respect to the treasures of the State Library of New South Wales: 'We know where the body of Australia is; most of us live in it. But if you want to converse with its soul, [...] the first and best place to start looking for it [...] is in the Mitchell and Dixson Collections.'

Is there a French component to this Australian soul? While there is research on the British dimensions of multicultural Australia, very little has been done on a possible French element. What role do rare French books and artefacts play in the cultural life of Australia? The following survey of the Australian 'treasures' galleries offers some insights.

French treasures in Australian libraries[22]
The State Library of New South Wales was the first Australian institution to give visitors a taste of its treasures, both Australian and international, by devoting the larger of the Dixson galleries to its Nelson Meers Foundation Heritage Collection. The State Library of South Australia followed suit shortly after, in 2003, when it created a Treasures Wall displaying objects from its collection. In 2014, the State Library of Victoria went further, opening a much bigger display, focused on Victoria, high in the dome of its original reading room.[23] Similarly, the Talbot Family Treasures Wall located in the State Library of Queensland showcases unique and rare heritage items from the past 200 years, and the Treasures Gallery, established in 2011, highlights the extraordinary holdings of the National Library of Australia. These prominent Australian libraries, together with the Northern Territory Library, the State Library of Tasmania, and the State Library of Western Australia, contributed to the touring exhibition 'National Treasures from Australia's Great Libraries', which opened in Canberra in December 2005.[24]

A close examination of the catalogues of such exhibitions reveals the existence of a variety of French treasures.[25] Two iconic items, for instance, appear in the National Library of Australia catalogue: a precious map by Philippe Buache, drawn in 1744 and engraved in 1757, 'With Two imaginary coastlines for E. and S.E. Australia'; and the minutes of the August 1789 French National Assembly with the Declaration of the Rights of Man and of the Citizen.[26] More modest items appear in the State Library of Victoria catalogue:

a hand-coloured lithograph dated 1833 showing seal fishers in Tasmania, and a first edition copy of an important Victorian goldfield account by French photographer and adventurer Antoine Fauchery (1857).[27] A Book of Hours (Use of Rome, Bourges, c. 1480), is the only French item in the State Library of New South Wales Treasures catalogue.[28] Select pages of this personal prayer book, splendidly illuminated, were digitised as part of the Nelson Meers Foundation Benefaction in 2002.[29]

The State Library of Western Australia, holding treasures in its Battye Library of West Australian History,[30] has several French items, most notably in the Freycinet collection (1801, 1818). Louis-Claude Desaulces de Freycinet was part of the scientific expedition headed by Captain Nicolas Baudin. A cartographer-surveyor, he surveyed the western Australian coast from King George Sound in the south round to Shark Bay and beyond in the north, on the *Naturaliste* (1801) and the *Casuarina* (1803); in a second expedition which he himself commanded, he again visited the Shark Bay area, this time on the *Uranie* (1818). The Freycinet collection contains material from both voyages. Among the French treasures is the original journal of Paul Joseph Gaimard, the surgeon and naturalist on the *Uranie*, a watercolour engraving of Shark Bay by Alphonse Odet-Peillon, an officer on the *Uranie*,[31] and the first detailed map of the Swan River, drawn by François Antoine Boniface Heirisson during the Baudin expedition's visit to the area.

The State Library of South Australia seems to nurture a strong connection with the French, as illustrated by the exhibition 'Chance Encounter: French influence in South Australia' of June-August 2016. Furthermore, the Treasures Wall regularly hosts French artefacts and provides virtual access to items from the State Library collections that would otherwise rarely be on display. Highlights include an exquisite sixteenth-century French Book of Hours, the memoir of an English cabin boy who met Napoleon as a prisoner of war, beautiful modern versions of the seventeenth-century French fairy tales of Charles Perrault, and the recently acquired photograph album and French souvenirs of an Adelaide man stationed in France during the First World War.

Jeu joyeux au Kangourou,
[State Library of South Australia, Children's Literature Research Collection]

Two of the French items featured in the Treasures Wall virtual exhibition are of particular interest: a beautiful prayer book and a children's game with a hopping tin kangaroo. The splendid fifteenth-century French Book of Hours, known as 'The Diocesan Book of Hours', has been on permanent loan to the State Library form the Anglican Diocese of Adelaide since 1983.[32] This medieval bestseller is a manuscript on paper with some leaves on vellum and offers a total of 58 brilliantly coloured miniatures. The modest *Jeu joyeux au kangourou* (*Joyful game with kangaroo*), is a children's game from the 1880s.[33] The label reads:

> This pinball or bagatelle-style tabletop game involves a kangaroo and an inclined board. The tin kangaroo hops down the incline to push a selection of balls into numbered sections at the base of the game. It would appear that the player who has the highest score wins. This children's game attests to the on-going French fascination with Australia's faunal emblem. [...] The French had access to live kangaroos from the early 1800s through specimens collected by the Baudin expedition.

This delightful item is emblematic of the State Library of South Australia and has been reproduced as merchandise sold by the Library shop.

Private collections in Australia also hold French treasures but are outside the scope of this article. Suffice to mention here the Kerry Stokes collection and its extensive French holdings, many of which were exhibited in 2015 at the Ian Potter Museum of Art (The University of Melbourne), together with the Rothschild Prayer Book, worth $15.5 million.

Concluding remarks

According to the definition used by librarians and curators, 'treasures' are 'icons of our national heritage' and 'landmarks [...] in the history of the nation';[34] they 'tell the story of the nation in all its intricacy over the course of the past centuries'.[35] As John Thompson writes, these items 'serve as a record of national life and endeavour, [...] reflect Australian society in all its strengths and weaknesses, in its ethnic and cultural diversity, and [...] provide the means by which the national memory is nourished and sustained'.[36]

How then do French artefacts fit into these definitions? The above-mentioned French treasures can be classified into different categories. First, there are 'universal' treasures that could be found in any exhibition of treasures around the world. The books of hours, for example, independently of their religious associations, are valuable for their rarity as well as their beauty, and items related to the French Revolution appeal as artefacts evoking a movement inspired by the universal values of democracy and human rights.

Secondly, there are heritage items that have shaped Australia's history and culture. Among these, of course, are items related to the exploration of Australia – maps, drawings, journals of explorers – but there are also less famous items. Certain books held in the Christ College collection of the University of Tasmania, for example, were collected by Rev. Robert Rowland Davies (1805–1880) to 'bring the European tradition to Australia'. A book such as Guillaume Budé's *Commentarii Linguae Graecae* (1529) (*Commentaries on the Greek Language*)[37] reveals the access Australian students had to the Classics. Another example of this introduction of a European tradition to Australia lies in the State Library of Victoria, which holds books donated by François Louis Nompar de Caumont Laporte, Comte de Castelnau (1810–1880), a French naturalist and diplomat. According to the *Australian Dictionary of Biography*, Castelnau arrived in Melbourne in 1862 and became Consul-General for France in 1864. He was an active member of the Zoological and Acclimatisation Society of Victoria and of the Entomological Society of New South Wales. Castelnau donated his own books to the Library, among them his monographs on insects collected under the title *Histoire naturelle des insectes* (1851).[38]

Included too in these heritage items are treasures with little monetary value. Antoine Fauchery's *Lettres d'un mineur/Letters from a Miner* is not especially rare – a dozen nineteenth-century editions, for instance, can be found in Australia – but the book nevertheless remains one of the best testimonies of the gold-rush period.

Finally, there are emotional treasures: 'things of small individual importance which nevertheless share in a large collective significance'[39]. A little book such as Arnaud Berquin's *L'Ami des enfans* (1787), held at the University of Melbourne's Baillieu library, tells the story of a girl, Isabella Broome, who came to Australia with her books – one of them a French handbook entitled 'The Gift of Grandpapa, 1800'.

Many items in the Australian collections are rare, and some represent the only known surviving copy in the world. As Leigh Hays writes of the Battye Library: 'the rarity, content and sometimes beauty of these artefacts give them a special place. But not all treasures in the collections are necessarily old and rare.'[40] Their significance rests with the information such treasures contain and the connection they have with the nation. The following quotation from Margaret Dent neatly sums it up:

> Treasures can arise from many sources and take many forms. Any collector, whether a private individual or an institution, has particular reasons for considering an item to be a treasure. Some of these are obvious, but not all. Like beauty, the unique quality that makes an object a treasure is often in the eye of the beholder.[41]

On Exploration

An examination of the map of Australia provides one answer to the question of what the French have done for us: they have given us a multitude of French place names, dotted principally along our coasts. For those unfamiliar with the mysteries of French pronunciation, some of these names pose a serious challenge – Kangaroo Island's Cape Gantheaume and Maupertuis Bay spring to mind. In practice, though, their pronunciation has been serviceably 'naturalised' to make them manageable.

Behind this legacy of place names is a story of prolonged scientific and geopolitical interest on the part of the French in the Indo-Pacific during the Age of Sail. It all began with the publication in 1663 of Jean Paulmier's *Memoirs Concerning the Establishment of a Christian Mission in the Austral Land*. In this work, Paulmier recounted the tale of a voyage purportedly undertaken in 1503 by his ancestor, Binot Paulmier de Gonneville, during which the latter claimed to have found the famed Terra Australis Incognita, or unknown south land – the hypothetical continent that ancient geographers had theorised must exist in the south to balance the landmass of the northern hemisphere. Jean Paulmier believed he was the descendant of an 'Indian' supposedly brought back to France by Gonneville. His aim in compiling these *Memoirs* was to obtain support for an evangelising mission to convert the inhabitants of this land. Whether or not anything in his story was true – and this is the subject of some debate – the publication of the *Memoirs* fuelled visions of a utopian paradise that captured the imagination of the

French and spawned a succession of voyages aimed at discovering, or rediscovering, Gonneville's Land. The fascination of the French with Terra Australis was all the more tenacious for having been founded on what may well have been a myth.

Their quest for its discovery was hampered by the belief, created by Paulmier's *Memoirs*, that the fabled southern land was to be found somewhere below and to the east of the Cape of Good Hope, between the meridiens of 60 and 80 degrees south. The discoveries made by the Dutch of lands they named New Zealand, New Holland and Van Diemen's Land created some confusion in this respect, but the Dutch charts were generally viewed with suspicion, as many considered them to have been inaccurately drawn with the purpose of putting off their European rivals. And so the French continued undeterred to look for Terra Australis in the general area beneath the Cape of Good Hope. In 1739, Jean-Baptiste Charles Bouvet de Lozier sighted a peak at 52° of latitude south which he believed to be part of Terra Australis and which he named Cape Circoncision – not because of its shape but because it came into view on 1 January, which happens to be the Feast of the Circumcision. The cape exists, and is part of the subantarctic island of Bouvetøya (or Bouvet Island), now a Norwegian dependency. Bouvet de Lozier believed that the snow and ice were just ramparts hiding a rich and fertile land.

Over the next decade or two, French scientists such as Georges-Louis Leclerc, Comte de Buffon, and Pierre-Louis Moreau de Maupertuis – he of the bay – began to question received wisdom about the configuration of the southern hemisphere. Buffon argued against the notion that the two hemispheres had to have balanced landmasses, whereas Maupertuis considered that the French should be looking for Terra Australis to the east of the Cape of Good Hope rather than to its south. Then in 1756 Charles de Brosses published what would prove to be one of the most influential works of the time, his *Histoire des navigations aux Terres australes*. In this book, he presented a history of the search for the *Terres australes* and speculated that these Southern Lands occupied not one but three separate zones, which he called Magellanie (lying below South America and the Cape of Good Hope), Australasie (incorporating the Spice Islands and New Holland, as well as the area south of India) and Polynésie (encompassing the South Pacific). In his view, Gonneville's Land was to be found in Australasie and so the French should shift their explorations to the areas on either side of New Guinea and work their way south. De Brosses also thought that the unknown land might harbour a superior civilised nation. The utopian strain in French imaginings of the Southern Lands was nothing if not persistent.

Inspired by the ideas propagated by de Brosses, a succession of French mariners visited the Indo-Pacific in the second half of the eighteenth century, getting ever closer to, and then zeroing in on what we now know as Australia. Their explorations led to major advancements in European knowledge about Australia – its geography, its peoples, its flora and its fauna. Beyond the place names, the French have thus left a lasting scientific legacy. They have also given us a rich trove of stories full of human interest, as the following account illustrates.

JWS

10

Jean Fornasiero and John West-Sooby

Tall tales and true from the history of French exploration in Australia

The 'Great South Land': A French obsession

The French obsession with Terra Australis Incognita – the 'unknown south land' – can be traced back to the publication in 1663 of the Abbé Jean Paulmier's *Memoirs Concerning the Establishment of a Christian Mission in the Austral Land.*[1] While the reliability of these *Memoirs* is contested by many scholars today, Paulmier's claim that his ancestor, Binot Paulmier de Gonneville, had discovered the mythical great south land below and to the east of the Cape of Good Hope sparked among his compatriots a keen and enduring interest.[2] There ensued a series of maritime voyages in search of 'Gonneville's Land' which eventually led the French to Australia's shores.

Louis Antoine de Bougainville and Jean-François Marie de Surville came close, Bougainville on 4 June 1768 when he encountered the Great Barrier Reef and wisely decided against trying to sail through it, and Surville on 4 December 1769 when, in the Tasman Sea in the approximate latitude of present-day Sydney, his officers reported the scent of land. In March 1772, Marc Joseph Marion-Dufresne, who had left the Île de France (Mauritius) five months earlier on a voyage in search of Gonneville's Land, arrived in Tasmania before sailing on to New Zealand. At around the same time, Louis François Marie Aleno de Saint Aloüarn, sailing in the

Gros ventre, arrived in Shark Bay in western Australia and claimed possession of New Holland in the name of King Louis XV. He was part of an expedition led by Yves-Joseph de Kerguelen de Trémarec which had left France in April 1771 in search of Gonneville's fabled land. Saint Alouärn had become separated from his commander in foggy weather after sighting land in the southern Indian Ocean and had decided to keep sailing east. He eventually made landfall at Cape Leeuwin on the south-western tip of Australia before heading north. His commander, meanwhile, returned to France where his wildly optimistic report of the misty coasts he had seen and their resources earned him command of a follow-up expedition designed to explore this land further and to colonise it. Kerguelen ended up in disgrace, however, when it was revealed that the land he had seen was simply a remote island that was anything but the hospitable and fertile land of lore.

James Cook's three Pacific voyages finally served to dispel the notion that there existed a great continent in the south. There nevertheless remained much to be determined, including the exact configuration of the Pacific, with its many islands. This was one of the chief aims of the maritime expedition led by Jean-François de Galaup, Comte de La Pérouse (1785–1788). His itinerary included an examination of the northern and western coastlines of New Holland, focusing on the 'torrid zone' as these coasts 'may also possess products associated with countries located in the same latitudes'.[3] He was also to visit Queen Charlotte Strait in New Zealand, to determine whether the British had established a settlement in the area. La Pérouse left France on 1 August 1785. On 6 September 1787, he arrived in Kamchatka where he received a dispatch advising him that the British were planning a settlement in New South Wales and instructing him to head forthwith to Botany Bay to investigate. He anchored in Botany Bay on 26 January 1788, just as Arthur Phillip was preparing to shift the First Fleet to Sydney Cove. Six weeks later, on 10 March, La Pérouse and his men set sail, never to be seen again.

As time went by and no news of La Pérouse was received in France, the governing authorities organised an expedition to search for him. Commanded by Antoine Raymond Joseph de Bruni d'Entrecasteaux, this expedition left France on 29 September 1791 and explored various parts of the Pacific, visiting Tasmania (twice) and the south-west coast of mainland Australia. Despite his extensive search, d'Entrecasteaux found no trace of La Pérouse, though his scientists achieved much in terms of cartography and natural history.

The actual Terra Australis, as opposed to the fabled south land, finally became the primary focus for the French with the voyage in 1800–1804 of Nicolas Baudin. This was a major scientific undertaking that aimed to resolve certain geographical questions – the definitive shape of the Australian mainland's southern coastline, which was still incomplete on European maps, along with some lingering mysteries surrounding the western, north-western and northern coasts – while at the same time allowing an impressive contingent of naturalists to study the land's flora, fauna and native peoples. France gained no geopolitical advantage from this expedition, but its scientific results were significant and it stands as a lasting testament to French interest in Australia.

Following the defeat of Napoleon in 1815 and the end of the Napoleonic wars, France resumed its explorations in the Indo-Pacific, sending first Louis Freycinet (1817–1820), then Louis Isidore Duperrey (1822–1825), Hyacinthe de Bougainville (1824–1826) and Jules Dumont d'Urville (1826–1829 and 1837–1840) to the region with instructions to call in at various parts of Australia.

There was thus no shortage of French visitors to Australia during the late eighteenth century and well into the nineteenth – a fact which has fuelled the enduring fantasy that parts of the country could almost have been French. As history shows, that was never likely to eventuate, due to a variety of factors and circumstances.[4] In terms of colonisation, the persistent explorations of the French did have one significant consequence, however: they served as a spur for the expansion of early British settlement.[5]

Humanising history: Reviving the lived experience

The above summary provides ample evidence of the sustained interest of the French in Australia and in the Indo-Pacific more generally. However, in providing that overview, we have done precisely the opposite of what we wish to achieve in this essay. For what is lost in this kind of broad-brush synthesis is the lived experience of the people who participated in these expeditions. If we simply state, for example, that Baudin took four months to sail from Tenerife to Mauritius, then we are glossing over the highs and lows of the voyage, the moments of excitement but also the sense of monotony created by the apparently endless days at sea, the frustration produced by periods of slow progress, the routine of shipboard activities, the friendships that developed or the quarrels that just as inevitably arose. In short, we risk dehumanising the individuals involved. Not only are their experiences and emotions interesting in themselves, they also provide a context that helps us to understand some of the more momentous events that took place during the voyage. The customary way of highlighting the human dimension of such expeditions is to focus on the drama and the tragedy that often beset them. A less common but equally useful approach is to highlight the lighter or more quirky moments of that lived experience. Our aim here, then, focusing on the expeditions led by d'Entrecasteaux and Baudin, is to shine a light on some of the less frequently mentioned incidents in order to remind ourselves that these explorers, who often come across as fixed and remote historical figures, were real people whose emotions and foibles are strikingly familiar.

1.   *Shipboard life*

There is no better starting point for capturing the colour of the lived experience on these maritime voyages than an examination of shipboard life itself. After all, it is not difficult to imagine that the cohabitation of over a hundred men for months and years on end within the small confines of a sailing ship would generate a variety of incidents large and small.[6]

(i)   *Conflicts*

As we might expect, many such incidents were conflictual in nature, sometimes brought about by professional or ideological differences, at other times simply the result of the pressures created by the harsh conditions or of personality clashes. An illustration of the latter is the confrontation between two of Baudin's officers regarding the zoologist François Péron. During dinner one evening when the expedition was in Sydney, sub-lieutenant Louis Charles Gaspard Bonnefoi (or Bonnefoy) de Montbazin, fully aware of lieutenant Henri Freycinet's friendship with the zoologist, began complaining about 'that peasant, your corporal Péron' (Péron had served in the revolutionary army before starting his medical studies). Henri Freycinet's response was just as cutting: 'a corporal like him is worth 10,000 officers like you!' The discussion went downhill from there. Bonnefoi, convinced that Péron had earlier insulted him, retorted by saying 'he is a pig'. To which Freycinet, summoning all his rhetorical skills, responded: 'You're the one who is a pig!'[7] Bonnefoi continued to criticise Péron, so Freycinet pulled rank and ordered him to his cabin, but Bonnefoi refused to go, claiming that their dispute had nothing to do with his official service. When this was reported to Baudin, he decided they were both to blame, and for good measure also reprimanded the engineer François-Michel Ronsard, who was on guard duty at the time and should have intervened to put an end to the quarrel. This incident might appear trivial, but as Nicole Starbuck has noted, it serves to illustrate why the two senior officers, Henri Freycinet and Ronsard, who were vying for the role of second-in-command on Baudin's ship, struggled to convince the commander that they were worthy of his trust – to the point where he finally deemed it impossible to delegate his authority.[8]

This kind of sensitivity to personal slights could, as in this case, be attributed to a commonly shared and heightened sense of honour. The rigours and stresses of the voyage, however, certainly exacerbated it. When Baudin arrived back in Tasmania after the long and arduous exploration of Australia's south coast, his helmsman, who had been accused of stealing some fish-hooks, was so offended that 'he kicked up a diabolical row'. Having tried to calm him down, Baudin returned to his cabin only to find that the helmsman had resumed his noisy protests. As Baudin noted: 'Tired of all this din, I gave the order for 12 strokes of the lash to be administered to him. This was about to be done when he jumped overboard to escape, even though the weather was none too good.'[9] Fortunately, the poor helmsman was not a good swimmer so they had no trouble fishing him out of the water. Baudin wanted him to be given 20 strokes with the cat-o'-nine tails when he was back on board, but the doctors advised that he was not in a fit state to receive them. Perhaps the bad weather had been a blessing after all.

Nothing was more likely to put the voyagers on edge than the question of food and drink. The tensions that arose among the officers and scientists on Baudin's expedition because of the table arrangements put in place by the government have been well documented.[10] D'Entrecasteaux, too, had his issues. When, during the long and difficult reconnaissance of Australia's south coast, midshipman François-Charles-Luc Achard de Bonvouloir announced during dinner in the great cabin that the water rations were being reduced, the botanist Jacques-Julien Houtou de Labillardière objected that he thought this measure premature. The conversation quickly degenerated, with Labillardière finally telling Bonvouloir that he did not trust him to report his thoughts honestly and accurately to the senior officers responsible for this decision. His honour insulted, Bonvouloir picked up the nearest object he could find, which happened to be a wine bottle, and hurled it at Labillardière, who was at that time eating his 'ragoût' (stew). Fortunately, the bottle flew over his head and smashed behind him. Undeterred, Bonvouloir picked up another bottle and flung it, this time with greater accuracy. Labillardière had anticipated this second missile, however, and was able to duck out of the way. The two men then went for each other and had to be separated. The records do not reveal whether the bottles thrown by Bonvouloir were full or empty. Given the reduction in water rations, his actions would be all the more reprehensible if they did contain such a precious commodity as wine.[11]

Food was, of course, just as vital a resource as wine and water. Complaints about the poor quality or insufficient supply of food were common on long sea voyages, but perversely, the sudden abundance of food in ports of call or as a result of successful fishing or hunting expeditions could also have unfortunate consequences. Such was the case for Baudin's cook, who, having been sick for three months and put on a diet, over-indulged in fish when the ship returned to Tasmania and died from indigestion.[12] Food could also be manipulated to quell trouble or curry favour. An illustration of this is provided by the obsequious note Lieutenant Alexandre d'Hesmivy d'Auribeau sent to d'Entrecasteaux on the *Recherche*: 'I expect to be scolded, general, for wishing to give you sausage and black pudding to eat. However, as this is a Provençal dish which I have sometimes seen you eat with pleasure, I hope this reason will find favour with you.'[13] D'Entrecasteaux was admittedly unwell at the time, so the gesture was not entirely self-serving. Whether or not a feast of his favourite sausage was actually good for his health at that point is uncertain.

Still on the topic of conflict, the old saying that one should never talk about politics or religion among colleagues and friends applies equally, it would seem, to ships of discovery. In the wake of the 1789 Revolution, religion had become a hot political subject in France. It is therefore no surprise to find that it was a divisive topic of conversation on the d'Entrecasteaux expedition. The naturalist Louis Ventenat, who was also the chaplain on board the *Recherche*, reported in a letter to the commander a discussion during which he was mocked and insulted for being a man of the cloth. He was sitting on the watch deck one day when two officers, Alexandre François de la Fresnay de Saint-Aignan and Alexis-Ignace de Crestin (or Crétin), joined him and began talking about the 'fake miracles of the holy shroud of Besançon, Gabriel and the virgin, the incredulity of Saint Thomas' and so on. Ventenat responded that it was precisely the fact that Thomas's doubts had been dispelled that should make believers of them. Tempers then became more heated:

– Oh! we only believe what we can see.

– In that case you should not believe that Louis XIV existed because you have not seen him.

– In faith, Abbé, said M. Saint-Aignan, it is the unworthy behaviour of ecclesiastics that influences my thinking. They publicly keep young women, they have horses and carriages, and that is not appropriate for them.

– [...] I admit that there are some bad subjects among our priests, but not all of them are bad.

– All of them, all of them, *without exception*, answered M. Saint-Aignan.

– Only a depraved imagination could conceive of such an idea.

– Depraved!

He stood up, swearing, then left me and I did not hear what he said after that. M. Crétin, who could see that the conversation was already heated and that there was no need to add further to it, said: 'Well! yes, Abbé (squeezing my arm), I am of the same opinion as Saint-Aignan, and it is surely not this particular voyage *which would give me any reason to change it.*' It seems to me that this is what we call creating a scandal, and you would need to have no blood in your veins not to feel the force of such language.[14]

In contrast to Ventenat, most of the other naturalists on the d'Entrecasteaux expedition were atheists – a reflection, perhaps, of the influence of the *philosophes* and of a certain strand of Enlightenment thinking. This devout disbelief was occasionally put to the test during the voyage, however. When the botanist Claude Antoine Gaspard Riche became disoriented and lost his way among the sand dunes during the expedition's brief stay in Port Esperance, he feared his race had been run. Thirsty and fatigued, he unexpectedly found a spring of fresh water – a piece of good fortune which, as he reported, almost made him believe in Providence. Almost, but not quite.

(ii)   Camaraderie

If there were numerous instances of conflict on these voyages, we can point to just as many examples of camaraderie and friendship. Baudin's young artist Charles-Alexandre Lesueur, for instance, developed what would prove to be a lifelong friendship with François Péron. Some of Baudin's comments suggest that he might have thought one or two of these relationships had developed into something more than friendship. We can speculate on the case of Lesueur and Péron, but there is reason to think the commander had firm suspicions with regard to his senior officer Alexandre Le Bas de Sainte Croix and sub-lieutenant Désiré Breton (*désiré* indeed!). In any event, he had plenty of other reasons to punish them: Le Bas provoked a duel with the engineer Ronsard and was disembarked from the expedition during the first stopover in Timor, while Breton, having slapped a gunner, was demoted for misconduct and transferred to Baudin's consort ship the *Naturaliste*.

The zoologist Stanislas Levillain, who sailed on the Baudin expedition, is one who showed a genuine attachment to his fellow travellers. When he was transferred from the *Géographe* to the

Naturaliste in Mauritius, he introduced himself to all the officers, 'who paid me the most flattering compliments [...]. From that moment I told myself that I might be leaving friends behind, but I have the hope of making new ones, and that is surely a pleasant and flattering perspective for such a long campaign.'[15] His affection for his dog, Kismy, is particularly endearing, and reminds us of the role animals played in terms of companionship. As Levillain wrote, his dog 'was loved by everyone on board and was so gentle that the entire crew adored him'. When the dog did not return from a shore excursion in Geographe Bay, Levillain was inconsolable:

> My poor dog Kismy [...], my most faithful friend for whom my attachment is without question, became frightened by the waves and would not let them catch him to put him in the boat. In the end they had to leave him. Alas, I cannot hold back my tears – you have to have had a pet such as this to feel the pain one feels when one is deprived of an animal to which one has become attached!!![16]

Levillain displayed a great capacity for friendship, with animal and human alike, but also an admirable degree of solidarity not just with the officers and his fellow scientists, but with the regular sailors as well. During the exploration of Shark Bay, he spent several days on Dirk Hartog Island in great discomfort and was much relieved when a boat finally arrived to collect him and his companions. To his frustration, the boatmen stopped to do some fishing on the way back to the ship, but he understood that 'the well-being and health of the crews demanded it'. This 'just consideration', he added, helped to cool his impatience.[17] On another shore excursion, likewise in Shark Bay, he took the defence of an unfortunate sailor whose leg had been injured in the course of his duties and who struggled to keep pace with the others. As Levillain recorded in his journal, the ship's captain, Emmanuel Hamelin, who was leading the march, showed no mercy to the sailor: 'That poor wretch was exhausted and could not go on. Well, our unctuous and honey-tongued captain treated him like the lowest of all men, in the most dreadful and cruel manner, because he could not walk.'[18]

Criticism of the captain, whether justified, as in this case, or not, as was also often the case, came with the territory. The gripes and resentments expressed by several of Baudin's officers and scientists with regard to his leadership are well documented. What is less well known is that for much of the outward journey the situation on board his ship was mostly harmonious and he enjoyed the strong support of many. The same Levillain who was so critical of Hamelin, for example, was very attached to Baudin. He had sailed from France to Mauritius with Baudin on the *Géographe* before being transferred to the *Naturaliste*, so was in a good position to compare the two.

(iii)   *Ceremonies and celebrations*

The commemoration of important dates and other ceremonial occasions often brought welcome relief from the monotony and hardship of shipboard life. An interesting point of contrast between Baudin and Hamelin, in this regard, is their attitude towards the traditional shipboard shenanigans conducted upon crossing the equator. Hamelin, fearing the quarrels that this ceremony sometimes created, did not allow it to take place on the *Naturaliste*. Baudin, on the other hand, not only allowed the ceremony to take place – provided that 'everything took place with the utmost propriety' – but donated eight piastres to the cause.[19] Even though he considered it to be an 'old and ridiculous custom',[20] he thought it would be instructive for his 'gentlemen' to 'obtain some idea of what it was like'.[21] So it was that, as recorded by the gardener Anselme Riedlé, at 4 o'clock on the afternoon of 12 December 1800, as everyone was dining, 'Neptune descended from the main top trembling with horror; he sent his messenger to deliver letters, one to the commandant [Baudin] and the other to the commander [Le Bas]. They were delivered; they requested permission to baptise those serving on his ship and all of those, officers and others, who had not yet been in the tropics, that is to say, who had not yet crossed the Line.'[22] The next morning:

> they began to beat the drum and at 8 am Neptune came down from the main top, wrapped in a sheep skin, along with his high priest and four others dressed up like savages, some white and some smeared with blacking. After paying a visit to the commandant they went around the ship twice and then they began to baptise all those who had not crossed the Line, starting with the officers, followed by the naturalists and then the sailors. They made you sit on a barrel filled with water, then they held you by the arm, lifting it a little above your head, and then they poured water down your sleeve with a funnel. They poured water on you, but in moderation; after this they made you say that you would never kiss a sailor's wife and made you kiss the crucifix. However, the sailors who gave no money were put into a barrel full of water. They had a rope tied around their waist to stop them getting out straight away. They had a large funnel to pour lots of water on them, then they took away the pole so that they fell into a barrel full of water and after that they threw a bucket of water or two over their head and daubed them with a kind of mortar made of chicken droppings and other filth they added. They made very rich pickings, about 60 piastres, that they received from the officers and naturalists.[23]

The leaders of these maritime expeditions were duty bound to maintain good morale on board their ships. Baudin, as we know, ordered his men to dance every evening between 6 and 8 in order to prevent 'melancholy'. D'Entrecasteaux, whatever he thought about the political upheavals that had taken place in France, was careful to ensure that important national dates were appropriately celebrated. As midshipman Pierre Gicquel noted: 'On 14 July the General had the Festival of Federation celebrated. He gave a double ration of his wine to the entire crew. They found it to be very good, for the campaign wine was like vinegar.'[24] As this observation suggests, the commander's largesse may have been appreciated on this occasion, but it also served to highlight the raw deal the crew had otherwise been given.

Nothing boosted morale as much as the arrival at an anticipated destination. Baudin was particularly bemused by the excitement generated on his ship when the island of Tenerife came into view, after only 13 days at sea:

> The moment we sighted land, all the scientists and even most of the officers were so overjoyed that they behaved like madmen. Each one called out to his friend or his neighbour in such a way that pandemonium reigned on board. If a stranger had witnessed what went on and had not known when we had left Europe, it would have been impossible for him not to think that we had just completed a voyage lasting at least six months and that we had been without all essential provisions. Towards evening, when the general curiosity had been satisfied somewhat, everyone went off to get his portfolio and his pencils and, to fore and aft of the ship, there was not a soul to be seen who was not busy sketching.[25]

As these examples demonstrate, life on board the ships provided many moments of pleasure that put into some perspective the more often cited periods of hardship.

(iv)   Professional duties

For a voyage of maritime exploration to be successful, everyone must show a high level of professionalism in the way they go about their business, whether that business is navigation and the running of the ship, in the case of the officers and the sailors under their command, or collecting specimens and making observations, in the case of the scientists. Failure to fulfil that duty, through inattention, laziness or incompetence, could have serious consequences – though not always.

One of the key responsibilities of the naval staff was to maintain a daily journal recording various navigational details – wind direction, barometer readings, weather conditions and so on – and noting the main happenings of the day, under the grandiose heading of 'historical events' (in keeping with naval practice, daily entries went from midday to midday, each new entry beginning with the readings from noon the previous day). Some performed this duty assiduously, while others took a more laconic approach to the task, especially when it came to recording events. Louis Freycinet was one of those in the latter category. For the 24 hours from 9 to 10 December 1800, for example, he simply noted: 'Tacked at mid-day. At 2 o'clock the commander signalled his bearings. We signalled ours.' A week earlier, all he could find to write under the heading 'historical events and remarks' was: 'Nothing new.'[26] Sub-lieutenant Jacques de Saint-Cricq had, if anything, an even more disdainful attitude, openly stating his hostility to the obligation to keep a journal: 'A nautical journal is, I believe, the most boring thing in the world, both to write and to read. However, it is customary to require one from each naval officer on duty, which is of the utmost uselessness, in my view'.[27] He then goes on to explain his point of view at great length, in apparent contradiction to his lack of commitment to writing. The other irony is that his is one of the more colourful and entertaining journals to have survived from the Baudin expedition.

To give Saint-Cricq his due, running the ship undoubtedly took priority over keeping a journal. Any professional shortcomings in the performance of navigational duties could have serious consequences – and attract the scorn of one's companions. When d'Entrecasteaux's ship the *Recherche* found itself heading for a reef off New Caledonia, a succession of officers attempted in vain to steer the ship away. Their ineffectual efforts drew sharp criticism and a certain amount of sarcasm from some on board. Here is how midshipman Gicquel described the incident:

> we found ourselves at dawn sailing close to windward of a large reef [...] heading directly for its end point. We failed at first on two

occasions to tack away through the fault of M. Rossel, who would not listen to the advice given to him by sailors who were more accomplished than he. He handed the watch over to M. Crestin on the pretext that he had a violent headache. The latter again failed to tack and left the deck suffering from a strong bout of colic. Finally, M. d'Auribeau, who had taken some medicine before daybreak, came up on deck and steered the ship away.[28]

Those aristocratic officers were apparently a fragile lot.

On another occasion, a combination of skill and good fortune helped to avert danger, and led to a new discovery. Having become trapped by a sudden wind change among a group of islands and islets off the south-west coast of Australia, d'Entrecasteaux's ships appeared doomed to be dashed on the rocks when a lookout on the *Espérance* spotted a narrow passage leading to what appeared to be a safe anchorage providing shelter from the winds. With skill and daring, the ship worked its way through this passage, and the *Recherche* followed suit. The bay they discovered now bears the name of Port Esperance. The group of islands was named the Recherche Archipelago.

Another important geographical discovery made by the d'Entrecasteaux expedition resulted not from a danger skilfully averted but from the simplest of errors. Rounding the southern tip of Tasmania with the intention of heading for Adventure Bay, the officer on watch inadvertently signalled an important marker, Eddystone, as lying south-west instead of south-east. The ships therefore headed north too soon, towards what appeared to be a broad indentation in the coast. Once the officers realised their error, they sent a boat to investigate and, inside the entrance to this apparent coastal indentation, a large bay offering safe anchorage was found. This was subsequently named Recherche Bay. Over the ensuing days, further excursions suggested that the stretch of deep and calm water they had entered was in fact a strait, which was named D'Entrecasteaux

Channel. The island it defined was also named after the General: Bruny Island. An officer's slip of the tongue had led to a significant discovery.

The naturalists, too, had to fulfil their professional duties with skill and efficiency. Most went about their tasks with zeal, and some went above and beyond the call of duty, as was the case with Baudin's mineralogists, Charles Bailly and Louis Depuch. During the expedition's stay in Sydney, the British governor, Philip Gidley King, made it known that he was keen to find out the geological composition of the foothills of the Blue Mountains. He suspected a survey might reveal the existence of coal deposits, but he had no mineralogists at his disposal in the colony. Depuch and Bailly duly took up the challenge and went to inspect the area, where they confirmed King's intuition. They were effectively working for the enemy.

In contrast to this example of generous collaboration, we might recall other incidents when competition arose between the naturalists. During the passage down the Atlantic, the men on Baudin's ship caught a large shark which, as the commander noted, proved to be a 'great distraction', especially for the scientists, 'who were seeing one alive for the first time'. Understandably curious, they wanted to get close in order to inspect it. But as Baudin observed with some bemusement, 'when it had thrashed its tail from side to side a few times, they were less eager to go near'. Péron and the surgeon François-Étienne Lharidon were more intrepid than the others and, once the shark had been tied down, both sought 'the glory of dissecting it'. This led to a serious dispute. Péron, dripping with blood, went to complain to Baudin that Lharidon had snatched the shark's heart from him, adding that he 'would not go on dissecting after such behaviour'. Baudin, suppressing the urge to laugh, tried to console Péron by promising that the next shark they caught would be his and his alone. As Baudin concluded: 'Doctor Péron was comforted by this promise and Surgeon

Lharidon was left the undisturbed possessor of the shark's heart.'[29]

The unfortunate Péron had earlier been the victim of another incident which, as Baudin noted, 'did not fail to delight all his scientific friends and most of the officers who witnessed it'. While taking thermometer readings in the port head, Péron thought he had been washed out to sea when a wave crashed over him, taking away his notebook and his thermometer. But when the water ran out, 'he was quite amazed not only to find himself alive, but still in the same place'.[30] Later on during the voyage, Baudin noted that Péron, who had taken responsibility for recording the levels of humidity with the hygrometer, had been neglecting this duty in preference for collecting shells. In response to a comment by his commander, Péron responded that, 'as his mother was no longer producing children and he was the family's sole hope, he did not want to kill himself taking observations at night'.[31] Baudin, as it happens, was just teasing Péron, but this emotional response struck him as being unprofessional.

2. *Encounters*

Encounters with other people, whether in ports held by European powers or in lands occupied by indigenous populations, were a natural and anticipated feature of maritime voyages of discovery. It was important for navigators to record these experiences in order to provide the authorities back home with information that might be useful in terms of trade or conquest. By the time of the Baudin expedition, the study of native peoples had also become an object of scientific interest, with formalised instructions issued on what should be observed and how the travellers should attempt to interact with them. These encounters have understandably been the subject of much scholarly debate, for they tell us a great deal about European attitudes and values, and provide important clues to indigenous agency. While some of these meetings – with other Europeans as with native peoples – were fraught and full of tension, there were also many moments of good-natured exchange and mutual curiosity.

(i)   The familiar other

In the late eighteenth century, Spain was a fading but still prominent maritime force, with outposts at various points around the globe. One of these was Tenerife, which was often the first port of call for ships on their way from Europe to the Indian and Pacific Oceans. Travellers were frequently struck by the unusual customs of the locals, in particular the curious contrast between strict religious observance and loose morals. The following observation made by one of d'Entrecasteaux's men is a case in point:

> I have noticed some windows opened wide, and this was simply to cater for the many fat monks who fill the island. A national assembly would be needed to prevent them from dying from apoplexy, which their portliness seems to threaten them with. The women have no scruples entertaining the priests in the open fields and no doubt earn their husbands a few indulgences in this way.[32]

As in all sea ports, some of the women in Santa Cruz had adopted this kind of activity as their profession. One of Baudin's gardeners, Antoine Sautier, gave a particularly colourful description of them:

> Most of the women went barefoot and barelegged and their heads were covered with a serge veil as if they would not deign to look at a man, and yet most were not too scrupulous, for most of their trade consisted of doing what a great many women in Paris do. Hookers, harlots, tarts, strumpets, such is their lovely profession. Still they scarcely tempted me for I myself found them too ugly. I think that if I had been obliged to marry and end my days there I would not have long to live but let's pass over that.[33]

Another of Baudin's gardeners, Riedlé, was particularly scathing in his assessment of the Spanish settlers on the island and their lack of work ethic:

The gardens that I saw in Tenerife were as parched as the countryside. Firstly, water is very scarce and all of these Spaniards are so averse to hard work. They prefer by far to sit in the shade rather than work and, in any case, how can you have any good gardeners in this country since they don't have any good ones in Spain? Not even in Madrid. The king's gardeners have never brought out a catalogue because it would be a disgrace to have so few plants. In Tenerife, all the wealthy people are French and English merchants or merchants of other nationalities, for the Spanish have no other occupation than to nurture their sloth.[34]

It is true that Riedlé, being Austrian, was of Germanic stock. Cultural stereotypes clearly go back a long way.

(ii)   The exotic other
Preconceived notions were certainly a factor in encounters with indigenous peoples, but the French voyagers also displayed a genuine curiosity and desire to learn about them and their customs. While these encounters were sometimes fraught with tension, there were also numerous interactions of an apparently more harmonious nature. There are many charming and even amusing incidents we could mention in this respect, but we will limit ourselves to one particular aspect: the use of music as a means of breaking down barriers.

Music was a feature of the encounters between the d'Entre-casteaux expedition and the Nuenonne and Lyluequonney people of south-east Tasmania. The botanist Labillardière reported that on one occasion, while walking back to their boat with a group of Aboriginal people, some of them 'attempted more than once to charm us by songs, with the modularity of which I was singularly struck, from the great analogy of the tunes to those of the Arabs in Asia Minor. Several times two of them sung [sic] the same tune at once, but always one a third above the other, forming a concord with the greatest justness.'[35] Lieutenant Saint-Aignan had earlier played the violin for them, but with less happy results: the Aboriginal people had covered their ears in pain. He would have more luck later, off the island of Buka in eastern New Guinea, where the locals were so captivated with his playing that they would have traded anything, even their canoe, to get their hands on his violin.[36] After an unsuccessful first attempt, the French eventually managed to persuade the Tasmanian Aboriginal people to dance in a circle with them. When the naturalist Ventenat played his flute for them, they apparently listened with great interest before trying to snatch the instrument from him.

When the Baudin expedition visited south-east Tasmania some ten years later, music was again used to facilitate contact with the Nuenonne people and to learn something about them, this time using a more systematic approach: by playing different types of music, Baudin's men were attempting to gain a better understanding of their listeners' emotions and ways of thinking. The Aboriginal audience became quite animated when the doctor, Jérôme Bellefin, sang the *Marseillaise*, whereas the French formed the impression that they were not as affected by the 'light, tender little airs' that were performed as a contrast.[37] Perhaps this apparent lack of reaction was in fact an appropriately reflective response to the gentler music.[38]

(iii)   *The natural world*

Encounters with the natural world also produced their share of anecdotes as the French travellers tried to come to grips with the many new and unusual animals and natural phenomena they found, at sea and on land. The kangaroo was a common source of fascination. According to one of d'Entrecasteaux's junior officers, there were two types of kangaroo, 'the large and the small'. It was just as well there were scientists on board to provide a more nuanced assessment. That same midshipman was completely mystified when he awoke one morning during an overnight shore excursion in Tasmania's Recherche Bay to find that the three fish and the parrot he had hung from a branch above his camp site had been eaten. He had neither seen nor heard the animal. He stayed up all the next night to try to see what it was, but to his disappointment it did not return and, as he concluded, he was 'obliged to surrender [his] supplies to it on credit'.[39]

* * *

There are countless other interesting and often amusing incidents we could recount from the stories of these two French maritime expeditions that visited the shores of Australia over 200 years ago. Individually, some of them reveal in microcosm certain issues of great import, and have consequently attracted the attention of historians; many others, however, have been overlooked or considered not worthy of mention because they appear to be anecdotal. What we hope to have shown here is that these moments have a real human interest and that, taken collectively, they serve to bring back to life the characters of the people who participated in these expeditions and the richness of their experiences. In that respect, these are not 'tall tales' at all but profoundly 'true'. Indeed, they all form part of the history of cultural exchange between our two worlds over the centuries. If the exploration of Australia was life-changing for the French mariners involved, it also contributed to developing a deeper knowledge and understanding of what makes Australia 'a world apart', even today. What the French have done for us thus goes much further than the legacy of place names dotted around our map.

Further reading

Plomley, Brian, and Josiane Piard-Bernier, *The General: The Visits of the Expedition Led by Bruny d'Entrecasteaux to Tasmanian Waters in 1792 and 1793*, Launcestion: Queen Victoria Museum, 1993.

Bruny d'Entrecasteaux, Antoine, *Voyage to Australia and the Pacific*, edited and translated by Edward Duyker and Maryse Duyker, Carlton: Melbourne University Press, 2001.

Baudin, Nicolas, *The Journal of Post-Captain Nicolas Baudin, Commander-in Chief of the Corvettes* Géographe *and* Naturaliste, *assigned by order of the government to a voyage of discovery*, translated by Christine Cornell, Adelaide: The Friends of the State Library of South Australia, 2004 (1974).

Fornasiero, Jean, Peter Monteath and John West-Sooby, *Encountering Terra Australis: The Australian Voyages of Nicolas Baudin and Matthew Flinders*, Kent Town: Wakefield Press, 2010 (2004).

Fornasiero, Jean, Lindl Lawton and John West-Sooby (eds), *The Art of Science: Nicolas Baudin's Voyagers 1800–1804*, Mile End: Wakefield Press, 2016.

Fornasiero, Jean and John West-Sooby (eds), *'Roaming Freely Throughout the Universe:' Nicolas Baudin's Voyage to Australia and the Pursuit of Science*, Mile End: Wakefield Press, 2021.

On Food

Gastronomy: from the Greek *gaster* ('stomach') and *nomos* ('law'). Etymologically speaking, then, 'gastronomy' signifies the art of managing or regulating the stomach. From the outset, however, the word was intended to encompass the all-important notions of excellence and pleasure, not just the prosaic practical aspects of food consumption. And in that respect, it is a concept unerringly associated with the French.

The term was indeed first used in its modern sense as the title of an 1801 poem by the French poet and humorist Joseph de Berchoux. The opening to 'La Gastronomie' immediately establishes the tone: in it, Berchoux announces that he will reveal how to 'embellish a meal' and 'augment the pleasures of an amiable banquet'; the gastronomic meal, he adds, offers an occasion for 'cementing friendships' as well as for 'endless pleasure' and for 'talking nonsense' while 'sweetly intoxicated'. Conviviality and a sense of indulgence have been associated with the concept of gastronomy ever since.

Berchoux's poem may have inaugurated the use of the term 'gastronomy', but the word gained worldwide currency thanks to the publication in 1825 of Jean Anthelme Brillat-Savarin's *Physiologie du goût* ('The Physiology of Taste'). In it, Brillat-Savarin defined gastronomy as the 'reasoned knowledge' of everything that relates to how we feed ourselves; its goal is to ensure our preservation 'by means of the best possible food'. For Brillat-Savarin, gastronomy had a fundamentally practical purpose but was also an intellectually driven activity predicated on the notion of excellence. How very French!

The gastronomic feast is normally reserved for special occasions, but the respect for food that it epitomises still permeates the planning and preparation of even the most humble everyday meal in France. Meal times likewise remain valued as moments of conviviality and enjoyment. Even in France, however, eating habits are evolving, in accordance with the demands and developments of modern life. It is now common to find shops devoted entirely to frozen foods in most French towns and cities, a sign of the shift towards more convenient modes of food preparation for the time-poor; and, for many urban dwellers at least, lunch is no longer the most important and substantial meal of the day, with many now preferring something light and easy such as a sandwich or a salad which can be eaten *sur le pouce* (literally: 'on the thumb' – on the go). But while the days of the long lunch might be diminishing, the respect for food is still very much a defining feature of French culture. Food, as Cath Kerry reminds us in the following account, is much more than a necessity for the French: it is one of life's essential preoccupations.

Throughout the world, French cuisine is usually associated with fine dining and chic restaurants. It has set the benchmark, in so many respects. But this was not always the case. In pre-modern times, the cuisine of France was in fact influenced by the culinary traditions of its neighbours. It was in the seventeenth century that François Pierre (de) La Varenne and other chefs codified French cuisine through the publication of influential books that recorded the many French innovations of the period and championed the use of indigenous produce, such as locally available herbs, used in preference to the costly exotic spices that were common in mediaeval and Renaissance times. In La Varenne's *Le Cuisinier françois* ('The French Cook', 1651), we find the first use of 'bouquet garni', 'fonds de cuisine' (stocks) and 'réductions', and of techniques such as the use of egg whites for clarification or of roux as the base for sauces. The book also contained the first mention of bisque and of Béchamel sauce, as well as the first recorded recipe for a mille-feuille. Many of the staple ingredients and techniques of what we know today as French cuisine have their origins here.

Beyond those ingredients and techniques, however, most of the best-known dishes that we might identify with French cuisine are regional specialties – with the possible exception of the quintessential *pot-au-feu* (from which the Vietnamese derived the phở, a reminiscence of colonial times). These regional dishes now have much wider circulation, but many still consider that it is more authentic to eat a *bœuf bourguignon* in Burgundy, a *choucroute* in Alsace, a *bouillabaisse* in Marseille, a *cassoulet* in Castelnaudary, or anything cooked in loads of cream and butter in Normandy. The richness of French regional cuisine combined with the advent of the motor car led to the creation of the Michelin guide, which was first published in 1900 as a form of advertising for Michelin tyres but which became the reference for gastronomic travel in France following World War I. With its detailed information on restaurants, the best of which receive highly valued stars (one, two or three), the Michelin guide serves as a de facto source of culinary criticism – which is something else the French have given us, dating back to Grimod de La Reynière's gastronomic criticism of the early nineteenth century. After all, if there is anything the French love (almost) as much as food, it is an animated debate!

JWS

11

Catherine Kerry

Live to eat – a very French pleasure

Beginnings ...

Food has been a feature of the shared history between France and Australia ever since the early French explorers first set foot upon the shores of 'Terra Australis'. Food, naturally enough, was a major preoccupation of mariners engaged in long sea voyages. Hunting and foraging in the places they visited was often a matter of survival; identifying new and productive sources of food also held the potential for economic gain. In the latter part of the eighteenth century, Enlightenment values ensured that such considerations were complemented by more philanthropic concerns, as travellers sought to improve the lot of the peoples they encountered – and of future mariners – by sowing plants and leaving animals that they thought would provide a more plentiful and beneficial source of sustenance – a practice which we might today consider presumptuous and patronising, but which was nonetheless inspired by a spirit of generosity, however misplaced that may have been.

One early French visitor to Australia's shores was Jean-François de La Pérouse, whose round-the-world discovery tour eventually took him to Botany Bay, where he anchored on 26 January 1788 just as the First Fleet was leaving for Port Jackson. La Pérouse was received cordially by the British officers, but they explained that they were not in a position to provide him with any essential items such as food, equipment or sails. As La Pérouse drily observed, this meant that 'their offers of help were limited to their good wishes for the success of our further travels'. He nevertheless replied that he fully understood the situation: 'I knew that ships sent to form a colony at such a great distance from Europe could be of no help to navigators'.[1] Besides, he added, he only needed to collect wood and water, which seemed to be in abundance in Botany Bay, and he was confident he had enough 'victuals' to get him to his next destination. All the same, it is hard to imagine that his crew would not have done any fishing, hunting or foraging during the six weeks or so that they spent in Botany Bay. Be that as it may, having taken on the necessary wood and water and gathered information on the activities of the British, La Pérouse left Australia in March 1788, never to be seen again.[2]

Three years and a revolution later, Antoine Bruni d'Entrecasteaux left Brest on a voyage to the Pacific in search of La Pérouse. In April 1792, as he rounded the southern tip of Van Diemen's Land (Tasmania) en route for the Pacific, a fortunate miscalculation led him to anchor his ships in a natural harbour that the French named Recherche Bay, after one of their ships. Exploring the area, they discovered a navigable body of water (subsequently named D'Entrecasteaux Channel) which separated the mainland from a significant island (Bruny Island). D'Entrecasteaux had with him a team of highly respected naturalists and hydrographers.

During this first, five-week visit to Tasmania, they observed, they collected, they surveyed – and they planted a garden. Their new maps of the area included the garden; it measured roughly nine metres by four metres. In 2003, a thorough survey around the Recherche Bay area confirmed the existence of stones and well-delineated beds – the layout of a real French kitchen garden, four squares in a square, *un vrai potager*. Records and diaries indicate what was planted (radishes, lettuce, chicory, cabbage, cress, potatoes ...), but these documents also show the intention behind the work: in addition to collecting local plant specimens to take back home, the French, in the philanthropic spirit mentioned above, wanted to leave something behind. (Tasmania's climate was in fact very similar to that of Brittany.) Fresh food, they hoped, might be of use to passing ships; but more importantly, the garden was seen as a gift from the French people to the indigenous people of this 'new' land.

No meaningful encounters took place during d'Entrecasteaux's first visit to south-east Tasmania, but that changed when he and his ships returned to the area in January 1793, following an unsuccessful first search for traces of La Pérouse in the south-west Pacific. The interactions between the French and the Lyluequonney and Nuenonne tribes during these meetings were mostly cordial; the visitors were interested in the food of the locals, how they gathered it, how they used their resources. They respected what could be learnt from the 'noble savage' – a popular French concept of the late eighteenth century. Could they in return offer the benefits of European plants and thus tempt or lure the Aboriginal people into cultivation? Might this help vary their diet choices? Might it lighten the load of Aboriginal women who spent laborious hours diving for crayfish and abalone? (Personally, I'll take the crayfish, hold the lettuce.)

Sadly, the garden had not flourished. In fact, not much had survived: wrong plants, wrong season, clay soil. The reasoning behind the planting of the garden was certainly paternalistic, but it was at the same time a kindly and well-intentioned gesture. Might this be an expression of France's desire to extend our horizon, the first attempt to reach out to Australia through food?

At table, we've always wanted to be French

From the late nineteenth century, it was 'classy' for menus to be written in French, even if what was on offer was fairly mundane. Lamb chops and boiled peas could be improved by being described

Cover and title page of *Oh, for a French Wife!* (New York: Abelard Press, 1953)

as *côtelettes aux petits pois à l'anglaise* (*à l'anglaise* referring to simply boiling in water).

In the early 1950s, the book *Oh, for a French Wife!* was a huge success, with eight reprintings into the early 60s. (One might even see it as an important piece of cultural history, a cult classic, a collector's item.) In it, Ted Maloney and Deke Coleman, two advertising men from the Sydney firm of J. Walter Thompson, offered encouragement and recipes (devised by four wives – theirs and two others). They went further than just food, discussing with a chatty urbanity the joys (and pitfalls) of entertaining. There were luncheons in the garden, cocktails and dinners; this at a time when dinner at home often meant black tie and a frock with some serious *décolleté*. The patronising and misogynistic tone of the book has a certain dated charm. The illustrations, by Hungarian immigrant, architect and cartoonist, George Molnar, of buxom, naked, cavorting cherubs in the kitchen, do it justice.

The Australian Hostess Cookbook (1970) and the magazine *Vogue Living*, which started around the same time, provided recipes from with-it hostesses in caftans – lamb chops *en cuirasse, pommes de terre fondantes, fraises dans la neige*, asparagus *fromage* (a gratin of tinned asparagus), scallops *en brochette*, apricot *plateau*. It was a delight to come across crayfish d'Entrecastreaux (cooked crayfish meat, two cups of evaporated milk, breadcrumbs, mixed mustard), cooked in individual ramekins and browned on top.

And let us note in passing *The Ipcress File*, Len Deighton's 1962 spy novel adapted for the screen in 1965, with Michael Caine in the lead role. The suave but troubled spy, Harry Palmer, likes to cook and chooses tinned *champignons* over button mushrooms.

We've always wanted to be French at table.

Food culture and language

The assimilation into everyday language of words and phrases taken from another language is usually a reliable indicator of cultural impact. In terms of food, how easily we have embraced the language of French! Today, the 'couch-potato' couple, eating their Uber-delivered *croque-monsieur* while watching Master Chef, have become quite at ease with the *sous-vide* technique, the *bain-marie* and the difference between a *beurre blanc* and a *beurre noisette*. Might they be tempted at the week-end to accompany their grilled steak with *julienned* vegetables, *sautéed* in butter, and some *béchamel*-coated macaroni – that is, a mac 'n' cheese, which is, let's face it, a delightful *gratin*? For the steak, a *demi-glace* might be going too far but a simple *jus* could suffice. Too complicated? Perhaps, then, just an *omelette*. A *fondue* is perhaps passé but if men still don't eat *quiche*, they certainly know what it is. Take care in offering a *coulis*, however. I've seen a raspberry *couille* in a food magazine; *couilles* is French slang for testicles.

French is everywhere. French vocabulary is certainly *de rigueur* in matters of food and hospitality. We want things to be French. We eat French fries, even though they were invented in Belgium. Stale bread, soggy with beaten egg and pan fried, is French toast, even though it is *pain perdu* (lost bread) in French. A long crusty loaf is French bread. A salad of greens is a French salad and has a *vinaigrette*, although the spelling sometimes eludes the menu writer – it is not a 'vinigerette'. (As an aside, the name for the sauce comes from the French word for vinegar: 'vinaigre', which literally means 'sour wine'.) For special occasions, a cake will not do; this self-same cake becomes a *gâteau*. A stew becomes a *casserole* or a *ragoût*, a fish soup becomes a *bisque*, possibly with *croûtons*, pancakes become *crêpes* and might be served with a *quenelle* of cream.

Eating out, whether in a *restaurant*, *bistro*, *brasserie* or *café* is a traipse through the French language. Even if we are eating Hungarian or Indian, we expect a restaurant to be a little structured with an *à la carte* menu (meaning there is a list from which we can choose). There will be a *maître d'* to tell us where to sit, perhaps even a *sommelier* to fetch and pour our wine. There will be a *chef* (even possibly a *chef de cuisine*) to cook our food. We ease into a meal with a *canapé* (a piece of fried or grilled bread in the shape of a 'canapé' – a couch or sofa – on which sits a tasty morsel) or possibly an *hors d'œuvre* or *amuse-bouche*. *Hors d'œuvre* is difficult to spell and difficult to pronounce for an English speaker but that has never stopped its use. It is a titbit, outside of ('hors de') the main 'work' ('œuvre'). A *croûton* with a sliver of smoked salmon is a *canapé*. Every *canapé* is an *hors d'œuvre* (and, one hopes, an *amuse-bouche* – a mouth pleaser), although not every *hors d'œuvre* is a *canapé*! We then happily move on to an *entrée* and end with a *dessert* (French terms used even when we order in a Thai or Mexican restaurant).

Returning to settings, a *brasserie* is a curious one. *Brasser* means to brew (beer). *Brasseries* used to brew beer on the premises as well as serve food, often with an Alsatian twist: lots of sausage and cabbage. A brasserie is a little less formal than a restaurant; cloths are generally still required but beer brewing and choucroute need no longer apply, even in France. The word remains, however. *Bistros* offer casual eating with simple service and atmosphere. They started as meeting places in Paris for coal merchants from the Auvergne region in the late nineteenth century. It is possibly our most popular form of dining, even with electricity now on hand and despite the fact that the Auvergne is an unknown territory to many. A *café* speaks for itself. A good cake shop has to be a *pâtisserie* where we confidently order our favourite *pâtisseries*: an *éclair au café* (so light it disappears like lightning – an 'éclair'), a *mille-feuilles* (a pastry of 'a thousand leaves'), a *croissant*, a *pain au chocolat* or an *escargot* (a bun curled like a snail).

Creations ...

In addition to the language of *cuisine*, we can attribute to the French a series of inventions and practical innovations which, over time, have completely revolutionised our approach to the preparation and preservation of food and drink. The following is just a sample.

French physicist Denis Papin worked with steam. His experiments led to the piston steam engine. In 1689, he also invented the steam digester or bone digester (we call it the pressure cooker), an enclosed cylinder with a tight-fitting lid that cooked food under pressure, drastically reducing cooking time. It was noted that ragoûts prepared using this method were tender and maintained deliciousness. (Where would bone broth be without it?)

In 1745, Charles-Marie de La Condamine published a record of his travels and observations in South America, which included an account of the use of *quinine* by the Amerindians (in what is now Ecuador) to stave off malaria. Later, in 1820, Pierre Joseph Pelletier and Joseph Bienaimé Cavetou, chemists, were able to extract quinine from the bark of the cinchona tree. Quinine gives the essential bitterness to tonic water as well as to *apéritifs* such as Dubonnet, Lillet, Campari and Angostura Bitters, essential to good digestion. (I once overheard two old French chefs discussing the digestive problems of a friend. It seems he was diligent in having an *apéritif* before a meal, but often forgot the post-prandial *digestif*. They shrugged. The fool – what could he expect?)

Nicolas Appert was a chef and pastry cook but he pioneered *tinned food*. 'An army marches on its stomach', said Napoleon. In 1795, encouraged by the army and a substantial prize, Appert devised a method to preserve meat, fruit and vegetables in air-tight containers. Up until then, anyone leaving home base had to rely on dried, smoked, fermented or pickled food. By 1810 he had perfected the method, first using wide-necked glass jars and later tins. He had no idea why the process worked; he left it to Pasteur to explain that.

Around the middle of the nineteenth century, Ferdinand Carré invented a method to make ice – big blocks of ice that could be used in ships for meat transportation from one continent to another, not to mention for chilling champagne and cocktails. He also invented the absorption refrigerator. This was improved upon by Abbot Marcel Audiffren. He devised a hand-cranked machine to cool the wine of his Cistercian monastery. He sold the patent and, by 1903, domestic refrigerators based on his designs were manufactured and became widely available (at great expense).

Charles Frédéric Gerhardt was a French chemist. The bark of a certain willow had been known as an analgesic for over 3,000 years. Identifying it as acetylsalicylic acid in 1853, Gerhardt needed to work on separating out unfortunate side effects. In 1899, it became available as *aspirin* (a help in dealing with a hangover). Almost a century earlier, a refinement to another pick-me-up was created by the Archbishop of Paris, Jean-Baptiste de Belloy, who, searching for a better way than just pouring boiling water over coffee, invented in 1800 the *dripolator*, which appears in various guises to this day.

Louis Pasteur, scientist, chemist, totally changed our under-standing of hygiene, public health and disease. He showed that food went bad when contaminated by 'germs'. He established the Pasteur Institute in 1888, by which time it was common practice to safeguard and preserve milk through *pasteurisation* (heating the milk just enough to kill bacteria without killing the essential nature of the milk). Even raw milk cheeses are safely possible now because of a better understanding of the behaviour of bacteria. (My mother continued to add a teaspoon of red wine to my water at table to 'kill the microbes'.)

Pierre Verdun, a butcher and catering salesman from Burgundy, worked on a machine that could take on the daily, time-consuming chores of the commercial kitchen. His *food processor*, the Robot-Coupe (1963), could chop, shred, purée, knead and blend, and was an instant hit. By 1971, a domestic version came out (at more or less the same time as 'nouvelle cuisine' hit the home market with books by Michel Guérard, the Troisgros brothers, Paul Bocuse, Roger Vergé *et al.*). We could not have produced the mousses and beautifully coloured purées and coulis that we know so well today without the Magimix. It was designed to be tough and last for 30 years, unlike the sad, noisy, trembling little battlers that tried to imitate it. It you weren't using your Magimix, you were working too hard. (It came out in America as the Cuisinart.)

And the best creation of all: The restaurant

The notion that restaurants sprang up in Paris only after the 1789 Revolution is a gross simplification. Establishments offering 'restorative' meals had already begun to appear in the French capital in the mid 1760s. It was after the Revolution, though, that the phenomenon really took off. Some chefs of large estates moved to the city, finding themselves out of a job when their aristocratic employers emigrated or went to the guillotine, but the habit of eating out grew in the atmosphere of *liberté, égalité et fraternité*.

Previously, one could eat at a tavern or find refreshment at an inn while travelling. But it was accepted that, at a *table d'hôte*, 'you ate what you got'. The fare was whatever the host chose to offer that day at tables generally shared with other people. Then, from around 1780, venues serving *restaurants*, a type of bouillon, began to come into prominence. At these establishments, one would be 'restored'.[3] Surroundings were pleasant. These venues came to be known by what they served – that is, as restaurants – and started offering more than soups. By the mid 1850s, they had become a Parisian institution, appreciated by a *beau-monde* eager to be sociable.

Later that century, a radical change was made to the way in which restaurants were run. Auguste Escoffier, perhaps the first celebrity chef, having honed his skills in Monte Carlo and Switzerland, accepted an offer in 1890 from Richard D'Oyly Carte (the English impresario responsible for bringing together Gilbert and Sullivan) to join the Savoy Hotel in London. Escoffier's military-style organisation made it possible to offer diners a choice. He codified menus (basic sauces, soups, desserts, etc.), standardised recipes and had kitchen brigades responsible for different elements of the menu. We take it for granted now that a table of four can order four different dishes over three courses – that is, twelve different dishes that all arrive at the right time, in the right order. Escoffier was tough but he certainly cleaned up the kitchen and its staff, ensuring they looked fresh in uniforms he had designed. (Cooks were known to work long hours, underground, in stifling conditions, and to gamble, smoke and drink too much.) The Escoffier story also includes an important, if anecdotal, Australian connection: in 1894, he invented a new dessert, the *pêche Melba*, named in honour of Australian soprano Nellie Melba. Paul Bocuse, 60 years later, further elevated the status of the chef, his sexy charisma giving the profession such a lift that a callow youth fresh from hospitality school might expect to be on the cover of *Gourmet* magazine any time soon. And as to training, it is the French method that is used universally. Although menus are now more likely to be written in the vernacular – even ironically ('Bangers and Mash' may have an elegant twist) – the language of the commercial kitchen is French.

Life basics ...

British and American bread took a drastic turn for the worse after World War II. Instead of the overnight process once standard in bread-making, the Chorleywood Bread Process (England c. 1960) made it possible to produce loaves, sliced and wrapped and out the door, in a couple of hours. This made it less flavoursome and less nutritious. The bread needed additives that were not necessarily required to be indicated on the label. The American Wonder Bread was soft and spongy (and unfortunately appealed to immature palates). The dough was so denatured that the makers were forced by government decree to 'enrich' it with vitamins and minerals.

French bread is made from flour, yeast, water and salt – four ingredients compared to the 10 to 12 ingredients listed on our industrial loaves. Bread in France must be sold under the sign of a *boulangerie* (be it a shop or a section in a supermarket). Other bread, heavily mechanised and often sold par-baked, frozen, to be finished at a later date, is available but must be labelled as such. (Some of this is sent to Australia. Don't be fooled.) The French love of good, real bread has caught on and has encouraged better, delicious, healthy bread made by artisan bakers, in Australia as elsewhere around the world. Lionel Poilâne's bread is certainly a benchmark for good bread all over the world. (At a price, Poilâne bread is even air-freighted from France to America and Japan.) Lionel and his wife were tragically killed in a helicopter crash in 2002. Their daughter, Apollonia, then 18, carried on the business. She has also continued her father's 'conversation' with the Vatican to have the word *gourmandise* (badly translated into English as gluttony) struck from the list of deadly sins. This shows a very French attitude to our daily bread and to the pleasures of the table.

Any country that uses milk makes cheese. It's what you do to preserve excess. While cheese is part of most diets, only the French have a whole, separate course taken after the main and before the dessert, if there is one. This might be one special cheese (very elegant) or a group showing different types – a creamy, a blue, a hard cheese. (Too many might seem vulgar; all creamy, dull.) As a regular meal-time habit, a French family takes out its box of cheeses and a bowl of fruit to finish a meal and calls it dessert. At a good dinner, likewise, there is a full cheese course, followed by dessert or simply replacing dessert. The renowned epicure and gastronome Jean Anthelme Brillat-Savarin (1755–1826) wrote: 'A dessert without cheese is like a beauty with only one eye' – admittedly not one of his best aphorisms. All the same, the importance of cheese in French culture is underlined by the fact that it is a point of reference for such pithy comments. When asked about the political divisiveness of France, President Charles de Gaulle commented wryly: 'How can you govern a country which has 246 varieties of cheese?'[4] France now produces over a thousand and the rest of us look and learn. We have expanded our knowledge of the vast variety on offer. Artisan cheese makers in Australia are now making brie-style, camembert-style, chèvres, etc. It is no longer just cheese to be grated on your pasta or *pommes dauphinoises*.

France, compared to other European countries, was late in taking to the potato, but after existing well on potatoes as a prisoner in a Prussian gaol, Antoine-Augustin Parmentier (1737–1813), pharmacist and agronomist, was determined to spread the news. He ran a strong campaign, from offering bouquets of potato flowers to hosting potato banquets for local and visiting dignitaries. Today, freeing us from the monotony of mash or chips, the *Larousse Gastronomique* has over 100 potato recipes. Potage Parmentier (potato soup), hachis Parmentier (cottage pie), gratin Parmentier (potatoes baked with cream), are only the beginning. Vegetables, more generally, form an especially important part of the meal in France and cooking methods are correspondingly varied. (At home, I have never had a straight, boiled vegetable, described in French as à l'anglaise, as previously noted.)

Three- or even four-course meals supplied to children and prepared on the premises are an accepted part of school life. An entrée might be carottes râpées (grated carrot salad dressed with a vinaigrette and light garlic), dessert simply a pastry, a cheese, a yoghurt or a piece of fruit. There is no waste. Vegetables are bought in small quantities so as to be eaten fresh and not lose their 'life force'. If meat is eaten, the whole beast is respected – 'nose to tail eating', as described by British chef Fergus Henderson. Liver, brains, sweetbreads are relished and seen as special treats. Meals are shared, which often means company. Meals are not rushed. Meals may seem ritualised – and what's wrong with that? In all, the French have a healthier attitude to eating.

Attitude ...

In 2010, UNESCO inscribed the French gastronomic meal and its rituals on the Representative List of the Intangible Cultural Heritage of Humanity, a list that includes Korean wrestling, the whistle language of Turkey and the watertight bulkhead technology of Chinese junks. The UNESCO website explains its recognition of this vital French cultural practice in the following terms: 'The gastronomic meal emphasises togetherness, the pleasure of taste, and the balance between human beings and the products of nature.'[5]

The 'pleasures of the table' is an expression which instantly evokes the tradition of the French table, with its more hedonistic and all-embracing attitude to food. Happiness at table comes when we live to eat rather than follow the Anglo-Celtic, Teutonic or Slavic view that we eat to live. (School friends in the sixties told me they were forbidden to talk during meals. It was usual that items of food were measured out onto each plate in the kitchen – a sausage, a potato, a piece of carrot and nine peas – rather than being offered together on a central dish.) The French know that we gather to share, to enjoy what we eat and to enjoy each other.

In France, this attitude dates back at least as far as the eighteenth century, which was retrospectively dubbed the Age of Enlightenment. It was a time of revolution in politics, a time of healthy scepticism of the established order, an age of discovery. Philosophers debated such weighty topics as human rights, human happiness and the meaning of life, but food and the table were an integral part of their discussions. It was not nutrition, wellness, allergies or the delights of the slow cooker that preoccupied them but the what and the why. Gastronomy spawned a vocabulary: *la gourmandise, gourmet* versus *gourmand, gastronome, épicure and connoisseur.*

Two men stand out in this respect; they wrote of gastronomy as art. Alexandre Balthazar Grimod de La Reynière (1758–1837) was a gourmet and a gourmand (the latter word not as crude in meaning as 'glutton' but designated someone who just loves eating). From 1803 to 1812, he published an eight-volume work, *L'Almanach des gourmands*, considered the foundational publication on gastronomy. He also wrote reviews of restaurants – a genre of critical writing that we continue to enjoy today – and set up panels of like-minded fellows to judge and rate prepared foods like cheese, pâtés and catered goods. He was ascerbic with a cruel wit. The previously mentioned Jean Anthelme Brillat-Savarin (1755–1826), more retiring, was a gentleman, gentle and encouraging. (They were acquaintances, rather than friends.) His book, *Phsyiologie du goût* ('The Physiology of Taste'), finally published in 1825 and never out of print, coaxed us to eat with pleasure and intelligence, suggesting that when we think of what we might eat, we should first consider with whom we will be eating.

The aphorisms and pronouncements of Grimod de La Reynière and Brillat-Savarin – which are sadly not featured in the UNESCO cultural heritage citation on the French gastronomic meal – are the expression of a veritable philosophy with regard to eating and drinking, as the following examples demonstrate:

Beware of people who don't eat; in general they are envious, foolish or nasty. Abstinence is an anti-social virtue.

To fold your napkin at table is tantamount to rudely hinting for another invitation.

It is an insult to your host to leave food on your plate or wine in your glass.

Grimod de La Reynière

Drunkards and victims of indigestion do not know how to eat or drink.

To entertain guests is to make yourself responsible for their happiness so long as they are beneath your roof.

The most indispensable qualification of a cook is punctuality. The same must be said of guests.

Jean Anthelme Brillat-Savarin

Epilogue

John Baxter, author and film maker, writes about food, French history and 'the movies'. A boy from suburban Australia who married into a redoubtable old French family, he has become so completely immersed into French life that for the last 30 odd years he has been in charge of the daunting family Christmas dinner. He writes: 'Whatever its reputation for rich sauces and flashy presentation, French cuisine, I'd come to understand through painful experience, is essentially simple. It relies on precisely isolating and emphasising the essential flavour of an ingredient, then juxtaposing two or more tastes in a pleasing or surprising harmony.'[6]

What have the French ever done for us? Like John Baxter, we have these days a deeper understanding of food – its preparation and its enjoyment – and have moved towards a more French manner and attitude to the table, no matter which cuisine we favour.

Increasingly, we seek out local and seasonal produce. We try to respect the land. We try not to waste food. We search for flavour. We aim to give pleasure. We share.

It is interesting to note that this principle was already in evidence over 200 years ago when the early French explorers visited Australia's shores – though it found expression in unexpected ways. D'Entrecasteaux admired the way in which the indigenous tribes of south-east Tasmania managed the land, moving on when necessary. He and his companions made several attempts to share their food with the Lyluequonney and Nuenonne people, but these were met with resistance – until they offered familiar indigenous foods such as lobster. The key to sharing was thus to find common ground. If only Félix Delahaye's garden had succeeded. How good would it have been for the French to sit down with their hosts and enjoy a meal of crayfish, abalone and oysters – locally sourced – with a little freshly grown lettuce and tiny radishes, in a spirit of mutual exchange and pleasure?

On Wine

In May 2022, the Cité internationale de la gastronomie et du vin – a vast exhibition, conference and training complex dedicated to French gastronomy and the terroirs of Burgundy – was inaugurated in Dijon. It is now part of a network of 'gastronomic cities' in France, the others being situated in Lyon, Paris-Rungis and Tours, but its distinctive mission is to promote wine culture alongside the culinary arts. It is an important reminder of the intimate link for the French between food and wine.

This is borne out by numerous surveys, all pointing to the fact that a large majority of French people associate wine with a good meal, and with conviviality more generally. These surveys also show that the old stereotypes – according to which the French are either discerning drinkers who only consume high-quality wines of exclusively French origin or indiscriminate consumers whose daily routine consists of quaffing a litre of any random red over lunch – no longer hold true ... if they ever did.

Habits have certainly changed. In 1975, the French consumed 100 litres of wine per head of population annually, but that figure has dropped to a little over 40 litres per capita per year in recent times and is on a downward trend. Illustrating this, only 16% of adults drink wine on a daily basis now, whereas in 1980 that figure was around 50%. A third of the population does not drink wine at all, or only on special occasions. Nevertheless, more people are apparently drinking wine in France these days, but they are doing it less frequently – and in some respects more thoughtfully. Wine is still seen as an accompaniment to food but people drink it these days as an apéritif, independently of the meal. This is a recent development which signals that wine is increasingly being appreciated for its cultural heritage status as much as for the pleasure it brings.

While not all French people would claim to be highly refined connoisseurs, they generally like to inform themselves before buying wine. Most consult family, friends or social media before making a purchase. The type and quality of the wine they will be drinking are naturally important to them, as is ensuring they get value for money; but the notion of quality now incorporates concerns regarding fabrication methods and the sustainability of cultivation practices, in addition to the age-old questions of origin and reputation. As a result, organic wines – 'vins bio' (short for 'biologiques') – and wines made with more modern, non-traditional techniques are rapidly gaining in popularity. Climate change, too, is having an impact. Warmer temperatures are leading to an increase in the sugar level in grapes, which is in turn producing a rise in the alcohol level of certain wines. In 1995, a bottle of côte-rôtie – the noted red wine from the Rhône region – contained 12.5% alcohol. That alcohol content rose to 14% in 2017, and to 14.5% in 2019. This is a matter of great consternation for a population used to drinking lighter wines!

That preference notwithstanding, it may come as a surprise to some that the French are less exclusive in their tastes these days than their reputation suggests. A considerable majority regularly enjoy wines from other countries – Italy and Spain, principally, but also the so-called 'new world' wines from vineyards in California, Chile and elsewhere. Australian wines are still hard to find in France, regrettably, though producers like Penfolds and Jacob's Creek are starting to make inroads. The market in France is highly competitive, so it will take a lot of patience and persistence to establish a stronger presence.

Conversely, the French, as Jackie Dutton documents in the following essay, have historically enjoyed many opportunities to contribute to the development of the Australian wine industry, from the earliest days of British colonisation. Reversing that trend, an Englishman by the name of Tony Laithwaite, who helped establish the Sunday Times Wine Club in England in the 1970s, came up with the original and provocative idea of engaging Australian winemaker Nigel Sneyd to supervise a vintage in the Dordogne, at the Saint-Vivien cooperative. The aim was to improve the consistency of the wine Laithwaite was importing to England by introducing to his French winemakers some of the modern techniques and procedures with which their Australian counterparts were more *au fait*. That was in the late 1980s. Other Australian winemakers soon made the same journey, as did vignerons from other parts of the world. And so the concept of the Flying Winemaker was born. After some initial resistance, the programme has proven highly successful and is an appealing example of cross-cultural exchange. It is also now a fully reciprocal undertaking. Some of the most prominent Flying Winemakers are French.

JWS

12

Jacqueline Dutton

An intercultural blend of French experience and Australian terroir

For many centuries, France has furnished the wine world with its language and ideals, its celebrations and style. The grape varieties, blends and methods favoured by the French have been exported everywhere vines are grown to make wine. Even more ancient wine regions like Italy's Barolo and Spain's Priorat have taken their lead from regions like Bordeaux in marketing their premium products to the world. The concept of *terroir* is a global phenomenon now, touted on wine websites from California to Thailand, no longer just the legacy of Burgundian monks in Clos Vougeot or Domaine Romanée Conti. French terminology and codification – *dosage*, *bâtonnage* and *méthode champenoise*, for example – are widely used in winemaking education[1] and Émile Peynaud's discourses on degustation remain the inspiration for winetasting courses.[2]

Some scholars date the 'Frenchification' of wine to the late nineteenth century,[3] but France's benchmarking influence on western European then trans-Atlantic and finally global wine industries certainly existed prior to that moment. Since Charlemagne's reign (800–814), Burgundian wines have been drunk in the region by the visiting leaders of the Catholic Church; converted kings and fashionable nobles subsequently transported them to the courts of Paris and beyond. During the Avignon Papacy (1309–1376), the Popes and their highly ranked European guests enjoyed both Burgundy and Rhône wines at the tastemakers' tables, adding to the renown and desirability of these quality wines. After shaping local ideals, French winemaking was then taken out into the New World.[4] When Jacques Cartier landed in 'la Nouvelle-France' – Canada – on his second voyage (1535–1536), he sighted abundant grape vines on an island in the Saint-Laurent River, which he immediately christened 'Isle de Bacchus' (now Île d'Orléans). The Recollet and Jesuit missionaries who followed in his footsteps in the early seventeenth century were the first to make wine there after their ecclesiastical supplies ran dry. Apparently the grapes resembled the varieties in Burgundy, but the wine, though passable, was not for the Pope's table.[5] Claret from Bordeaux graced the palates of the English from 1152, when the region passed to English rule following the marriage of Eleanor of Aquitaine to the Duke of Normandy and soon-to-be King Henry II of England. Even after Aquitaine was reclaimed by the French during the Hundred Years' War, in 1453, the taste for fine French wine persisted in the English upper classes, although fortified wines from Portugal, Madeira and the Canary Islands dominated middle and lower class consumption. The British colonial ruling elite in North America therefore sought to produce fine French-style wines, which did not travel so well, rather than the export-ready non-French fortified wines. Not much changed in British wine tastes, as a similar tendency was witnessed in Australia around 200 years later. Unlike America, though, which had its own native grape vines, *Vitis labrusca* and *Vitis rotundifolia*, Australia needed to bring in grape vines from Europe in order to begin its wine industry.

From the plants and the people to the knowledge and the practice, everything wine-related had to be imported across the globe to Australia. The French, more than any other European community, were the most influential in the foundational stages as well as the breakthrough moments in Australian winemaking success. The Germans in the Barossa, the Italians in the Hawkesbury and

Riverina, the Swiss in Geelong and Yarra Valley regions have all contributed immensely to Australia's viticultural identity. However, the unique role played by the French derives from a fascinating interplay between the specific nature of the expertise on offer and the superior status of the French in the global wine industry.

In some instances, French expertise does not measure up to that stellar reputation. In others, Australian expertise in leadership, education or business is necessary to catalyse French know-how. A few examples taken from the very early efforts to make wine in Australia illustrate these situations perfectly. The first French winemaker imports were prisoners of war François de Riveau and Antoine L'Andre, cousins from Nantes, who were reportedly vinedressers. They were invited to travel to Australia in 1800 as free settlers on condition that they spend three years cultivating vines and making wines for the Crown, in other words for Governor Philip Gidley King, as well as promoting winemaking in the colony. In Governor King's opinion, their efforts in growing vines were reasonable but they were so unsuccessful in making wine that no samples would be sent back to England for tasting. L'Andre was allowed to remain in Australia, as he made passable cider from peaches, but Riveau left for Calcutta. Neither was knowledgeable enough about winemaking to tackle the task. In the absence of adequate guidance from France or elsewhere, entrepreneur John Macarthur and his sons James and William went to France and Switzerland in 1815–1816, walking through the vineyards and talking with winemakers to gain knowledge and cuttings, notably from Burgundy, to bring back to plant at Elizabeth Farm in Parramatta. James and William Macarthur would subsequently produce the first commercial wine from their vineyards at Camden Park in 1844, and later entered their wine into competition at the 1855 Paris Universal Exhibition. Their fact-finding missions took the random nature out of the provision of French expertise as they sought out the superior source in France for themselves. James Busby adopted a similar attitude. He spent several months studying winemaking and collecting cuttings in France before arriving in Australia from Scotland in 1824. Busby eventually planted a vineyard on his Hunter Valley property but his contributions were more educational than practical. He taught viticulture and published a number of treatises on vine and wine (1825, 1830, 1833) based in large part on French manuals that he translated to promote the wine industries in Australia and New Zealand.[6]

There are many stories of French connections in the Australian wine industry, ranging from viticulturalists and oenologists to tastemakers and restaurateurs, as evidenced by a major historical thesis on the topic by Mikaël Pierre.[7] Barbara Santich has commenced compiling an ambitious database on 'French-Australian Exchanges in Viticulture and Winemaking' which promises to add granular detail to the biographies of many vital figures.[8] Julie McIntyre's and David Dunstan's work on the history of winemaking in Australia has unearthed many foundational links to French vines, wines and people.[9] Various scholarly articles have traced certain paths through the French-Australian wine journey,[10] and esteemed wine writers contribute important observations on the constant interactions between individuals and industries across the two countries.[11] In this short piece on what France has done for the Australian wine industry, I want to continue musing on the interplay between the specific nature of the expertise on offer – whether French or Australian – and the superior status of the French in the global wine industry. I will focus on a few key moments related to some of our iconic red, white, sparkling and rosé wines born of French-Australian exchanges in some of Australia's most respected wine regions.

Red wine
Whether the very first Australian wines produced were red or white is debatable – most likely they were a mix of the various grape

varieties brought from the Cape of Good Hope with the First Fleet in 1788. Governor Sir Arthur Phillip reported that his vines were flourishing and laden with fruit in 1791, as were those planted on Norfolk Island. A German ex-convict, Phillip Schaeffer, planted the first productive vineyard around the same time, described by Captain Watkin Tench as 'unrivalled' in 'beauty of form and situation'.[12] The botanist from James Cook's first voyage to the Pacific, Sir Joseph Banks, was following this early progress in winemaking from London, and despite the dismal winemaking experiment with the inept Frenchmen, encouraged his entrepreneurial friend Gregory Blaxland to emigrate to the new colony in the hope that he might take up the challenge. Arriving in 1806 as one of the few free settlers at the time, Blaxland quickly established himself in livestock farming and by 1820 had settled at Brush Farm where he planted blight-resistant vines – he thought them to be claret but Busby identified them as Burgundy.[13] While John Macarthur and his sons were researching and touring France's vineyards, Blaxland was already exploiting Swiss-French experience in practice. Having borrowed Jean-Jacques Dufour's 1802 treatise on making wine in colonial Kentucky from Macarthur's wife, Elizabeth, he made what many consider to be the first Australian wine and in 1822 took it to London's Society for the Encouragement of Arts, Manufactures and Commerce (later The Royal Society) and won a silver medal for it.[14] According to the Society's judges, this wine was light but sound, 'with much of the odour and flavour of ordinary claret, or rather holding an intermediate place between that wine and the red wine of Nice'.[15] Clearly, it was a red wine, but it may have been made from any number of grapes available in the colony at the time.

The origins of red winemaking in Australia were therefore tenuously linked to French methods and compared – relatively favourably – to French benchmarks of claret, Burgundy and Provence. Throughout the nineteenth century, advocates of the healthful and civilising properties of red wine promoted its production and consumption, including French-naturalised Swiss winemaker Hubert de Castella. His brother Paul had arrived in Melbourne from Neuchâtel in 1849, purchasing Yering Station in the Yarra Valley for sheep farming and winemaking in 1850. Hubert visited him there in 1854 and proceeded to establish his own business, running cattle on a neighbouring property in partnership with another Swiss settler, Guillaume de Pury. Both de Castella brothers were successful winemakers: Paul was a pillar of the Victorian wine industry and won a Grand Prix at the Paris Exhibition in 1889, while Hubert was a master of marketing and storytelling, publishing *Notes d'un vigneron australien* in 1882 for a French winemaking readership – especially in the Bordelais – and *John Bull's Vineyard* in 1886 for a more general public. Hubert had bought part of Yering Station to create his own winery, St Hubert's, in 1862, inspired by Bordeaux-style wines, but planting pinot noir (Burgundy) and syrah (Rhône) vines to produce prize-winning wines.[16] Despite the dominance of Swiss-French winemakers who emigrated to Victoria – from Geelong to Great Western and the Yarra Valley – their reliance on French varieties, methods and technical advancement points to France's superior status in the wine industry.[17]

After achieving relative success both locally and internationally, dry red table wines struggled to find their place in Australia during the first half of the twentieth century. The vineyards of Victoria and New South Wales had been ravaged by the phylloxera infestation, an imported aphid which had also killed off vines in Europe and could only be kept at bay by grafting onto American vine rootstock. Furthermore, the domestic and export market demanded stronger wines – brandy, sherry, port and tokay – rather than table wines. But French expertise and status again came to the rescue of red wine in the form of Maurice O'Shea. The son of an Irish wine and spirit merchant and a French mother, O'Shea was born in Sydney but attended a lycée in Montpellier, then the prestigious École nationale supérieure agronomique de Grignon, near Paris, completing his studies in viticulture and chemistry at the University of Montpellier. He returned to Australia in 1920 and persuaded his widowed mother to purchase a small vineyard near Pokolbin in the Hunter Valley, which he named Mount Pleasant. O'Shea's contemporary viticultural and winemaking knowledge drawn directly from France helped cement his reputation as the country's leading red wine maker of both single varietal wines – especially shiraz and pinot noir – and unorthodox but successful blends of the two. The McWilliams family invested in his vineyard and eventually took it over in 1941, leaving O'Shea to manage it.[18] He continued to consult widely in the Hunter Valley region until his death in 1956, leaving a celebrated legacy of wines and prizes named after him, as well as books in tribute by Campbell Mattinson and Peter McAra.[19]

White wine

'Hock' was undoubtedly the most widely consumed white wine in Australia until products like Lindeman's Ben Ean Moselle edged into the marketplace in the 1960s and 70s, followed by chardonnay in the 1980s and 90s and sauvignon blanc in the 2000s.[20] Commonly used in Britain to refer to German white wine from the Rhine Valley region, hock was also popular in Australia, made mostly from riesling vines probably gathered up randomly by the First Fleet in the Cape, but planted with intent and expertise by William and James Macarthur at Camden Park in the 1830s. These second-generation colonial winemakers brought German vinedressers to work in their vineyards from 1838. Their success in planting and harvesting riesling led to the variety taking root in the fledgling vineyards of the Barossa Valley in the late 1830s and 40s, encouraged by Bavarian migrant Johann Gramp, who founded Orlando Wines, Joseph Gilbert of Pewsey Vale and William Jacob of Jacob's Creek. Though some French winemakers in South Australia, Victoria and New South Wales included riesling in their vineyards, there was no particularly evident French influence in most white table wine in Australia until Jack Mann took over his father's role as chief winemaker at Houghton Wines in the Swan Valley, north-east of Perth, in 1930.

Mann had been learning and experimenting with a wide range of styles and grape varieties since working his first vintage in 1922, producing prize-winning sweet wines in the early 1930s. He created a distinctive dry white wine that won first prize in the open class at the Royal Melbourne Wine Show in 1936 and 1937, lauded by one of the judges as 'like one of the great white burgundies of France'. It was released for commercial sale in 1938 as Houghton White Burgundy, becoming one of Australia's only iconic dry white wines to rival riesling for the next 50 years. Made mainly from chenin blanc, a French grape variety likely imported with the First Fleet from the Cape, this wine may have also contained some chardonnay, which is the principal grape variety allowed in Burgundian white wines. In 2005, Houghton White Burgundy was reborn as Houghton White Classic, as European Union legislation on naming rights no longer allowed the use of 'Burgundy' for wines made outside Burgundy's Protected Designation of Origin (or French AOC).

Western Australia's white wine production has since moved further south to Margaret River. Founding winemaker of the region – Perth cardiologist Tom Cullity – planted his Vasse Felix vineyard there in 1967, naming it after Timothée Vasse, a French sailor on the Baudin expedition who was lost in the surf in Geographe Bay in 1801. Although Bordeaux-style semillon-sauvignon blanc blends are more commonly produced for domestic consumption and export, premium chardonnays from Vasse Felix, as well as from Leeuwin Estate, Cullen Wines, Moss Wood and Lenton Brae, are often compared to Burgundian chardonnay and certainly rival the best, according to Jancis Robinson, Andrew Caillard and other internationally recognised wine critics.

Sparkling wine

Unsurprisingly, Australia's sparkling wine industry took longer to develop than its still or fortified wines, given the technical skills and specialised equipment required. Two maverick French couples started the bubbly flowing in Victoria in the 1860s but it took until the 1980s to really establish commercial sparkling wine production using the *méthode champenoise*. Siblings Anne-Marie and Émile Blampied emigrated from the Lorraine region in eastern France to Beechworth in Victoria in 1852 to try their luck in the goldfields, where they met Jean-Pierre Trouette from the winemaking region of Gers in south-western France. He married Anne-Marie and they all moved to Great Western, a village between Ararat and Stawell, to continue recruiting miners for work in the goldfields. When the gold rush slowed down, they began to explore other activities, which included planting small plots of vines. These thrived, so they bought more land from another Frenchman – Monsieur Durand – in 1863 and called it St Peter's.[21] By 1867, they had 50,000 vines and realised that the most expensive and sought-after wine to celebrate Victoria's boom in the nineteenth century was French champagne.[22] Adding another French name to the family, Émile married Louise Metzger and it appears that these enterprising couples were the first to produce sparkling wines in Australia, winning fifth place at the Melbourne International Exhibition of 1880–1881 with their 1875 vintage sparkling wine.

In second place was Dr Louis Lawrence Smith's 1879 vintage Crème de Bouzy made from grapes grown at Nunawading, blended and fermented in his half-acre cellars on the corner of Bourke and Exhibition Streets in the centre of Marvellous Melbourne. He floated his Victorian Champagne Company on the sharemarket in 1881, attracting several celebrity shareholders after his second prize and ensuring future success with his expert French champagne maker, Auguste D'Argent, who claimed to have worked for over 40 years in a prestigious Champagne house.[23] D'Argent's flagship 'recipe' for Crème de Bouzy used pinot, riesling and chasselas blended in equal portions, but he also produced a drier sparkling called Perle d'Australie, a rose coloured sparkling burgundy, and Sillery, a fine dry champagne. These wines became the benchmark for Australian sparkling production, taking gold, silver and bronze medals in Bordeaux and Amsterdam in 1882–1883.[24] Despite its evident success and very positive reception in Australia and abroad, the Victorian Champagne Company went into voluntary receivership in 1884 shortly before D'Argent died from a lingering illness. Clearly, the Frenchman was the cornerstone of this fountain of sparkling wine, which did not outlive him.

Other French efforts to produce sparkling came and went. Bordelais winemaker François Gaston Léonce Frère's efforts dating from 1875 had already failed in the Albury district at St Hilaire. But a few more stars blazed bright before phylloxera and wars took away their champagne dreams. In 1887, Trouette and Blampied sold St Peter's to Hans Irvine, who found an excellent replacement winemaker from near Reims, Charles Pierlot, a former employee of Pommery and Moët et Chandon. Beginning in 1890 with an annual production of around 2,000 bottles of bubbly, Pierlot and Irvine worked hard – if not well – to increase and improve their sparkling wine production over a twenty-year period. They planted more pinot meunier, chardonnay, and pinot noir to emulate more closely the blends for French champagne. Pierlot experimented with various chemicals, yeasts and sugars following research from France, and Irvine imported expensive French equipment to refine their methods. However, there seems to have been some intercultural conflict, as the two men did not get along well. Pierlot left in 1895 to make some excellent sparkling wine at Wooroora Vineyard in Riverton, South Australia. At around the same time, in the eastern Adelaide suburb of Auldana, another Frenchman, Léon Edmond Mazure, was making sparkling red wine and producing champagne on a large scale. Around the turn of the twentieth century, other French winemakers also produced bubbly in South Australia: Joseph Foureur, who arrived from Moët et Chandon to work with Thomas Hardy and who then consulted more widely as a sparkling wine specialist; and Émile Bernier, who joined Mazure at Auldana after some time with Irvine in Great Western. Pierlot returned to work with Irvine and they maintained their partnership alongside several other French winemakers until Pierlot retired in 1912. Irvine eventually sold the winery to Benno Seppelt in 1918.[25]

Seppelt and sons maintained sparkling wine production in Great Western through the difficult first half of the twentieth century. South Australia fortunately remained phylloxera free and, in 1956, Orlando began producing Barossa Pearl, a light fruity sparkling wine which launched a new wave of similar German style *perlweins* made from riesling and semillon sweetened with muscatel and frontignan juice in the secondary fermentation process. The French *méthode champenoise* came back in the 1970s as Great Western reignited the flame, followed by newcomer Dominique Landragin from the Champagne village of Verzenay, who established the highly successful Yellowglen label in Smythesdale near Ballarat with Ian Home, producing their first vintage in 1982. By 1984, Yellowglen's exponential growth required greater investment – which Mildara Wines provided – and the company promptly replaced the French expertise with Australian talent.[26] Moët et Chandon's chief winemaker, Philippe Coulon, visited Victoria in 1982 to check out sites in the Yarra Valley after starting the company's first international ventures in Argentina and California. The French dominance in Australian sparkling wine continued to assert itself from Domaine Chandon's first vintage in 1989 until Tasmania's House of Arras began to win international sparkling wine competitions, beating the French at their own game with their 1995 vintage and maintaining high levels of success and accolades.[27]

Rosé wines

Pink wines from Massalia – modern-day Marseille – were renowned in the Mediterranean even before the Romans arrived. Made from field blends of red and white grapes, rosé wines were therefore already inextricably linked to the south of France in ancient times, though their popularity rose in the modern era in the early twentieth century, when the French Riviera became a major destination for European and American tourists and phylloxera had faded as a distant nightmare. In Australia, lighter style red wines were often referred to in winemakers' journals and letters during the early colonial times, suggesting that rosé wines were produced from the outset, as winemaking techniques were being perfected. One of the first intentionally produced rosé wines, however, was made by Serbian winemaker George Kolarovich at Kaiser Stuhl, the Barossa cooperative, in 1962. It won many medals in the Montpellier wine shows, and was even awarded the Montpellier Cup in 1966. The squat bottle was subsequently adorned with a French tricolore ribbon around its neck and became known as the Gold Medal Rosé. Although it evolved into a sweeter lolly-pink drink in the late 1970s, it was a much drier 100% grenache in the early years of production.[28]

The global popularity of Mateus sparkling rosé from Portugal and other such sweet pink wines waned in the late 1980s and 90s when the only Australian rosés on the shelves were the dark pink Rockford's Alicante Bouchet and Charlie Melton's Rose of Virginia. It was a Frenchman from Bordeaux not Provence who made pale pink dry rosé for the Australian market in the early 2000s: Dominique Portet with his Fontaine Rosé from the Yarra Valley. The phenomenal renaissance of rosé over the past twenty years has brought a flood of French imports into Australia, but also sparked a trend for French-style labelling and naming of Australian produced rosé. One of the most well received Provence-style wines is Jacob's Creek's Le Petit Rosé, which was launched in 2017 to coincide with the Australian Open Tennis Tournament. Other such

French-Australian associations include De Bortoli's La Bohème and Vinoque, Paige Cooper's Poppie the Frenchie – named after the winemaker's French bulldog – and Parlez-Vous Rosé, which appeared briefly in 2018.[29] Though clearly the most recent of French-Australian wine exchanges, the rosé example demonstrates that Australia is still keen to learn from French models of winemaking and wine marketing, whenever that superior French status is perceived to be an advantage.

An intercultural blend of French experience and Australian terroir
Over the 200 years during which Australia has been producing wine, French experience has certainly influenced perception and investment in Australian terroir. The four major sectors of the wine industry explored here have each displayed differing levels of French intervention ranging from deep engagement in sparkling wine production and red wine refinement to more allusive strategies for differentiation in the case of white wine. Rosé wines continue to leverage French connections as do various sub-sectors of the Australian wine industry. Cool-climate pinot noir makers from Mornington Peninsula, the Adelaide Hills, the Yarra Valley, and Tasmania often reference Burgundy; cabernet sauvignon-merlot blends from Coonawarra and Margaret River might benefit from associations with Bordeaux; shiraz from Heathcote and the Grampians could use comparisons to the Rhone Valley as shorthand for their diverse terroirs. Fortified wines and brandies, which were a key component of Australia's early wine industry, have not been considered here, even though some French migrants did work at Rutherglen and the Goulburn Valley. In general, French expertise and influence were more aligned with the production of fine table wines than with the consumption of stronger alcoholic beverages.[30]

Examining the specific nature of the expertise on offer – whether Australian or French, in business or in technique, enacted in theory or in practice – reveals the diverse ways in which actors in the Australian wine industry engage with the received idea of France's superior status in the global wine industry. In the end, this intercultural blend of French experience and Australian terroir can take credit for wines like Dr John Middleton's Mount Mary Quintet and may be indirectly responsible for such bold experiments as Max Schubert's Grange Hermitage at Penfolds, even though the mixing of shiraz and cabernet sauvignon might make a contemporary French winemaker's toes curl ...

Notes

Chapter 1 – French and English: Deluge, reversed deluge, and what comes after us

1   Melvyn Bragge, *The Adventure of English: The Biography of a Language*, London: Hodder & Stoughton, 2003, p. 3.
2   Geoffrey Hughes, *A History of English Words*, Oxford: Blackwell, 2000, pp. 91–108.
3   Roland Sussex and Paul Cubberley, *The Slavic Languages*, Cambridge: Cambridge University Press, 2006, pp. 66–69.
4   David Crystal, *The Cambridge Encyclopedia of the English Language*, Cambridge: Cambridge University Press, 1995, p. 46.
5   https://en.wikipedia.org/wiki/Ayenbite_of_Inwyt (consulted 30 June 2020).
6   Joseph Addison, *The Spectator*, 8 September 1711. Available online at: http://www.gutenberg.org/files/12030/12030-h/12030-h/SV1/Spectator1.html#section165 (consulted 30 June 2020).
7   Ibid.
8   Samuel Johnson, *Dictionary of the English Language*, London: W. Strahan, 1755, Preface.
9   See https://en.wikipedia.org/wiki/List_of_English_words_of_French_origin (consulted 30 June 2020).
10 See Joseph M. Williams, *Origins of the English language: A Social and Linguistic History*, New York: Free Press, 1975.
11 Winston S. Churchill, *Winston Churchill's Speeches*, online at: https://www.nationalchurchillmuseum.org/winston-churchills-speeches.html (consulted 30 June 2020).
12 See https://en.wikipedia.org/wiki/Languages_of_France (consulted on 30 June 2020).
13 See http://www.academie-francaise.fr/linstitution/statuts-et-reglements (consulted 30 June 2020). All translations are my own.
14 See https://fr.wikipedia.org/wiki/Politique_linguistique_de_la_France (consulted 30 June 2020).

15 Quoted in Rodney Ball, *The French Speaking World: A Practical Introduction to Sociolinguistic Issues*, London & New York: Routledge, 1997, p. 211.

16 For further discussion of these issues, see Rodney Ball and Dawn Marley, *The French Speaking World: A Practical Introduction to Sociolinguistic Issues*, London & New York: Routledge, 2017 (second edition).

17 See https://www.conseil-constitutionnel.fr/le-bloc-de-constitutionnalite/texte-integral-de-la-constitution-du-4-octobre-1958-en-vigueur (consulted 30 June 2020).

18 See Sussex and Cubberley, *The Slavic Languages*, Chapter 2.

19 See https://www.coe.int/en/web/european-charter-regional-or-minority-languages/languages-covered (consulted 30 June 2020).

20 See Michael Clyne (ed.), *Pluricentric Languages: Differing Norms in Different Nations*, Berlin & New York: Mouton de Gruyter (Contributions to the Sociology of Language, 62), 1992.

21 See https://www.francophonie.org/la-langue-francaise-dans-le-monde-305 (consulted 30 June 2020). See also Emmanuel Macron, *Journée internationale de la Francophonie: Discours prononcé par M. Emmanuel Macron, Président de la République*, Académie française, 20 March 2018, available online at http://www.academie-francaise.fr/discours-prononces-sous-la-coupole-lors-de-la-venue-de-m-emmanuel-macron-loccasion-de-la-journee (consulted 12 May 2020).

22 For more extended discussions, see Adrian Battye, Marie-Anne Hintze, & Paul Rowlett, *The French Language Today: A Linguistic Introduction*, London & New York: Routledge, 2003; Zsuzsanna Fagyal, Douglas Kibbee & Frederic Jenkins, *French: A Linguistic Introduction*, Cambridge: Cambridge University Press, 2006; R. Anthony Lodge, *A Sociolinguistic History of Parisian French*, Cambridge: Cambridge University Press, 2004; R. Anthony Lodge, *French: From Dialect to Standard*, London & New York: Routledge, 2013; R. Anthony Lodge, Nigel Armstrong, Yvette M.L. Ellis & Jane F. Shelton, *Exploring the French Language*, London & New York: Routledge, 2016 (e-book edition); Peter Rickard, *A History of the French Language*, London: Routledge, 1989 (second edition); Carol Sanders, (ed.), *French Today: Language in its Social Context*, Cambridge: Cambridge University Press, 1993.

23 Bragge, *The Adventure of English*, p. 3.

24 See, for example, Josette Rey-Debove & Gilberte Gagnon, *Dictionnaire des anglicismes: les mots anglais et américains en français*, Paris: Robert, 1980.

25 See http://www.globish.com/.

26 See http://www.academie-francaise.fr/dire-ne-pas-dire/neologismes-anglicismes.

27   See Clyne (ed.), *Pluricentric Languages*.
28   See Robert B. Kaplan & Richard B. Baldauf, *Language Planning from Practice to Theory*, Clevedon, UK & Philadelphia, USA: Multilingual Matters, 1997.
29   See Clyne (ed.), *Pluricentric Languages*.
30   Georg Bossong, 'Normes et Conflits Normatifs', in Hans Goebl, Peter H. Nelde, Zdenek Sary & Wolfgang Wölck (eds), *Kontaktlinguistik. Ein Handbuch der internationalen Forschung*, Berlin: de Gruyter, 1996, pp. 609–624 (p. 614).
31   Maurice Grevisse, *Le Bon Usage: Grammaire française*, 13ème édition revue/refondue par André Goosse, Paris: Duculot, 1993.
32   Ruth Kircher, 'How pluricentric is the French language? An investigation of attitudes towards Quebec French compared to European French', *Journal of French Language Studies*, vol. 22, no. 3, 2012, pp. 345–370.
33   Georges Lüdi, 'French as a pluricentric language?', in Clyne (ed.), *Pluricentric Languages*, pp. 149–178; Georges Lüdi, 'Traces of monolingual and plurilingual ideologies in the history of language policies in France', in Matthias Hüning, Ulrike Vogl & Olivier Moliner (eds), *Standard Languages and Multilingualism in European History*, Amsterdam and Philadelphia: John Benjamins, 2012, pp. 205–230.
34   Anu Bissoonauth, 'Pluricentricity and sociolinguistic relationships between French, English and indigenous Languages in New Caledonia', in Rudolf Muhr & Dawn Marley, in collaboration with Heinz L. Kretzenbacher and Anu Bissoonauth, (eds), *Pluricentric Languages: New Perspectives in Theory and Description*, Frankfurt/Main & Vienna: Peter Lang Verlag, 2015, pp. 255–270

Chapter 2 – France and the French in Australia's growth to nationhood: 1914–1945

1   The text of the agreement is still available on the website of Australia's Department of Foreign Affairs and Trade: https://www.dfat.gov.au/geo/france/joint-statement-of-enhanced-strategic-partnership-between-australia-and-france (consulted 16 August 2022).
2   A theme taken up by the French press at the time. *Paris Match*, for example, in the by-line of its 3 May 2016 article announcing the agreement, proclaimed that the contract represented a 50-year marriage ('un "mariage" pour cinquante ans'). Seven months later, when the agreement was signed, the financial daily, *Les Échos*, used the same metaphor in the title of its article: 'Sous-marins: célébration du mariage franco-australien' (20 December 2016).
3   The analysis presented here is a partial response to the agenda I flagged in an earlier article, in which I argued for a more in-depth historical synthesis of Australia's relations with France, particularly in

areas – diplomacy being a case in point – which offer scope for further study. See Colin Nettelbeck, 'French-Australian Relations: Towards an Historical Perspective', *The French Australian Review*, 57, Australian Summer 2014–2015, pp. 3–27.

4   As noted by Richard James, *Australia's War with France: The Campaign in Syria and Lebanon, 1941*, Newport (NSW): Big Sky Publishing, 2017 (back cover summary): 'The Australians won the war, but at the price of more than 400 young men, sons of Anzacs who had fought to defend France in the trenches of the western Front. The British were embarrassed, the campaign was forgotten, and the Australians who fought were dubbed "the silent men".' On this campaign, see also Daniel Seaton, 'Fighting against the French: Australians in the Allied invasion of Lebanon and Syria, 1941', Australian War Memorial website: https://www.awm.gov.au/tobruk/learnmore

5   Alexis Bergantz, 'French Connection: the culture and politics of Frenchness in Australia, 1890–1914', PhD thesis, Australian National University, December 2015, p. 54.

6   Bergantz, 'French Connection', p. 2.

7   As demonstrated by Christopher Allen in his contribution to this volume.

8   Éric Berti and Ivan Barko (eds), *French Lives in Australia*, North Melbourne: Australian Scholarly Publishing, 2015.

9   Jean Fornasiero and John West-Sooby have sought to debunk this myth, in the case of South Australia at least. See their essay 'A Contested Coast? Revisiting the Baudin-Flinders encounter of April 1802', in Carolyn Collins and Paul Sendziuk (eds), *Foundational Fictions in South Australian History*, Mile End: Wakefield Press, 2018, pp. 13–27.

10 On Péron's proposed invasion plan, see Jean Fornasiero and John West-Sooby, *French Designs on Colonial New South Wales. François Péron's Memoir on the English Settlements of New Holland, Van Diemen's Land and the Archipelagos of the Great Pacific Ocean*, Adelaide: Friends of the State Library of South Australia, 2014.

11 Source: Australian War Memorial.

12 E.J. Rule, *Jacka's Mob*, Sydney: Angus & Robertson, 1933 (emphasis added).

13 Colin Nettelbeck, 'Not Just a Nostalgic Farewell: The "Dernière Heure" as a Landmark Document in Franco-Australian Friendship', *The French Australian Review*, 59, 2015, pp. 55–77.

14 J.R.W. Taylor, 'France has attracted Australia by her glorious spirit', in J.R.W. Taylor and Cyril Leyshon White (eds), *The "Dernière Heure"*, Rouen: L. Wolf, 1919, p. 16.

15 Final two stanzas of a poem entitled 'Past and Gone', signed by 'Pioneer' (*The "Dernière Heure"*, p. 43).

16 The letter is preserved in the Australian Red Cross Archives, University of Melbourne, Box 211.

17 Peter Brown, 'Augustine Soubeiran (1858–1933): Innovative Educator and Dynamic Secretary of the French-Australian League of Help', *French Lives in Australia*, pp. 319–337; Colin Nettelbeck, 'Charlotte Crivelli (1868–1956): Patriot and Fund-Raiser', *French Lives in Australia*, pp. 338–352.

18 See, for example, Melanie Oppenheimer, 'Gifts for France: Australian Red Cross Nurses in France, 1916–1919', *Journal of Australian Studies*, vol. 17, issue 39, 1993, pp. 65–78; Melanie Oppenheimer, 'Shaping the Legend: The Role of the Australian Red Cross and Anzac', *Labour History*, no. 106, 2014, pp. 123–142.

19 Goods and cash raised in Australia by the Australian Red Cross are estimated at £1,375,000 (exclusive of France and Egypt); goods and cash raised by Augustine Soubeiran and Charlotte Crivelli directly for France are estimated at between £500,000 and £700,000.

20 *Argus* (Melbourne), 7 June 1916, p. 9.

21 *Argus*, 27 August, p. 19.

22 Robert Aldrich, 'La Mission Française en Australie de 1918: l'Australie et les relations franco-australiennes au lendemain de la guerre', in André Dommergues and Maryvonne Nedeljkovic (eds), *Les Français et l'Australie: voyages de découvertes et missions scientifiques de 1756 à nos jours*, Paris: Université de Paris X Nanterre, pp. 295–305.

23 Romain Fathi, *Our Corner of the Somme: Australia at Villers-Bretonneux*, Cambridge: Cambridge University Press, 2019.

24 The text of the cable is reproduced on the website of the Australian Government's Department of Foreign Affairs and Trade (DFAT): https://www.dfat.gov.au/about-us/publications/historical-documents/Pages/volume-03/331-mr-r-g-menzies-prime-minister-to-mr-p-reynaud-french-prime-minister

25 Margaret Barrett, 'Jean Trémoulet, the Unloved Consul-General', *Explorations*, no. 51, December 2011, pp. 15–32.

26 On Australia's role in installing Sautot as governor of New Caledonia, see Denise Fisher, 'Supporting the Free French in New Caledonia: First Steps in Australian Diplomacy', *Explorations*, no. 49 Part 1, December 2010, pp. 18–37.

27 P.G. Edwards, *Prime Ministers and Diplomats: the Making of Australian Foreign Policy 1901–1949*, Melbourne: Oxford University Press, 1983, p. 180.

28 Edwards, *Prime Ministers and Diplomats*, p. 150. Hodgson's initial title was Minister; this was changed to Ambassador in 1948.

29 William Hodgson to Norman Makin (Acting Minister for External Affairs), Dispatch 12, Paris, 1 December 1945. National Archives of Australia, A1066, IC45/64/3/1. Extracts available on the DFAT

website: https://wragge.github.io/dfat-documents-web/volumes/
volume-8-1945/423-hodgson-to-makin/

30 'L'avenir, tu n'as point à le prévoir mais à le permettre.' Antoine de Saint-
Exupéry, *Citadelle*, Paris: Gallimard, 1948, p. 167.

Chapter 3– Some Australian artists in France: 1890–1930s

1 This paper was originally delivered as a relatively informal reflexion on
a broad topic, and it would be contrary to its spirit to attempt to turn it
into a fully referenced academic text. Consequently l have resisted the
temptation to include too many footnotes, except in the case of Agnes
Goodsir, who is both significant and little known, so I wanted to be as
accurate as the available information allowed. For other more familiar
figures, the sources for most of the information I mention will be found
in the short reading list that follows the essay.

2 According to Karen Quinlan, *In a Picture Land over the Sea*, Bendigo:
Bendigo Art Gallery, 1998, p. 42, Sylvia Beach also resided at no. 18.

3 Quinlan reproduces a photograph of this portrait, *In a Picture Land*,
p. 17, but the location of the work is unknown.

4 Quinlan, *In a Picture Land*, p. 15.

5 Rachel's *acte de décès*, in the registers of the 6th *arrondissement*, states
that she was born on 4 April 1886, in West Chester, Pennsylvania, to
Thomas Dunn and Kate Cobb, and that she died at 5:00 in the morning
on 13 April 1950 in her apartment. Accessed online 8 June 2019.

6 Email message from Karen Quinlan, 11 June 2019.

7 Quinlan, *In a Picture Land*, p. 17.

8 Quinlan, *In a Picture Land,* p. 66.

Chapter 4 – Languephile

1 François-René de Chateaubriand, *Memoirs from Beyond the Grave: 1768–
1800*, introduction by Anka Muhlstein, translation by Alex Andriesse,
New York: New York Review of Books, 2018, p. xx.

2 https://www.youtube.com/watch?v=TPiv0EKzd8k

Chapter 5 – The polos of Michel Foucault (and other tales of French literary life)

1 Roland Barthes, *Mythologies*, New York: Farrar, Straus & Giroux, 1972,
p. 28.

2 Priscilla Parkhurst Ferguson, *Literary France, The Making of a Culture*,
Berkeley: University of California Press, 1987, p. 203.

3 Alain Viala, 'The Theory of the Literary Field and the Situation of the
First Modernity', *Paragraph*, vol. 29, no. 1, 2006, pp. 81–82.

4   Pierre Bourdieu, 'But Who Created the "Creators"?', in Pierre Bourdieu, *Sociology in Question*, London: Sage, 1993, p. 139.

5   Olivia Rosenthal and Lionel Ruffel, 'Introduction', in Olivia Rosenthal and Lionel Ruffel, *La Littérature exposée. Les écritures contemporaines hors du livre, Littérature*, vol. 4, no. 160, 2010, p. 3 (my translation).

6   Henry James, *French Poets and Novelists*, London: Macmillan and Co, 1884.

7   Clémentine Mélois, *Cent titres*, Paris: Grasset, 2014.

8   For the images of Foucault alongside the autumn/winter collection of polos, see Clémentine Mélois's web site : https://twitter.com/Clemelois/status/559101581036380160 (posted on 25 January 2015).

9   Sylvie Ducas, 'Prix littéraires en France: consécration ou désacralisation de l'auteur?', *COnTEXTES* (online), no. 7, 2010 (my translation). Accessed on 23 January 2020.

10   ASA Cultural Tours website: https://www.asatours.com.au/tours/literary-tour-of-france-2016/

11   'Flaubert, c'est le patron'; 'Flaubert, moi c'est mon Dieu', quoted by Sylvie Ducas, 'Roman auctorial et fiction biographique: L'Écrivain-lecteur ou le paradigme de la lecture dans la rhétorique de la vocation littéraire', *La Lecture littéraire*, Université de Reims, no. 5/6, April 2002, p. 189.

12   Pierre Michon, *Le Roi vient quand il veut*, Paris: Albin Michel, 2007, pp. 348–349.

13   Roland Barthes, *Writing Degree Zero*, translated by Annette Lavers and Colin Smith, Michigan: Jonathan Cape, 1967, p. 63.

14   Jean-Paul Sartre, *Words*, translated by Irene Clephane, Great Britain: Penguin Books, 1964, p. 40.

15   Pierre Michon, *Les Vies minuscules*, Paris: Gallimard, 2005, p. 157 (my translation).

16   Dominique Viard and Laurent Demanze, *Fins de la littérature: Esthétiques et discours de la fin,* Paris: Armand Colin, vol. 1, 2011, p. 31.

Chapter 7 – 'To the depths of the unknown in search of the New!': How French composers accepted Baudelaire's 'Invitation au voyage'

1   Vincent D'Indy, *Ma vie: journal de jeunesse, correspondance familiale et intime*, ed. Marie d'Indy, Paris: Séguier, 2001, p. 143 (diary entry for 26 September 1871).

2   Roger Delage, *Emmanuel Chabrier*, Paris: Fayard, 1999, p. 172.

3   Fauré, *Correspondance*, ed. Jean-Michel Nectoux, Paris: Fayard, 2015, p. 128 (letter to Hugues Imbert, August 1887).

4   Debussy, *Correspondance (1872–1918)*, eds François Lesure and Denis Herlin, Paris: Gallimard, 2005, p. 43 (letter to Henri Vasnier, 19 October 1885).

5   See his 1913 reviews of d'Indy's *Fervaal* and Erlanger's *La Sorcière*, in Arbie Orenstein (ed.), *A Ravel Reader: Correspondence, Articles, Interviews*, New York: Columbia University Press, 1990, pp. 355–358.

6   Fauré's op. 22 cantata *Le Ruisseau* appears to be set to his own words. See Roy Howat, 'Fauré the practical interpreter', in Stephen Rumph and Carlo Caballero (eds), *Fauré Studies*, Cambridge: Cambridge University Press, 2021, pp. 170–191.

7   See Margaret Cobb, *The Poetic Debussy*, Boston: Northeastern University Press, 1992, *passim*.

8   Orenstein, *A Ravel Reader*, p. 412.

9   The bassoon obbligato in this song was almost certainly written for the bassoonist (and occasional composer) Désiré Dihau, of the Opéra. Around this time, Dihau and Chabrier were both featured in a famous painting by their mutual friend Edgar Degas, *L'Orchestre de l'Opéra* (c. 1868–1870). Dihau appears front and centre, in the concertmaster's place, while Chabrier – the only visible auditor – peers from the box at the top left corner of the painting.

10 Regarding the dating of Fauré's Baudelaire settings, see Roy Howat and Emily Kilpatrick (eds.), *Gabriel Fauré: Complete Songs*, London: Peters, vol. 1, 2014.

11 Lawrence Porter, *The Crisis of French Symbolism*, Ithaca: Cornell University Press, 1990, p. 25.

12 Baudelaire, *Œuvres complètes*, ed. Marcel Ruff, Paris: Seuil, 1968, p. 159.

13 Baudelaire, *Œuvres complètes*, p. 124.

14 David Evans, *Rhythm, Illusion and the Poetic Idea: Baudelaire, Rimbaud, Mallarmé*, Amsterdam: Rodopi, 2004, p. 99, n. 5.

15 Joseph Acquisto points out the thoroughly Baudelairean imagery in a passage in Wagner's *Lettre sur la musique*, which celebrates a sunset walk in the forest as prompting the discovery of a (new) melody, an 'eternal resonance', one that offers redemption and illumination in its turn. Acquisto, *French Symbolist Poetry and the Idea of Music*, Aldershot: Ashgate, 2006, p. 29.

16 Verlaine was later to write that Chabrier and others 'set our words to music, without damaging or prettifying them – a great act of beneficence, one acknowledged with the boundless gratitude and goodwill of those listeners who knew nothing of harmony but were well schooled in beauty in all its forms!' Verlaine, *Mémoires d'un veuf, Œuvres complètes*, Paris: Vanier, vol. 4, 1904, pp. 297–298.

17 According to Ravel. Orenstein (ed.), *A Ravel Reader*, p. 450.

18 Richard Strauss and Romain Rolland, *Correspondance, Fragments de Journal. Cahiers Romain Rolland* 3, Paris: Albin Michel, 1950, p. 53 (letter dated 2 August 1905).

19 Strauss and Rolland, *Correspondance*, pp. 55–56 (letter dated 9 August 1905).

20 Mimi Daitz describes Fauré's early songs as 'for the most part faulty in this regard [text-setting]', singling out 'S'il est un charmant gazon' as containing 'patent examples of faulty prosody'. See Daitz, 'Les manuscrits et les premières éditions des mélodies de Fauré: Étude préliminaire', *Études fauréennes*, vols 20–21, 1983–1984, p. 21. For more detailed consideration of syllabification and variants in Fauré's early songs, see Roy Howat and Emily Kilpatrick, 'Editorial Challenges in the Early Songs of Gabriel Fauré', *Notes*, vol. 68, no. 2, 2011, pp. 239–283.

21 See Roy Howat, *The Art of French Piano Music*, London and New Haven: Yale University Press, 2009, pp. 265–268, and Howat and Kilpatrick, 'Editorial Challenges', pp. 265–267.

22 Mary Garden and Louis Biancolli, *Mary Garden's Story*, London: Michael Joseph, 1952, p. 64.

23 Linda Laurent, 'Jane Bathori, interprète de Ravel', *Cahiers Maurice Ravel*, vol. 2, 1986, p. 64.

24 Hélène Abraham, *Un art de l'interprétation: Claire Croiza: les cahiers d'une auditrice*, Paris: Office de centralisation d'ouvrages, 1954, *passim*.

25 Baudelaire, *Œuvres complètes*, vol. 1, pp. 275–276.

26 Orenstein, *A Ravel Reader*, p. 338.

27 Debussy, *Correspondance*, p. 43 (letter, 19 October 1885).

28 Porter, *The Crisis of French Symbolism*, p. 24.

29 Porter, *The Crisis of French Symbolism*, p. 25.

30 Across 1885–1887, Debussy composed six further Verlaine settings, which he published as *Ariettes* in 1888, later revising and republishing them as *Ariettes oubliées* (1903).

31 Most of them remained unpublished in Debussy's lifetime. See the *Œuvres complètes de Claude Debussy*, Series 2, vol. 2 (*Mélodies*, 1882–1887), ed. Marie Rolf, Paris: Durand, 2016.

32 Outside this group, only Debussy's setting of Paul Bourget's *La Romance d'Ariel* includes similar textless vocalising. The two Spanish-themed songs (the duet 'Chanson espagnole' and the Gautier setting 'Séguidille'), also include significant vocalising; in both, however, this is implicit in the text (Musset's poem includes the lines 'Ah! Ah!'; 'Séguidille', by its repeated 'Alza! olà!', similarly suggests it).

33 'L' sounds proliferate in the next strophe too: 'Cependant *l*'excel*l*ent docteur / Bo*l*onais cuei*l*le avec *l*enteur / Des simp*l*es parmi *l*'herbe brune' ('Meanwhile the excellent doctor / From Bologna is leisurely picking / Medicinal herbs in the brown grass').

34 Strauss and Rolland, *Correspondance*, p. 158. See Emily Kilpatrick, *The Operas of Maurice Ravel*, Cambridge: Cambridge University Press, 2015, pp. 5–6.

35 Fauré, 'Sous la musique que faut-il mettre', *Musica*, no. 101, 1911, p. 38.

36 Fauré, *Correspondance*, p. 195 (letter to the Princesse de Scey-Montbéliard, late July 1891).

37 Reported by Fauré's son Emmanuel. Fauré, *Correspondance*, p. 213, n. 6.

38 Questions of tonality and transposition in the 'Venetian' songs are explored in Howat and Kilpatrick, 'Gabriel Fauré's Middle-Period Songs, Editorial Quandaries and the Chimera of the "Original Key"', *Journal of the Royal Musical Association*, vol. 139, no. 2, 2014, pp. 303–337.

39 Similar qualities can also be found in Fauré's last work of 1894, the song 'Soir' (on a text by Albert Samain), composed in December. Here again, a D-flat tonality facilitates kinetic and gestural affinities.

40 Nina Gubisch, 'Les Années de jeunesse d'un pianiste espagnol en France (1887–1900): journal et correspondance de Ricardo Viñes' (PhD thesis), Paris: Conservatoire de musique, 1971, p. 219. The six poems were censored two months after the original 1857 publication of *Les Fleurs du mal*. They were subsequently published in *Les Épaves* (Amsterdam, 1866), but were officially suppressed in France until 1949.

41 Gubisch, 'Les Années de jeunesse', p. 266.

42 Baudelaire, *Œuvres complètes*, p. 146.

43 Vlado Perlemuter and Hélène Jourdan-Morhange, *Ravel according to Ravel*, trans. Frances Tanner, London: Kahn and Averill, 1990, p. 35.

44 Howat, 'Ravel and the piano', in Deborah Mawer (ed.), *The Cambridge Companion to Ravel*, Cambridge: Cambridge University Press, 2000, pp. 81–87.

45 Edgar Allan Poe, 'The Philosophy of Composition', first published in *Graham's Magazine*, vol. 28, no.4, April 1846, pp. 163–167.

46 Orenstein (ed.), *A Ravel Reader*, p. 394. See also the unsigned interview printed in *New York Times* on 6 January 1928; Orenstein (ed.), *A Ravel Reader*, p. 454.

47 Orenstein (ed.), *A Ravel Reader*, p. 433. Poe's poetry and prose respectively had been translated into French by Ravel's two literary lodestars, Mallarmé and Baudelaire, the former's volume illustrated by Édouard Manet (Ravel's favourite of the Impressionist painters).

48 Banville, *Petit traité de poésie française*, Paris: Charpentier, 1883, p. 245.

49 Newbould, 'Ravel's Pantoum', *The Musical Times*, vol. 116, no. 1585, 1975, p. 228.

50 Howat, *The Art of French Piano Music*, pp. 176–183.

51 Henriette Faure, *Mon maître Maurice Ravel*, Paris: ATP, 1978, p. 61.

52 Poe, 'The Philosophy of Composition'.

53 Ravel's second choice of text, 'Placet futile', offers another fascinating literary rabbit warren, involving several characters already encountered in these pages. The sonnet is something of a pastiche, in the classical sense: it traces the lines of an earlier poem, which was first published

under the name of Privat d'Anglemont, in the journal *L'Artiste*, managed at the time by Arsène Houssaye. This poem, titled 'À Madame du Barry', was in fact by Charles Baudelaire. Mallarmé dedicated his poem to Houssaye, a gesture that suggests he may have been well aware of the true authorship of 'À Madame du Barry' (which remained in dispute until the end of the nineteenth century). See Emily Kilpatrick, 'Ravel's *Trois Poèmes de Stéphane Mallarmé*: A Philosophy of Composition', *Music & Letters*, vol. 101, issue 3, 2020, pp. 512–543.

54 Orenstein (ed.), *A Ravel Reader*, p. 32.

55 Michel Edwards, 'Ravel et Mallarmé: Poésie et musique', *Conférence*, vol. 28, 2009, p. 268.

56 This is most obvious in Mallarmé's stunningly modernist 'Un coup de dés' of 1897, which employs different typefaces and font sizes and distributes text across each double page, with generous use of blank space.

57 Orenstein (ed.), *A Ravel Reader*, p. 393.

58 Roger Marx, *Maîtres d'hier et d'aujourd'hui*, Paris: Calmann-Lévy, 1914, p. 292.

Chapter 8 – Re(viewing) French cinema

1 I shall be indicating academic sources of interest if the reader wishes to follow up on any aspect. A general source book for French cinema is Michael Temple and Michael Witt (eds), *The French Cinema Book*, London: BFI, 2008. An important collection on contemporary French cinema covering a range of approaches is Alistair Fox, Raphaëlle Moine, Hilary Radner and Michel Marie (eds), *A Companion to Contemporary French Cinema*, Chichester: Wiley-Blackwell, 2015.

2 See Phil Powrie, '"I'm Only Here for the Beer": Post-tourism and the Recycling of French Heritage films', in David Crouch, Felix Thompson and Rhona Jackson (eds), *The Media and the Tourist Imagination: Converging Cultures*, London: Routledge, 2005, pp. 143–153.

3 For more on Besson see Susan Hayward, *Luc Besson*, Manchester: Manchester University Press, 1990; Susan Hayward and Phil Powrie (eds), *The Films of Luc Besson: Master of Spectacle*, Manchester: Manchester University Press, 2006.

4 Carrie Tarr with Brigitte Rollet, *Cinema and the Second Sex: Women's Filmmaking in France in the 1980s and 1990s*, New York: Continuum, 2001, p. 1.

5 Carrie Tarr, 'Introduction: Women's Film-Making in France 2000–2010', *Studies in French Cinema*, vol. 12, no. 3, 2012, p. 190.

6 See Julia Dobson, *Negotiating the Auteur: Cabrera, Lvovsky, Masson and Vernoux*, Manchester: Manchester University Press, 2012.

Notes

7   See Mary Harrod, *From France with Love: Gender and Identity in French Romantic Comedy*, London: I.B. Tauris, 2015.

8   For this film, see Isabelle McNeill, 'Virtual Homes: Space and Memory in the Work of Yamina Benguigui', *L'Esprit Créateur*, vol. 51, no. 1, 2011, pp. 12–25; Leslie Kealhofer, 'Veiled Voices in the Films of Yamina Benguigui', *Studies in French Cinema*, vol. 11, no. 3, 2011, pp. 207–221.

9   Eva Jørholt, 'Banlieue Chronicles: A "Demigrantising", Historical Look at Cinematic Representations of the Ill-Famed French Suburbs', *Studies in European Cinema*, vol. 14, no. 3, 2017, pp. 249–267; Isabelle McNeill, '"Shine Bright Like a Diamond": Music, Performance and Digitextuality in Céline Sciamma's *Bande de filles* (2014)', *Studies in French Cinema*, vol. 18, no. 4, 2018, pp. 326–340.

10 See Tim Palmer, 'Crashing the Millionaires' Club: Popular Women's Cinema in Twenty-First Century France', *Studies in French Cinema*, vol. 12, no. 3, 2012, pp. 201–214.

11 See Carrie Tarr, *Reframing Difference: Beur and Banlieue Filmmaking in France*, Manchester: Manchester University Press, 2005.

12 See Will Higbee, *Post-beur Cinema: North African Émigré and Maghrebi-French Filmmaking in France Since 2000*, Edinburgh: Edinburgh University Press, 2013.

13 Among the many articles on Kechiche, see: Colin Nettelbeck, 'Kechiche and the French Classics: Cinema as Subversion and Renewal of Tradition', *French Cultural Studies*, vol. 18, no. 3, 2007, pp. 307–319; Ari J.Blatt, '"The Play's the Thing": Marivaux and the Banlieue in Abdellatif Kechiche's *L'Esquive*', *The French Review*, vol. 81, no. 3, 2008, pp. 474–487; Dana Strand, 'Être et parler: Being and speaking French in Abdellatif Kechiche's *L'Esquive* (2004) and Laurent Cantet's *Entre les murs* (2008)', *Studies in French Cinema*, vol. 9, no. 3, 2009, pp. 259–272; Mary Jean Matthews Green, 'All In the Family: Abdellatif Kechiche's *La Graine et le Mulet* (*The Secret of the Grain*)', *South Central Review*, vol. 28, no. 1, 2011, pp. 109–123; Claudia Esposito, 'Ronsard in the Metro: Abdellatif Kechiche and the Poetics of Space', *Studies in French Cinema*, vol. 11, no. 3, 2011, pp. 223–234; Panivong Norindr, 'The Cinematic Practice of a "cinéaste ordinaire": Abdellatif Kechiche and French Political Cinema', *Contemporary French and Francophone Studies*, vol. 16, no. 1, 2012, pp. 55–68; Louisa Shea, 'Exit Voltaire, Enter Marivaux: Abdellatif Kechiche on the Legacy of the Enlightenment', *The French Review*, vol. 85, no. 6, 2012, pp. 1136–1148; Jim Morrissey, 'Objectification and Resistance: Dance Performances in Abdellatif Kechiche's *La Graine et le mulet* (2007) and *Vénus noire* (2010)', *French Cultural Studies*, vol. 24, no. 3, 2013, pp. 306–318.

14 As is the case with Kechiche, the films of Bouchareb have also received considerable academic attention: Michael F. O'Riley, 'National Identity and Unrealized Union in Rachid Bouchareb's *Indigènes*', *The French*

Review, vol. 81, no. 2, 2007, pp. 278–290; Alec G. Hargreaves, '*Indigènes*: A Sign of the Times', *Research in African Literatures*, vol. 38, no. 4, 2007, pp. 204–216; Panivong Norindr, 'Incorporating Indigenous Soldiers in the Space of the French Nation: Rachid Bouchareb's *Indigènes*', *Yale French Studies*, no. 115, 2009, pp. 126–140; Anne Donadey, '"Wars of Memory": On Rachid Bouchareb's *Hors la loi*', *L'Esprit Créateur*, vol. 54, no. 4, 2014, pp. 15–26; Eva Jørholt, 'To Remember in Order to Be Able to Forget: Rachid Bouchareb's *Outside the Law* and the Construction of a New, Inclusive French National Identity', *Studies in European Cinema*, vol. 13, no. 1, 2016, pp. 1–14; Anne Donadey, 'Gender, Genre and Intertextuality in Rachid Bouchareb's *Hors la loi*', *Studies in French Cinema*, vol. 16, no. 1, 2016, pp. 48–60; Bennet Schaber, 'Missing Children: Merzak Allouache and Rachid Bouchareb or, 2005 Ten Years Later', *Journal of North African Studies*, vol. 22, no. 5, 2017, pp. 741–760; Anne Donadey and Wissem Brinis, 'Multilingual Strategies in Rachid Bouchareb's *Hors la loi*', *Contemporary French and Francophone Studies*, vol. 22, no. 2, 2018, pp. 178–186; Ipek A. Celik Rappas, 'Tracing a History of Terrorism in Rachid Bouchareb's Films: *London River* (2009), *Hors la loi* (2010) and *La Route d'Istanbul* (2016)', *Studies in French Cinema*, vol. 19, no. 3, pp. 179–193. Bouchareb has made films outside of France: *London River* (2009) focuses on the aftermath of the 7/7 London bombings, and he followed with two films in the USA, *Just Like a Woman* (2012) with Sienna Miller and Golshifteh Farahani, and *Two Men in Town* (2014) with Forest Whitaker and Harvey Keitel.

15   See Joseph McGonagle, 'Gently Does It: Ethnicity and Cultural Identity in Olivier Ducastel and Jacques Martineau's *Drôle de Félix* (2000)', *Studies in European Cinema*, vol. 4, no. 1, 2007, pp. 21–33; Thibaut Schilt, 'Hybrid Strains in Olivier Ducastel and Jacques Martineau's *Drôle de Félix* (2000)', *Contemporary French and Francophone Studies*, vol. 11, no. 3, 2007, pp. 361–368; Denis M. Provencher, 'Tracing Sexual Citizenship and Queerness in *Drôle de Félix* (2000) and *Tarik el hob* (2001)', *Contemporary French and Francophone Studies*, vol. 12, no. 1, 2008, pp. 51–61; Nick Rees-Roberts, *French Queer Cinema*, Edinburgh: Edinburgh University Press, 2008; Neil Archer, *The French Road Movie: Space, Mobility, Identity*, Oxford: Berghahn, 2012; Michael Gott and Thibaut Schilt, *Open Roads, Closed Borders: The Contemporary French-Language Road Movie*, Chicago: University of Chicago Press, 2013.

16   For a general introduction to contemporary French comedies, see Mary Harrod and Phil Powrie, 'New Directions in Contemporary French Comedies: From Nation, Sex and Class to Ethnicity, Community and the Vagaries of the Postmodern', *Studies in French Cinema*, vol. 18, no. 1, 2018, pp. 1–17. On the three films mentioned here, see Raphaëlle Moine, 'Stereotypes of Class, Ethnicity and Gender in Contemporary French Popular Comedy: from *Bienvenue chez les Ch'tis* (2008) and *Intouchables* (2011) to *Qu'est-ce qu'on a fait au Bon Dieu?*', *Studies in*

French Cinema, vol. 18, no. 1, 2018, pp. 35–51. On *Intouchables*, see Charlie
Michael, 'Interpreting *Intouchables*: Competing Transnationalisms in
Contemporary French Cinema', *Substance*, vol. 43, no. 1, 2014, pp. 123–137;
David Pettersen, 'Transnational Blackface, Neo-Minstrelsy and the
"French Eddie Murphy" in *Intouchables*', *Modern & Contemporary France*,
vol. 24, no. 1, 2016, pp. 51–69; Gemma King, 'No Laughing Matter?
Navigating Political (In)correctness in *Intouchables*', *Francosphères*, vol.
7, no. 1, 2018, pp. 1–14; Emine Fişek, 'Rethinking *Intouchables*: Race and
Performance in Contemporary France', *French Cultural Studies*, vol. 29,
no. 2, 2018, pp. 190–205. On *Bienvenue chez les Ch'tis*, see Mary Harrod,
'Linguistic difference as ontological sameness in *Bienvenue chez les Ch'tis*
(2008)', *Studies in French Cinema*, vol. 12, no. 1, 2012, pp. 75–86; Mackenzie
Leadston, 'Happily Never After: The Visual Politics of Contemporary
French Interracial Romantic Comedy', *Studies in French Cinema*, vol. 19,
no. 4, 2019, pp. 335–352.

17 Alexandre Garcia, '17 millions de Français touchés par *Intouchables*',
   Le Français et vous, no. 71 (February 2017), http://www.cia-france.com/
   francais-et-vous/sur_les_paves/108-millions-de-francais-touches-par-
   intouchables.html; accessed 7 February 2019. My translation.

18 Gérard Lefort, Didier Péron and Bruno Icher, '*Intouchables*? Ben
   si ...', *Libération*, 14 November 2011, https://next.liberation.fr/
   cinema/2011/11/14/intouchables-ben-si_774456; accessed 7 February
   2019. My translation.

19 Jay Weissberg, 'Film Review: *Untouchable*', *Variety*, 29 September 2011,
   https://variety.com/2011/film/reviews/untouchable-1117946269/;
   accessed 7 February 2019.

20 Sylvie Granotier, 'J'ai aimé *Intouchables*, et alors?', *Libération*, 5
   December 2011, https://next.liberation.fr/cinema/2011/12/05/j-ai-aime-
   intouchables-et-alors_779451; accessed 7 February 2019. My translation.

Chapter 9 – Treasured possessions in Australian rare book collections

1 Tim Bonyhady, 'Introduction', in *National Treasures from Australia's Great
  Libraries*, Canberra: National Library of Australia, 2005, p. 1.

2 Editorial, *The Burlington Magazine*, vol. 99, no. 656, November 1957,
  p. 361. On this exhibition, see the extensive catalogue written by
  William Bürger (pseudonym of Théophile Thoré), *Trésors d'art exposés
  à Manchester en 1857 et provenant des collections royales, des collections
  publiques et des collections particulières de la Grande-Bretagne*, Paris, Vve
  J. Renouard, 1857, and Gustav Waagen, *A walk through the Art-Treasures
  Exhibition at Manchester: under the guidance of Dr Waagen [...] A
  companion to the official catalogue*, London: John Murray, Albemarle
  Street; and W.H. Smith & Son, Strand, 1857.

3 Bonyhady, 'Introduction', p. 1.
4 Bürger, *Trésors d'art*, p. viii (my translation).
5 See, for example: *The Perth Gazette and Independent Journal of Politics and News*, Friday 14 August 1857, pp. 3–4; *The Inquirer and Commercial News*, Wednesday 2 September 1857, p. 3; *Empire*, Friday 24 July 1857, pp. 6–7; *Hobart Town Daily Mercury*, Wednesday 22 July 1857, p. 3.
6 According to Bonyhady, since Hobart did not have a public library, art gallery or museum, the organisers used the Tasmanian Parliament, which had already housed an exhibition a decade before.
7 *Hobart Town Daily Mercury*, Saturday 10 July 1858, p. 4.
8 *Hobart Town Daily Mercury*, Saturday 10 July 1858, p. 4.
9 *Argus*, Tuesday 21 May 1861, p. 5.
10 *Argus*, Tuesday 21 May 1861, p. 5.
11 *Examiner and Melbourne Weekly*, 20 November 1859 and 21 May 1859. Cited by Kathleeen M. Fennessy, 'For "Love of Art": the Museum of Art and Picture Gallery at the Melbourne Public Library 1860–70', *La Trobe Journal*, no. 75, Autumn 2005, p. 6.
12 Alison Inglis, 'The Empire of Art', in Martin Hewitt (ed.), *The Victorian World*, London: Routledge, 2012, p. 594.
13 Christine Downer and Jennifer Phipps, *Victorian Vision: 1834 Onwards, Images and Records from the National Gallery of Victoria and State Library of Victoria*, Melbourne: National Gallery of Victoria, 1985, p. 38.
14 Bonyhady, 'Introduction', p. 5. Many of the visitors enjoyed the modest admission price on Saturday nights (six pence).
15 Bonyhady, 'Introduction', p. 2.
16 Bonyhady, 'Introduction', p. 2. It was a Colt revolver from the Burke and Wills expedition.
17 Inglis, 'The Empire of Art', p. 594. She adds: 'Furthermore, as technological advances like chromolithography and photography produced even more accurate replicas, copies began to be valued by museum officials as a means of achieving more comprehensive collections, formed along art historical lines.'
18 An example would be the fabulous treasure that was found in September 2017 at the Abbey of Cluny in France. It included 2,200 silver coins, 21 gold dinars, and a gold signet ring.
19 See the 'Telling stories – Tiny treasures' workshop held at the State Library of Victoria.
20 An example would be the *Trésor de la langue française*, a 16-volume dictionary of nineteenth- and twentieth-century French published from 1971 to 1994, and from which these definitions of 'treasure' are taken.
21 Anne Robertson, *Treasures of the State Library of New South Wales: the Australiana Collections*, Sydney: Collins Australia in association with the State Library of New South Wales, 1988, p. viii.

22　In this essay, the definition of 'French' is understood to be very broad and includes books published in Francophone countries such as Switzerland, Belgium or the Low Countries, by francophone authors, and written in French or in Latin (in particular, books of hours published during the Middle Ages or the Renaissance).

23　This exhibition, which is renewed every year, has a different approach today. It does not seek to showcase 'treasures', but 'rare, beautiful and historically significant' books (2019).

24　This exhibition was curated by Margaret Dent. A catalogue has been issued (introductory text by Tim Bonyhady, essays by John Clark, essay introduction texts by Margaret Dent). See note 1.

25　Anne Robertson, *Treasures of the State Library of New South Wales: the Australiana collections,* Sydney: Collins Australia in association with the State Library of New South Wales, 1988; John Thompson (ed.), *The People's Treasures. Collections in the National Library of Australia,* Canberra: National Library of Australia, 1993; *Library of Dreams: Treasures from the National Library of Australia,* compiled by Jennifer Gall and past and present members of the National Library of Australia, Canberra: National Library of Australia, [2011]; Anne Glover, *Victorian Treasures from the La Trobe Collection,* South Melbourne: Macmillan, 1980.

26　Philippe Buache, *Carte physique de la Grande Mer: ci-devant nommée Mer du Sud Pacifique ... Avec la représentation de ce que l'on conjecture sur la Mer Glaciale Antarctique. Dressée et présentée à l'Acad. des Sc. le 5 septbre 1744. Par* Philippe Buache; gravée par Desbruslins, pere, 1757. *Procès-verbaux de l'Assemblée nationale contenant les articles qu'elle a adoptés de la déclaration des droits de l'homme & du citoyen, & ceux pour la constitution & l'organisation du pouvoir legislatif,* Paris: Au bureau du journal général de la cour & de la ville, 1789 (séances des 20, 21, 22, 23, 24, & 26 août 1789).

27　Louis Auguste de Sainson (after), *Habitation de pêcheurs de phoques au port Western* (Nouvelle Hollande); Antoine Fauchery, *Lettres d'un mineur en Australie par Antoine Fauchery; précédées d'une lettre de Théodore de Banville,* Paris: Poulet-Malassis et de Broise, 1857.

28　*Book of Hours*, Bourges, c. 1480, Safe 1/7c. Manuscript on vellum, produced in the workshop of Jean Colombe of Bourges. The text is in Latin, with a calendar in French.

29　http://digital.sl.nsw.gov.au/delivery/DeliveryManagerServlet?embedded =true&toolbar=false&dps_pid=IE1069599

30　See https://slwa.wa.gov.au/treasures/

31　Odet-Peillon depicts the *Uranie* encampment at Shark Bay with the fresh water distillery in the centre and, on the right, Rose de Freycinet, the commander's wife, sitting next to her tent with a mixed-race companion. Since Rose had stowed away in Toulon, and should not have been there, she was removed from the print of this picture and does not feature in the official publication of the voyage.

32 394 pages (16 lines), bound: colour illustrations, 17 cm, catalogue no. 096.1 C363. The text is in Latin, with a calendar in French, and is written in a Gothic hand. See https://digital.collections.slsa.sa.gov.au/nodes/view/2536

33 Game, colour, paper on board, in box 22 x 43.5 x 5 cm, [Paris?]: [s.n.], [188–?]. See https://digital.collections.slsa.sa.gov.au/nodes/view/782

34 Thompson, *The People's Treasures*, p. 2, citing *Treasures of the British Library*, compiled by Nicolas Barker, London: The British Library. 1988, p. 11.

35 Treasures Gallery, Canberra.

36 Thompson, *The People's Treasures*, p. 2.

37 Budé, *Commentarii Linguae Graecae*, Paris: Josse Bade, 1529.

38 *Histoire naturelle des insectes, coléoptères, par M. le comte de Castelnau [...] avec une introduction renfermant l'anatomie et la physiologie des animaux articulés, par M. Brullé*, Paris: Société Bibliophile, 1851. Catalogue no. RARES 595.76 C27H.

39 Thompson, *The People's Treasures*, p. 2

40 Leigh Hays, *Worth telling, worth keeping: a guide to the collections of the J.S. Battye Library of West Australian History*, Perth: Library Board of Western Australia, 2002, p. 15.

41 Margaret Dent, 'Time's Treasures', in *Treasures from the world's great libraries*, Canberra: National Library of Australia, 2001, p. 9.

Chapter 10 – Tall tales and true from the history of French exploration in Australia

1 The full title in French is *Mémoires touchant l'établissement d'une mission chrestienne dans le troisième monde, autrement appellé la Terre australe, méridionale, antarctique & inconnuë*. A critical edition of the text produced by Margaret Sankey was published in Paris by Champion in 2006.

2 Margaret Sankey has written extensively on the enduring legacy of the Gonneville story and the debates it has generated. See, for example: 'The Abbé Jean Paulmier and French Missions in the *Terres australes*: Myth and History', *Australian Journal of French Studies*, vol. 50, no. 1, 2013, pp. 3–15; 'The Abbé Paulmier's *Mémoires* and Early French Voyages in Search of *Terra Australis*', in John West-Sooby (ed.), *Discovery and Empire: the French in the South Seas*, Adelaide: University of Adelaide Press, 2013, pp. 41–68; and 'Jean Paulmier, Gonneville and Utopia: the Making and Unmaking of a Myth', *Australian Journal of French Studies*, vol. 58, no. 1, 2021, pp. 8–23.

3   La Pérouse's instructions are reproduced in English translation in *The Journal of Jean-François de Galaup de La Pérouse 1785–1788*, edited by John Dunmore, London: The Hakluyt Society, 1994, 2 vols, vol. I, pp. cx–cl (see p. cxxxvii for the quotation).

4   As indicated in note 9 to Colin Nettelbeck's essay, above, we have attempted to debunk this myth, as far as South Australia is concerned, in our essay 'A Contested Coast? Revisiting the Baudin-Flinders encounter of April 1802', in Carolyn Collins and Paul Sendziuk (eds), *Foundational Fictions in South Australian History*, Mile End: Wakefield Press, 2018, pp. 13–27.

5   On this, see Jean Fornasiero, Peter Monteath and John West-Sooby, *Encountering Terra Australis: The Australian Voyages of Nicolas Baudin and Matthew Flinders*, Kent Town: Wakefield Press, 2010 (2004), p. 384.

6   On the d'Entrecasteaux expedition, 113 men sailed from France on the *Recherche* (36.4 m in length, beam of 9.1 m) while there were 106 men on the *Espérance* (length 37 m, beam 8.3 m). For the Baudin expedition, there were on departure from France 133 men on the *Géographe* (length 40.3 m, beam 9.7 m) and 125 men on the *Naturaliste* (length 39 m, beam 8.8 m).

7   Ronsard, Journal nautique, vol. I, Archives Nationales de France (ANF), série Marine, 5JJ 29, entry dated 4 Vendémiaire Year II (26 September 1802). All translationa are our own, unless otherwise indicated.

8   Nicole Starbuck, *Baudin, Napoleon and the Exploration of Australia*, London: Pickering and Chatto, 2013, p. 56.

9   Nicolas Baudin, *The Journal of Post-Captain Nicolas Baudin, Commander-in Chief of the Corvettes* Géographe *and* Naturaliste, *assigned by order of the government to a voyage of discovery*, translated by Christine Cornell, Adelaide: The Friends of the State Library of South Australia, 2004 (1974), p. 411.

10   See Frank Horner, *The French Reconnaissance: Baudin in Australia, 1801–1803*, Carlton: Melbourne University Press, 1987, pp. 60–61, 87, 92. See also Jean Fornasiero and John West-Sooby, 'An Appetite for Discovery: The Culinary Adventures of Matthew Flinders and Nicolas Baudin in Terra Australis', in A. Lynn Martin and Barbara Santich (eds), *Gastronomic Encounters*, Brompton: Eastside Publications, 2004, pp. 21–34.

11   On this episode, see the reports of the naturalist Louis Ventenat, who was a witness to the scene, and of Achard de Bonvouloir himself, ANF, série Marine, 5JJ 4.

12   Baudin, *Journal*, p. 409.

13   D'Auribeau to d'Entrecasteaux, ANF, série Marine, 5JJ 4.

14   Ventenat to d'Entrecasteaux, in Ventenat, Journal, ANF, série Marine 5JJ 4, Cahier 1.

15 Levillain, Journal, Muséum d'Histoire naturelle, Le Havre, Collection Lesueur (MHNH CL), dossier 07 008, entry dated 5 Floréal Year 9 (25 April 1801). Another copy of his Journal, with slight variations, is kept in the National Archives in Paris.

16 Levillain, Journal, MHNH CL, dossier 07 008, entry dated 19–23 Prairial Year 9 (8–12 June 1801).

17 Levillain, Journal, ANF, série Marine, 5JJ 32, p. 37.

18 Levillain, Journal, ANF, série Marine, 5JJ 32, p. 44. For more on Levillain's sensibilities, see John West-Sooby, 'An Emotional Voyager: Stanislas Levillain (1774–1801), Trainee Zoologist on the Baudin Expedition', in Jean Fornasiero and John West-Sooby (eds), *'Roaming Freely Throughout the Universe': Nicolas Baudin's Voyage to Australia and the Pursuit of Science*, Mile End: Wakefield Press, 2021, Chapter 14.

19 Baudin, *Journal*, p. 54.

20 Baudin, *Mon voyage aux Terres Australes*, edited by Jacqueline Bonnemains, Paris: Imprimerie Nationale, 2000, p. 134.

21 Baudin, *Journal*, p. 54.

22 Riedlé, Journal, Muséum national d'Histoire naturelle, Paris, Bibliothèque centrale, ms. 1688, entry dated 21 Frimaire Year 9 (12 December 1800).

23 Riedlé, Journal, entry dated 22 Frimaire Year 9 (13 December 1800).

24 Gicquel, Journal, ANF, série Marine, 5JJ 14, entry for 14 July 1792.

25 Baudin, *Journal*, p. 20.

26 Louis Freycinet, Journal, ANF, série Marine, 5JJ 49, entries dated 18–19 Frimaire and 10–11 Frimaire Year 9 (9–10 December and 1–2 December 1800).

27 Saint-Cricq, Journal, ANF, série Marine, 5JJ 48, opening page.

28 Gicquel, Journal, ANF, série Marine, 5JJ 14, entry for 20 June 1792.

29 Baudin, *Journal*, p. 46.

30 Baudin, *Journal*, p. 37.

31 Baudin, *Journal*, p. 277.

32 Anonymous journal, ANF, série Marine, 5JJ 6A, entry titled 'Description of the island of Tenerife'.

33 Sautier, Journal, Muséum national d'Histoire naturelle, Paris, Bibliothèque centrale, ms. 1687, p. 8 (unnumbered pages).

34 Riedlé, Journal, p. 26.

35 Labillardière, *Voyage in Search of La Pérouse, Performed by Order of the Constituent Assembly, During the Years* 1791, 1792, 1793, *and* 1794, unnamed translator, London: John Stockdale, 1800, 2 vols, vol. 2, p. 50.

36 As reported by Gicquel, Journal, entry for 15 July 1792.

37 See François Péron, *Voyage of Discovery to the Southern Lands*, translated by Christine Cornell, Adelaide: Friends of the State Library of South Australia, vol. 1, 2006, pp. 181–182 and 200.

38 On these musical experiments, see Jean Fornasiero and John West-Sooby, 'Cross-Cultural Inquiry in 1802: Musical Performance on the Baudin Expedition to Australia', in Kate Darian-Smith and Penelope Edmonds (eds), *Conciliation on Colonial Frontiers: Conflict, Performance, and Commemoration in Australia and the Pacific Rim*, London: Routledge, 2015, pp. 17–35. On the importance of the song tradition to the Aboriginal people of south-east Tasmania, see Skye Krichauff, 'Baudin and the Nuenonne: Exploring Encounters between the French and the People of Lunawanna, Alonnah, 1802', BA Honours thesis, University of Adelaide, 2003, p. 45.

39 Anonymous journal, ANF, série Marine, 5JJ 6A, entry for the night of 5–6 May 1792.

Chapter 11 – Live to eat – a very French pleasure

1 L.A. Milet-Mureau, *Voyage de La Pérouse autour du monde*, Paris: Imprimerie de la République, 1797, t. III, p. 265.

2 While on his way to the guillotine, Louis XVI is purported to have asked: 'Is there any news of La Pérouse?' It was only in September 1827 that the wrecks of La Pérouse's two ships were discovered in Vanikoro, by an Irish trading captain named Peter Dillon. In more recent times, marine archaeologists have conducted detailed surveys of the wreck site. In 2005, a shipwreck on the reef of Vanikoro in the Solomons was formally identified as *La Boussole*. Maritime exploration was a risky occupation at the time: d'Entrecasteaux likewise perished in the Pacific – near the Bismarck Archipelago off the north-east coast of New Guinea, not that far away, in relative terms, from Vanikoro. He died of scurvy on 21 July 1793, aged 55.

3 It follows that someone who restores you is a 'restaurateur', not a 'restauronteur'.

4 The number of cheeses referred to when this phrase is quoted is subject to variation: 258, 365, 400…

5 UNESCO website: https://ich.unesco.org/en/RL/gastronomic-meal-of-the-french-00437

6 John Baxter, *Cooking for Claudine: How I Cooked My Way to the Heart of a Formidable French Family*, London: Short Books, 2011. Published in America as *Immoveable Feast: A Paris Christmas*, New York: Harper Perennial, 2008.

Chapter 12 – An intercultural blend of French experience and Australian terroir

1   See Isabel Negro, 'Wine Discourse in the French Language', *Revista Electrónica de Lingüística Aplicada*, no. 11, 2012, pp. 1–12.
2   Émile Peynaud, *Le Goût du vin: le grand livre de la dégustation*, Paris: Éditions Dunod, 1980.
3   Julie McIntyre, *First Vintage: Wine in Colonial New South Wales*, Sydney: New South Publishing, 2012, pp. 36–38.
4   Jacqueline Dutton, 'Postcolonial Vine and Wine', in C. Forsdick, E. Achille and L. Moudileno (eds), *Postcolonial Realms of Memory: Sites and Symbols in Modern France*, Liverpool: Liverpool University Press, 2020, pp. 373–382.
5   Catherine Ferland, 'La Saga du vin au Canada à l'époque de la Nouvelle-France', *Anthropology of Food*, vol. 3, 2004, http://aof.revues.org/245
6   James Busby, *Treatise on the Culture of the Vine*, Sydney: R. Howe Government Printer, 1825; *A Manual of Plain Directions for Planting and Cultivating Vineyards and for Making Wine in New South Wales*, Sydney: R. Mansfield, 1830; *Journal of a Tour through some of the vineyards of Spain and France*, Sydney: Stephen and Stokes, 1833.
7   Mikaël Pierre, '"France of the Southern Hemisphere": Transferring a European Wine Model to Colonial Australia', PhD thesis, University of Bordeaux-Montaigne and University of Newcastle, 2020.
8   Barbara Santich, 'ISFAR Research Project: French-Australian Exchanges in Viticulture and Winemaking', *The French Australian Review*, no. 72, 2022, pp. 20–37. Website: https://www.isfar.org.au/france-australia-wine/
9   McIntyre, *First Vintage*; David Dunstan, *Better than Pommard! A History of Wine in Victoria*, Kew: Australian Scholarly Publishing, 1994.
10 See, for example: Amie Sexton, 'The French in the Australian wine industry: 1788–2009', *International Journal of Wine Business Research*, vol. 23, no. 3, 2011, pp. 198–209; Éric Bouvet and Chelsea Roberts, 'Early French migration to South Australia: preliminary findings on French vignerons', in S. Williams, D. Lonergan, R. Hosking, L. Deane and N. Bierbaum (eds), *The Regenerative Spirit: (Un)settling, (Dis)location, (Post-) colonial, (Re)presentations – Australian Post-Colonial Reflections*, Adelaide: Lythrum Press, 2004, pp. 86–92.
11 For example: James Halliday, *A History of the Australian Wine Industry 1949–1994*, Adelaide: Australian Wine and Brandy Corporation in association with Winetitles, 1994; Max Allen, *The History of Australian Wine: Stories from the Vineyard to the Cellar Door*, Melbourne: Victory Books, 2012.
12 McIntyre, *First Vintage*, p. 77.
13 McIntyre, *First Vintage*, p. 92.

14 McIntyre, *First Vintage*, p. 92.

15 *Transactions of the Society, Instituted at London, for the Encouragement of Arts, Manufactures, and Commerce*, London, 1823, vol. 41, p. 285.

16 Pierre, '"France of the Southern Hemisphere"', p. 85.

17 Cf. Dunstan, *Better than Pommard!*, and Pierre, '"France of the Southern Hemisphere"', p. 86.

18 Nicholas Faith, *Liquid Gold: The Story of Australian Wine and its Makers*, Sydney: Pan Macmillan, 2002, pp. 136–137.

19 Campbell Mattinson, *The Wine Hunter: The Man Who Changed Australian Wine*, Sydney: Hachette Australia, 2006; Peter McAra, *The Vintner's Letters*, Chatswood: Mira Books, 2007.

20 Julie McIntyre and John Germov, '"Who Wants to be a Millionaire?" I Do: Postwar Australian Wine, Gendered Culture and Class', *Journal of Australian Studies*, vol. 42, no. 1, 2018, pp. 65–84.

21 Pierre, '"France of the Southern Hemisphere"', p. 114.

22 Dunstan, *Better than Pommard!*, pp. 127–131.

23 Dunstan, *Better than Pommard!*, pp. 132–133.

24 Dunstan, *Better than Pommard!*, pp. 134–135.

25 Dunstan, *Better than Pommard!*, p. 143.

26 'The Rise of the Land Dragon', interview with Alex Landragin by Richard Fidler, ABC Radio, 10 June 2019. Online: https://www.abc.net.au/radio/programs/conversations/alex-landragin/11175264

27 'House of Arras: Australia's most awarded sparkling wine', sponsored feature on the World of Fine Wine website, 2 December 2021, https://worldoffinewine.com/2021/12/02/house-of-arras-australias-most-awarded-sparkling-wine/

28 See Angela J. Steinberner, *Kaiser Stuhl, the Growers' Winery: A History of the Barossa Co-operative Winery Limited, 1931–1982*, Beulah Park, South Australia: Crito Press, 1994.

29 See Jacqueline Dutton, Colin Jevons and Nadine Normand-Marconnet, 'Generation Z Perceptions of Rosé Wine in Australia: From Packaging to Product', *Proceedings of the 12th Conference of the Academy of Wine Business Research*, 2021, pp. 70–80. Online: http://academyofwinebusiness.com/wp-content/uploads/2021/11/1.-Generation-Z-Perceptions-of-Rose-Wine-in-Australia-From-Packaging-to-Product.pdf

30 Pierre, '"France of the Southern Hemisphere"', pp. 116–117, 204.

Contributors

Christopher Allen is an art critic and historian who graduated from the University of Sydney, has worked at the Collège de France in Paris and lectured for many years at the National Art School in Sydney. He is the author of *Art in Australia: From Colonisation to Postmodernism* (1997), *French Painting in the Golden Age* (2003), *Charles-Alphonse Dufresnoy, De Arte Graphica* (2005) and several other works including *Jeffrey Smart: Unpublished Paintings 1940–2007* (2008). In 2021, he published *A Companion to Australian Art*, an edited collection of essays on the history of Australian artforms from colonisation to postmodernism. He was art critic for the *Australian Financial Review* from 2005–2008 and since 2008 has been national art critic for the *Australian*. He is also Senior Master in Academic Extension at Sydney Grammar School, where he teaches Art History and Classical Greek.

Brian Castro was born in Hong Kong and is of Portuguese, Chinese and English parentage. He lives in the Adelaide Hills and is the author of eleven novels. He has received eight major Australian awards for literature, beginning with The Australian/Vogel Literary Award for his first novel, *Birds of Passage* (1983), and culminating in the Prime Minister's Award for Poetry in 2018, for *Blindness and Rage: A Phantasmagoria. A Novel in Thirty-Four Cantos* (2017). He was the winner in 2014 of the Patrick White Award for Literature. From 2008 to 2019 he held the Chair of Creative Writing at the University of Adelaide.

Véronique Duché is the A.R. Chisholm Chair of French Studies at the University of Melbourne. Her research centres on European literature of the Renaissance. She is recognised as one of the leading experts on the history of translation in fifteenth- and sixteenth-century France, with a particular focus on the impact and circulation in France of Spanish literature of the period. She directed the first volume of the *Histoire des Traductions en Langue Française. XVᵉ et XVIᵉ siècles (1470–1610)* (Paris: Verdier, 2015). She also has a strong interest in rare books and in the historical and cultural links between France and Australia.

Jacqueline Dutton is Professor of French Studies at the University of Melbourne. She is a leading researcher on contemporary French and Francophone culture and identity, specialising in literature, food, wine, travel and utopia as intercultural products of regional, national and international geopolitics. She has published widely in all of these areas, including a monograph in French on the representations of utopia in the work of 2008 Nobel Laureate in Literature J.M.G. Le Clézio, *Le Chercheur d'or et d'ailleurs* (2003), and co-edited books *Wine, Terroir, Utopia: Making New Worlds* (2020) and the *Routledge Handbook of Wine and Culture* (2022). She is currently working on a cultural history of wine in Bordeaux, Burgundy and Champagne.

Jean Fornasiero is Professor Emerita of French Studies at the University of Adelaide. She is a Fellow of the Australian Academy of the Humanities, an Officier of the Palmes Académiques and a life member of the Australian Society for French Studies and of the Institute for the Study of French–Australian Relations. She has worked extensively on Nicolas Baudin's voyage of discovery to Australia and has published several books on the subject, as co-author or co-editor, including *Encountering Terra Australis: The Australian Voyages of Nicolas Baudin and Matthew Flinders* (2004; 2010), *French Designs on Colonial New South Wales* (2014), *The Art of Science: Nicolas Baudin's Voyagers (1800–1804)* (2016) and '*Roaming Freely Throughout the Universe': Nicolas Baudin's Voyage to Australia and the Pursuit of Science* (2021). She was a chief investigator on two major research projects funded by the Australian Research Council: 'The Baudin Legacy' (2005–2009) and 'Revolutionary Voyaging' (2014–2016). Her other research interests include the history of ideas in nineteenth-century France, from the Revolutionary period to the Second Empire, and crime fiction.

Françoise Grauby was Associate Professor of French at the University of Sydney from 1994 to 2019. She has published extensively on French literature from the nineteenth century to the present, with a particular focus on the representation of the writer at work. Her book, *Le Roman de la création, Écrire entre mythes et pratiques/The Novel of Creative Writing: Between Myth and Practice* (2015), examines the impact of creative writing programs in France and their growing popularity. She has also worked on various aspects of French culture and literature, including 'autofiction' and Aids literature, crime fiction, Michel Houellebecq and medical discourses and popular beliefs about the body, the latter of which led to a book-length study: *Le Corps de l'artiste: discours médical et représentations de l'artiste au XIXᵉ siècle*. She is the author of two novels published by Maurice Nadeau: *Un cheval piaffe en moi* (2004) and *Les Îles* (2007).

Catherine (Cath) Kerry was born in Algeria; French mother and English father. She was a teacher (French, English and Cinema) before becoming a chef and restaurateur. While director of the Art Gallery of South Australia Restaurant, she received the National Restaurant and Catering Lifetime Achiever Award for Commitment and Service to the Industry in 2006. She has a strong academic interest in food, in why, how and what we eat, believing that at the table, we learn a protocol that curbs natural savagery and greed and cultivates a capacity for sharing, and thoughtfulness. She became a trained Art Gallery Guide in 1992. Out of the kitchen, she is interested in architecture and design from the Viennese Secession to the mid twentieth century. She has a weakness for collecting vintage and antique tableware. She is an amateur cheese-maker.

Contributors

Emily Kilpatrick is an Associate Professor of the Royal Academy of Music, London, where she lectures in Academic Studies. A graduate of the University of Adelaide, she previously taught at the Elder Conservatorium of Music (Adelaide) and the Royal Northern College of Music (Manchester). Emily has published widely on French music, her research exploring performance and staging practice, musical analysis, text-music interchanges, and documentary and cultural history. Her warmly received first book, *The Operas of Maurice Ravel* (Cambridge, 2015), was followed in 2022 by the monograph *French Art Song: History of a New Music, 1870–1914* (Rochester). With Roy Howat, Emily is co-editor of the first complete critical edition of Fauré's songs (Edition Peters); and his 45 *Vocalises*, published for the first time in 2013. Her recordings include Fauré's piano duets (with Roy Howat) and, with tenor Tony Boutté, the first recording of Fauré's song cycle *La Bonne Chanson* after the new Peters critical edition.

Stephen Muecke is a Fellow of the Australian Academy of the Humanities, Emeritus Professor at the University of New South Wales and Professor in the Nulungu Research Institute of the University of Notre Dame Australia. He is a cultural theorist and has worked at the University of Technology Sydney, the University of Western Australia, the University of Adelaide and Flinders University. He has worked for many years with the Goolarabooloo people of the Kimberley region in Western Australia. An early result of that collaborative work was the book *Reading the Country: Introduction to Nomadology* (1984), co-authored with Krim Benterrak and Paddy Roe, which explored the meaning and politics of place through Aboriginal narratives, songs and paintings. More recently, again with Paddy Roe, he published *The Children's Country: Creation of a Goolarabooloo Future in North-West Australia* (2021). He is also a creative writer (*The Mother's Day Protest and Other Fictocritical Essays* was published in 2016) and has translated several books from French into English, notably *Another Science is Possible* (2018), by Belgian philosopher Isabelle Stengers, *The Wandering Souls* (2019), by French ethnopsychiatrist Tobie Nathan, and *Our Grateful Dead: Stories of Those Left behind,* (2021) by Belgian ethologist Vinciane Despret.

Colin Nettelbeck was Emeritus Professor of French Studies at the University of Melbourne, where he served as Head of the School of Languages (2000–2005) and held the A.R. Chisholm Chair of French from 1994 until his retirement in 2005. He was a Fellow of the Australian Academy of the Humanities and a life member of the Australian Society for French Studies as well as of the Institute for the Study of French Australian Relations, which he founded in 1985, and of the Alliance Française de Melbourne, having served as President of all three. With Wallace Kirsop and Dennis Davison, he co-founded the journal *Explorations* (now *The French Australian Review*), devoted to the study of the historical and cultural links between France and Australia. He was an Officier of the Palmes Académiques and a Chevalier de la Légion d'Honneur. He wrote extensively about twentieth-century and contemporary French literature, cinema and cultural history, with a special focus on the French experience of World War II. He published many books and articles, including *Forever French: Exile in the United States 1939–1945* (1993), *A Century of Cinema: Australian and French Connections* (with Jane Warren and Wallace Kirsop, 1996), and *Dancing with de Beauvoir: Jazz and the French*, published by Melbourne University Press in 2004. He was a jazz fan and sometime practitioner and, like Cole Porter, loved Paris in any season. He sadly passed away following a long battle with illness on 21 October 2022.

Phil Powrie is Emeritus Professor of Cinema Studies at the University of Surrey. He has published a number of books mainly on French cinema, including *French Cinema in the 1980s: Nostalgia and the Crisis of Masculinity* (1997), *Jean-Jacques Beineix* (2001), *Pierre Batcheff and Stardom in 1920s French Cinema* (2009), *Music in Contemporary French Cinema: The Crystal Song* (2017), *The French Film Musical* (2020, with Marie Cadalanu). An edited collection, *When Music Takes over in Film*, was published in 2023. He was Chief General Editor of the journal *French Screen Studies* (formerly *Studies in French Cinema*) from 2010 to 2020 and Chair of the British Association of Film Television and Screen Studies (2014–2017).

Roland (Roly) Sussex OAM is Emeritus Professor of Applied Language Studies at the University of Queensland. He is a specialist in comparative linguistics, particularly of the European languages, and has co-authored with Paul Cubberley a book on *The Slavic Languages* (2006). He is also keenly interested in the changes experienced by different languages, the evolving nature of Australian English, and the role of English internationally, especially in Asia: see Andy Kirkpatrick and Roland Sussex (eds) 2012, *English as an international language in Asia: Implications for language education,* Berlin and London: Springer-Verlag; and Andy Curtis and Roland Sussex (eds) (2018), *Intercultural communication in Asia: Education, language and values,* Berlin and London: Springer Verlag. His current research focus is on communication and pain, including pain in intercultural communication. He has presented a weekly ABC radio language talkback program for over 20 years in Queensland and South Australia. He is a Chevalier des Palmes Académiques, a Fellow of the Queensland Academy of Arts and Sciences, an honorary life member of the Alliance Française, and patron of the Institute of Professional Editors, and of Communication and Speech Performance Teachers Inc. He is currently president of the English-Speaking Union (Queensland), and co-editor of the journal *Intercultural Communication Studies.*

John West-Sooby is Emeritus Professor of French Studies at the University of Adelaide, where he served for many years as Head of the Department of French Studies and convenor of the University's language programmes. His research interests include the nineteenth-century French novel and French and Australian crime fiction. He has also worked for many years on the history of French maritime exploration in the Indo-Pacific, and notably on Nicolas Baudin's voyage of discovery to Australia. As co-author or (co-)editor, he has published several books on the subject, including *Encountering Terra Australis: The Australian Voyages of Nicolas Baudin and Matthew Flinders* (2004; 2010), *French Designs on Colonial New South Wales* (2014), *The Art of Science: Nicolas Baudin's Voyagers (1800–1804)* (2016) and *'Roaming Freely Throughout the Universe': Nicolas Baudin's Voyage to*

Australia and the Pursuit of Science (2021). He was a chief investigator on two major research projects funded by the Australian Research Council: 'The Baudin Legacy' (2005–2009) and 'Revolutionary Voyaging' (2014–2016). He is an Officier of the Palmes Académiques.

Index

Wakefield Press is an independent publishing and
distribution company based in Adelaide, South Australia.
We love good stories and publish beautiful books.
To see our full range of books, please visit our website at
www.wakefieldpress.com.au
where all titles are available for purchase.
To keep up with our latest releases, news and events,
subscribe to our monthly newsletter.

Find us!

Facebook: www.facebook.com/wakefield.press
Twitter: www.twitter.com/wakefieldpress
Instagram: www.instagram.com/wakefieldpress

Milton Keynes UK
Ingram Content Group UK Ltd.
UKHW020756070624
443893UK00002B/191